Safety at Work

Ellis Amdur, M.A., N.C.C., C.M.H.S.
William Cooper, M.B.A., M.P.A.

Skills to Calm and De-escalate Aggressive and Mentally Ill Individuals

A Comprehensive Guidebook for Corporate Security Managers,

Human Resources Staff, Loss Prevention Specialists, Executive Protection,

and others involved in Threat Management Professions

An Edgework Book
www.edgework.info

Notes and Notices

Safety at Work: Skills to Calm and De-escalate Aggressive and Mentally Ill Individuals

By Ellis Amdur, M.A., N.C.C., C.M.H.S and William Cooper, M.B.A., M.P.A. © 2011

ISBN: 978-1-950678-03-7

A Message to Our Readers

Edgework is committed to offering the best of our years of experience and study in the interest of professional and public safety. We ask that you express your respect for these intentions and honor our work by adhering strictly to the copyright protection notice you'll find below. By choosing NOT to reproduce these materials, you're supporting our work and making it possible for us to continue to develop materials that will enhance the safety of both the professionals for whom this book is written and the public. We thank you sincerely for your vigilance in respecting our rights!

Credits

Photographs by: Dreamstime.com
Illustrations by: Shoko Zama
Design: Soundview Design Studio
Cover photograph by: Brad Mering, Wikimedia Commons

Contents

Books by the Author (and Co-Author)

Published by Edgework www.edgework.info

On the De-escalation of Aggression

EVERYTHING ON THE LINE: Calming and De-escalation of Aggressive and Mentally Ill Individuals on the Phone
A Comprehensive Guidebook for Emergency Dispatch (9-1-1) Centers
Ellis Amdur

FROM CHAOS TO COMPLIANCE: Communication, Control, and De-escalation of Mentally Ill, Emotionally Disturbed and Aggressive Offenders
A Comprehensive Guidebook for Parole and Probation Officers
Ellis Amdur & Alan Pelton

GRACE UNDER FIRE: Skills to Calm and De-escalate Aggressive and Mentally Ill Individuals in Outpatient Settings: 2nd Edition
A Comprehensive Guidebook for Health and Social Services Agencies, and Individual Practitioners
Ellis Amdur

GUARDING THE GATES: Calming, Control and De-escalation of Mentally Ill, Emotionally Disturbed and Aggressive Individuals
A Comprehensive Guidebook for Security Guards
Ellis Amdur & William Cooper

IN THE EYE OF THE HURRICANE: Skills to Calm and De-escalate Aggressive and Mentally Ill Family Members: 2nd Edition
Ellis Amdur

SAFE BEHIND BARS: Communication, Control, and De-escalation of Mentally Ill and Aggressive Inmates
A Comprehensive Guidebook for Correctional Officers in Jail Settings
Ellis Amdur & Chris De Villeneuve

SAFE BEHIND THE WALLS: Communication, Control, and De-escalation of Mentally Ill and Aggressive Inmates
A Comprehensive Guidebook for Correctional Officers in Prison Settings
Ellis Amdur & George Galaza

SAFE HAVEN: Skills to Calm and De-escalate Aggressive and Mentally Ill Individuals: 2nd Edition
A Comprehensive Guidebook for Personnel Working in Hospital and Residential Settings
Ellis Amdur

SAFETY AT WORK: Skills to Calm and De-escalate Aggressive and Mentally Ill Individuals
A Comprehensive Guidebook for Corporate Security Managers, Human Resources Staff, Loss Prevention Specialists, Executive Protection, and others involved in Threat Management Professions
Ellis Amdur & William Cooper

THE THIN BLUE LIFELINE: Verbal De-escalation of Mentally Ill and Emotionally Disturbed People
A Comprehensive Guidebook for Law Enforcement Officers
Ellis Amdur & John Hutchings

On Martial Arts

DUELING WITH OSENSEI: Grappling with the Myth of the Warrior Sage
Ellis Amdur

HIDDEN IN PLAIN SIGHT: Tracing the Roots of Ueshiba Morihei's Power
Ellis Amdur

OLD SCHOOL: Essays on Japanese Martial Traditions
Ellis Amdur

In Gratitude for Expert Critique

In each draft, of this book we have corrected errors of fact, added new information, and fine-tuned the manuscript. One of the qualities of a good Security Professional is the understanding that the task supersedes the protection of someone's feelings; therefore, we have appreciated all the direct criticism. The professionals listed below have closely reviewed this book.

All responsibility for this book, however, must lie in our hands. Any errors, in particular, are our responsibility. Given that lives can be on the line in work such as this, please do not hesitate to contact us if you believe that any part of this book is inaccurate or requires additional material. The book will be revised as necessary in future editions.

David Behar. He is currently the Senior Manager for Security and Emergency Management for Snohomish County Public Utility District. David has 25-years of experience in the electrical utility industry, is a certified business continuity planner, a member of the Association of Threat Assessment Security Professionals, and has successfully managed several hundred workplace violence cases.

Fatuesi Fatuesi is a senior Site Supervisor for Guardsmark. Fatuesi is a retired Master Sergeant after 24-years in the United States Army. In his distinguished career, Fatuesi received the Bronze Star and Meritorious Service Medal. He has been with Guardsmark for five years, and received the World Class Leadership Award. He earned an Associate Degree from Troy State in Education. He has led and managed Security Professionals through many workplace violence events, including assisted security terminations, and has personally and successfully interacted with individuals showing most of the behaviors described in this book.

Jeffrey Slotnick, CPP, PSP. President of Setracon, Inc. a Consultancy focused on the professional development and training of security, law enforcement, and military personnel, the provision of quality security services, protective services, investigations, and the conduct of risk, vulnerability, and threat assessments. Slotnick is a security industry consultant with more than 27-years of experience.

Introduction

This book is for Security Professionals who will potentially interact with emotionally unstable, hostile, mentally ill, and/or criminal individuals. Among those for whom this book is written are corporate security managers, security directors, loss prevention specialists, executive protection managers, workplace violence specialists, and human resources personnel, to name only a few. For the sake of clarity and consistency throughout the text, we will use the term "Security Professionals" to denote anyone that works in these areas.

To be absolutely clear, "Security Guards," those usually uniformed individuals who provide basic protection services: patrol, checking site security, bag and I.D. checks, shop-lifting protection, etc. are not included in this category. Although there is certainly considerable overlap in the subject matter addressed, the needs of those in the Security Guard profession are specifically covered in another book, Guarding the Gates, by the same authors.

There will to be some sections of this book that may discuss subjects that are not something you would encounter on a daily basis. For example, the sections on mental illness may appear to be less relevant to those who work in upper echelons of the corporate world. Nonetheless, there are times when employees have psychotic breaks or manic episodes, or have used drugs that, during the period of intoxication, cause them to act in ways analogous to short-term mental illnesses.

We also present policies that should be incorporated at an organizational level. Managers, administrators, support staff, and the professionals who work directly with problematic individuals must be part of a team that is committed to creating and maintaining a safe environment. Therefore, we strongly recommend a read-through of the entire book.

This book is also for trainees entering the field of security. Such individuals are given a large amount of information in training. Then they are deployed on assignment, and the abstract information in books, computer training modules, and role-plays become real, sometimes frighteningly so. This book, which encompasses over 60 years of direct experience with aggressive, mentally ill, and emotionally disturbed individuals, will be invaluable in readying you for such encounters.

We have all read about or watched the results of workplace violence; it is covered extensively in the media, whether it occurs at a corporation, a small business enterprise, a school, a mall, or other facility. There is considerable discussion about who the perpetrators are and why the incident occurred: a troubled childhood, a disgruntled worker, or a mentally ill person. Whatever the circumstances, there is little discussion on how to recognize such individuals before a crisis occurs, much less how to prevent such events. For this reason, the primary focus of this book deals will be the recognition of aggression from the first triggering event, and the verbal de-escalation of such unstable individuals before violent acts occur.

Security Professionals, regardless of assignment, are often considered the police of their organization and function at various times as first responders, detectives, executive protection specialists, or as security consultants. In most cases, professionals find their work to be straightforward and unambiguous. However, circumstances can suddenly change, and such events can be very dangerous, especially when dealing with angry, erratic, or unstable people. This work provides a broad overview of such people, not only who they are, but how to work with them and succeed.

This book has two primary aims. The first is to augment your abilities in dealing with the most puzzling individuals, those suffering from serious mental illness. We wish to highlight anything that a professional can do while interacting with a mentally ill or otherwise emotionally disturbed individual that will establish the kind of interaction most likely to lead to a safe resolution. We also intend to make the reader aware of anything that would make things worse: that is, escalate the situation. The second aim is to hone your ability to recognize dangerous and manipulative behaviors, as well as enhancing your skills in de-escalation and the control of people using such tactics.

Rather than being concerned about "what if " situations that you concoct in your own imagination, something that many people do when confronted by the strange or unfamiliar, you will become more skilled in assessing if someone is truly dangerous. In many situations, you will have the ability to calm them as well. You will then embody a trait that can be termed "grace under fire," that ability to become the center of gravity within a crisis situation so that it coalesces into an ordered system around you. You will find your presence alone often calms a situation. In a surprising number of situations, aggressors will become willing to comply with directives, even anxious to meet your approval or gain your respect.

You may find that reading this book is not sufficient. In varying capacities, the authors offer direct training, traveling to site locations to provide not only basic de-escalation training, but also advanced training in such areas as strategic communication with individuals with character disorders or anti-social traits, predictive analytics, and management models to allow for an intelligence-based, proactive set of strategies. We also offer consultation on difficult cases, and discuss options as well as formulate the best strategies to ensure safety for everyone, based on the presenting behaviors of the people of concern. Inquiries about such training can be directed to www.edgework.info.

SECTION I

Core Requirements

CHAPTER 1

The Development of a Safety Mindset:
Systems Issues

The job of a Security Professional carries a significant possibility for unpleasant human interaction or even danger. There is always a potential of risk to personal safety, whether on the worksite or off. This is not to say that you must go through your day in a state of hyper-vigilance, constantly on guard against an attack. Instead, you develop a "safety mindset," maintaining a general awareness of your surroundings while always being prepared to protect yourself and others. This accomplished, you will not have to switch yourself on when you start your working day. The development of a safety mindset is based upon the following fundamental assumptions:

- Being pro-active about safety issues must be a primary concern of all security staff: managers and supervisors, as well as those in direct service positions, extending all the way to support staff.
- There must be consistency and a common understanding in the application of safety procedures and emergency protocols at all levels of the agency.
- Adequate staff safety preparedness is not a once-and-done training event. A regular review of safety protocols, crisis response processes, physical site safety issues, and ongoing safety training for all staff is crucial.

Although this book centers on verbal de-escalation skills, we must start at a more basic level, because the cause of many critical incidents can be attributed to a lack of attention to fundamental safety precautions. This must begin *before* you start your workday.

First and foremost, always be mentally prepared to attend to your duties in a professional manner. Failing to do so can place not only yourself, but also your co-workers and the subject of your concern in appallingly dangerous situations. Explosive acts of violence rarely occur without some recognizable precursors, and an unfocused mind will impair your ability to notice these early warnings signs. Anything that distracts you puts everyone at risk. Therefore, professionals cannot allow personal or familial issues to intrude upon their ability to focus on the job at hand.

Staff also needs to be mindful that employees often do not pose the greatest threat to our safety. Upset family members of employees or complete strangers may pose a much greater danger on the worksite, in the office parking lot, or in areas around your facility.

Figure 1.1 It Is Not Safe to Avoid the Subject of Safety

In an effort to avoid creating what they believe to be an atmosphere of fear, some managers attempt to deal with safety concerns by attempting to avoid these issues altogether. This approach is wrong-minded, even dangerous. Experience suggests that heightened awareness and a pro-active approach to safety through planning, developing procedures, training, and on-going communication contribute to a much safer and happier environment.

To foster safety and enhance effectiveness, it is imperative that everyone (including clerical and support staff) who engages with potentially confrontational individuals has a sense of control over their situation, grounded in the knowledge that appropriate agency support systems are in place. The following will be helpful:

- **Follow standard procedures.** Given the fluid nature of human relationships, you will never be limited in your opportunities for creativity. Nonetheless, there <u>must</u> be standardized procedures for dealing with potentially or actually aggressive individuals, including those who are mentally ill. It is true that one sometimes has to make an exception and go outside the rules, but you must understand that, in doing so, you are taking personal rather than institutional responsibility for your actions. It may be the right thing to do, but you will have to prove it: not only by positive results, but also by your explanation. In any event, this must be the most unusual of occasions.
- **Adaptability.** Notwithstanding the necessity for a predictable environment with standardized procedures, such procedures must also be flexible. Standardization must never become rigidity. In many cases, the situation may evolve or deteriorate, requiring you to be agile enough to accommodate the changes.
- **Solid boundaries.** All individuals must have an assurance that Security Professionals are vigilant in maintaining an exemplary level of professionalism. You must not act in any way among yourselves that will negatively affect either the company or the security team.
- **Good training and regular practice.** It is your professional and moral responsibility to be well-versed and skilled in de-escalation methods. This certainly requires an effort on the part of the individual Security Professional, but even more so, it must be agency policy that good training is made available and that times are set-aside on a *regular* basis to practice these skills.

Figure 1.2 Ongoing Training

Ongoing training specific to your responsibilities is essential. There are a variety of methods for accomplishing this. One of the most effective is regular "table-top" exercises of short duration, covering everything from disaster preparedness to workplace violence and other safety concerns.

- **Integrity.** Beyond all else, Security Professionals must be persons of dignity and integrity, who are rightly held to a higher moral and ethical standard than the average citizen. All who have any reason to have professional interaction with Security Professionals must also be absolutely confident that they are vigilant in maintaining ethical and moral relationships. Without this, all the de-escalation methods in the world are just empty words.

Staff Meetings Should Always Include a Focus on Safety Concerns

Supervisors and administrators should ensure that regular staff meetings include a focus on safety concerns. The regular discussion of these issues will serve to increase morale and foster unit cohesion. While thoughtful preparation cannot prevent every critical incident from occurring, an alert and well-trained staff can reduce the impact of such an event through a well-coordinated response.

Debriefing meetings are particularly important in the wake of a critical incident, in the review of a planned action (such as a termination of an employee or escorting an enraged spouse off the premises), as well as inter-departmental operations with law enforcement or social service agencies. Termed "After Action Reviews" (AAR), these meetings are very important in refining or revising existing procedures. AARs are not to be used as an attempt to lay blame for problems or difficulties during an operation. Some things are likely to not go as planned or anticipated even in a successful operation. Improvement begins with a thoughtful discussion among those involved. Therefore, AARs must focus solely on what can be done to improve the process and enhance everyone's safety for future operations.

CHAPTER 2

Threat Assessment

Figure 2.1 Objective and Subjective Factors of Risk Assessment
Proper risk assessment of any individual entails a balanced mixture of objective and subjective data. Paradoxically, "objective" data is not objective until it has undergone a subjective review. Risk assessments must be qualitative, highlighting what is unique about each situation and each individual.

Intake: Gathering Critical Information

Some companies have rather extensive intake and reporting procedures, and newly assigned cases will contain many pieces of information vital to the Security Professional. All too often, however, you receive a bare minimum of information. In these instances, Security Professionals must conduct their own background checks via human resources and any other avenue prior to making that initial first contact. Objective data will allow the Security Professional to conduct a preliminary risk assessment prior to the first meeting. Indeed, this preliminary information may dictate the time, place, and method of that initial contact.

Threat Assessment

A more detailed assessment, beyond record review, should be conducted by the Security Professional during face-to-face and sometimes, collateral interviews. All information has a context. For example, you may become aware that an individual used to own several knives. By itself, that tells you little. You need to know why he owned them: for cooking, for a collection, or as part of a festering obsessive fantasy life, etc.

If you are aware that an individual is associated with any of the items in the list below, you will have a much better idea who to really be concerned about, and what to watch out for. Such a list is not an absolute predictor of aggression or violence. Instead, it is an "alert," to follow-up with further information gathering.

- **A past history of violence.** This is one of the most important factors. Violence is not only innate: it is a trained behavior, which becomes easier and easier to use as a problem-solving strategy. Furthermore, it is rewarding: some people feel most powerful when they are violent. Power over others is the best experience of their lives.
- **History of bullying or intimidation.** This is the psychological counterpart of physical violence. Bullies and intimidators typically reveal themselves over a period of time in a workplace environment.

- **Prior arrest.** Any arrest is a heightened risk factor even if it was for a non-violent crime. The individual may be terrified or outraged at the idea of being arrested again or even having more contact with law enforcement or other authorities. Furthermore, with the prevalence of physical and sexual assault within correctional institutions, the non-violent arrestee may have come out a very different person than they went in.[1]
- **Possession of weapons, fascination with weapons, or a past history of weapon use.** In particular, we must be concerned when the individual has a history of brandishing or using weapons, or talking about weapons and their use in menacing terms, a fascination with weaponry, or fantasizing about weapons in a pathological manner. *The latter two are a concern even if the individual does not possess weapons.*

Figure 2.2 Example: Fascination With Weapons

A recent case in a major telecommunications firm had a 4-month employee frequently speak of his guns. He was also a poor performer and was to be terminated for performance issues. He came to work the day of the termination discussion armed with a shotgun, intending to kill employees. Law enforcement required nearly 2 hours to negotiate him out of his vehicle.

- **History of physical abuse or the witnessing of physical abuse and violence.** Beyond a history of personal victimization, it is particularly traumatic to have witnessed abuse of a family member. The victim of abuse often hates his own weakness, and begins hating weakness in others as well. Once this occurs, it is a natural move for some people to begin victimizing what they hate: the weak.[2]
- **Head injury.** This is associated with impulse control problems. Many of our young soldiers are coming home from 21st century combat with closed head injuries. It is also endemic among violent felons.[3] Those who have suffered from head injuries can present an increased risk of assaultive behavior because such damage can impair the brain's natural capacity to inhibit violent impulses.
- **Dementia.** Elderly people with Alzheimer's disorder or other degenerative brain illnesses can show some of the same impulse control problems as those with traumatic brain injuries. Although not a major portion of a Security Professional's responsibilities, worksites will occasionally have elderly employee who have begun to deteriorate or even someone who has just wandered on the worksite.
- **Fear of attack or invasion of personal space.** Paranoid and fearful individuals may lash out in defensive violence. If you are properly "tracking" the individual, you should be aware if they become increasingly agitated or stressed when in close physical proximity to you.
- **Low frustration tolerance.** This is the inability or unwillingness to tolerate limit setting—"I want what I want and I want it now and you'd better not keep me from it." This is something that the subject will often verbalize.
- **Recent stressors and losses.** Bereavement, separation, divorce, job loss, incarceration, etc. can make an individual more willing to become violent. In some cases the individual may feel as if

they have nothing left to lose. *The threat of job loss is, of course, particularly acute in these difficult economic times.*

- **A feeling of victimization and grievance.** Certain individuals may feel victimized by society in general, or hold a grudge against "the company." They regard their current predicament as someone else's fault and maintain this attitude no matter what evidence is presented to the contrary. The Security Professional becomes the "face" of the system for the individual, and as a result, an available target.

- **Excessive use of intoxicating substances.** Almost all intoxicating substances can be disinhibiting to both impulse control and moral sensibilities. Intoxicants act like solvents, dissolving the internal barriers that hold us back from our base desires, among them aggression. This does not only concern alcohol and illegal drugs. More and more people are abusing prescription medications that may have been originally prescribed for a genuine medical need.

Figure 2.3 Example: A Typical Incident With an Intoxicated Subject

Chaotic and irrational at a company picnic:

An employee reported a woman wearing a company badge becoming enraged at two people inside a car whom she thought were blocking the entrance to a building. The woman staggered, and otherwise appeared intoxicated. She started screaming obscenities and kicking their car, then got into her own vehicle and tore out of the parking lot, almost crashing into other vehicles.

- **Physical pain or discomfort.** Chronic pain and illness can make people irritable, frustrated, and/or desperate.

- **The individual has already given up.** Expecting the interaction to be difficult or absolutely negative, their response can be, "What the hell. Nothing will help. If I'm aggressive, at least I can make my mark on the world ... or on you." This fact, alone, should provide impetus to remove unnecessary institutional obstacles to people achieving their goals legitimately.

- **Severe psychopathological symptoms:**
    a. Rapid mood swings: such a person is unpredictable, and can suddenly flare into rage just when the Security Professional thinks he/she has solved the problem.
    b. Hallucinations, particularly command hallucinations: auditory hallucinations may tell the individual to do something terrible. If you think someone is hearing voices, ask what they are hearing.
    c. Mania: this is a state of extreme excitement, typified by rapid speech, grandiose thinking, very poor judgment, and impulsive behavior. It is a behavior we see in people with bipolar disorder (manic-depression), as well as intoxication on stimulants such as methamphetamine or cocaine, and not infrequently, alcohol.
    d. History of predatory or manipulative behaviors.

- **Interactional factors between an aggressor and victim.** Particularly in domestic violence situations, the aggressor views the victim as having power over him/her, views them as being inflexible or controlling, or denying them what they are owed. In short, the aggressor usually believes themself to be the victim.

All of these can also occur in the interpersonal dynamics between an employee and management, HR, or Security Professionals.

Figure 2.4 Protecting the Target of Aggression Driven by "Interactional Factors"

When considering a potential victim:
- Consider situational factors such as working alone, working after-hours, transporting someone in one's car.
- Consider if your agency is actually doing everything that could help keep the person safe.
- Consider any behaviors on the part of the victim that make them more vulnerable, or if their behaviors, however inadvertent, make the situation more dangerous for themselves.

- **Religious and cultural clashes.** Culture is any set of rules and customs that orders the relationships between people. Avoid any religious, political, or cultural debates with employees or others on the worksite. However, Security Professionals should also make an attempt to be aware of others' cultural mores and religious practices, so that they do not inadvertently insult them. You should also be aware that some cultures sanction violence under different circumstances from our own mainstream culture, and take this into account in any threat assessment
- **Post Traumatic Stress Disorder (PTSD).** When in a panic engendered by PTSD, the brain believes that one is in a survival situation. Survival demands simplicity; therefore, the only options the brain in survival mode offers are fight, flight, freeze, or faint. Obviously, "fight" becomes our biggest concern. Even more central are any events that evoke memories, or worse, re-experiencing the traumatic event. Smells, more than any other sense, seem to be tied directly to memory and hence, are particularly likely to evoke such an episode. Due to the circumstances of the current wars in the Middle East, where the biggest threat was Improvised Explosive Devices (IED), veterans will be particularly stressed in crowds, in traffic, or in other circumstances where they are blocked from freely moving. PTSD among veterans may also evoked during certain holidays or events associated with loud, popping noises such as the 4th of July or Memorial Day.

A Review of Aggressive Encounters

Take some time to reflect on the aggressive and/or violent incidents that have occurred in the past with individuals involved with your agency. Try to learn more about the patterns of behavior that might have preceded their aggression, as well as any actions on the part of the Security Professional that were either unhelpful or contributory towards the individual becoming violent. Security Professionals should note the following:

- What were the circumstances that led to the aggressive encounter?
- What was the *first* sign that indicated that the situation was getting volatile or dangerous?
- What did the individual say in the moments just before the aggressive incident?
- People are generally able to control their verbal expressions better than their non-verbal signals, so recall the individual's body language prior to the incident. Tension can also create a change in the quality of the voice such as rate of speech, pitch, and/or volume.
- Consider what your thoughts were at that time. We very frequently have some advanced warning of an assault, such as, a stray thought that we mistakenly discount as being unfounded. Did you minimize, contextualize, or otherwise resist looking at the situation head-on?
- Consider what you felt, physically and emotionally, at each stage of the encounter. The sensations evoked within the context of an encounter with another person are physical expressions of intuition. When you next experience that same sensation be aware that it is an early warning sign that a similar situation may be developing.
- What do you believe you should have done differently?
- What planning did you do in regard to that individual subsequent to the aggression? How did that plan work?
- Did you report the encounter, and if so, to what degree do you believe your agency backed you up? Security Professionals are encouraged to report any incident in which they felt threatened in any fashion. Over time, these reports will provide data for:
  a. A general representation of the more common threats that Security Professionals face when performing their duties, which enables you to fine-tune safety protocols on an ongoing basis.
  b. Illuminating a pattern of behaviors that precede aggressive encounters with an individual. Understanding of the pattern helps security preemptively intervene, before the individual is once again, in full crisis.

Core Interview Questions Regarding Potential Violence During Interviews

Whenever possible, ask a person of concern direct questions about their previous history and potential for violence. The best predictor of future behavior is past behavior. Be sure to hold yourself in a calm, relaxed, manner, offering a direct gaze. You have to convey that you are asking for the information to ground your understanding, not because you are afraid. You are also trying to convey that you are able to handle anything they might mention, even angry or threatening statements. You accomplish this through an air of quiet confidence and genuine interest in the person, not through challenge or trying to appear tough. Reminder: the quality of their answer—tone of voice, body language, and facial expression—is as important, or more so, than the specific answer they give.

Questions can include (NOTE: This is not a complete list. These are some examples to help you understand the scope and nature of the questions you need to ask):

- "Have you hit anyone within the last six months?" "Have you done anything else violent in that time period?" "How about the last year"? "Have you ever been arrested for assault?" "How about for fighting with someone?" "When was the last time you had to physically defend yourself?"

Notice the nuanced levels of the questions. You are able, here, to assess the individual's familiarity with the legal system. (What if they deny assault, but endorse an arrest for "fighting."). By asking "six months," you may get a more manipulative person, who otherwise might lie, to say, "Not in six months," because they think that's all you care about. Or, they deny assault, but endorse fighting, which indicates that they went through an entire trial without either paying attention to the charges, or with no particular interest in the proceedings. Or, the individual will launch into a long story how they were the actual victim of the assault, or that their action was blown far out of proportion, and they only pled guilty to get out of jail.

- "Tell me what happened?" "Why do you think this situation occurred?" "Was there anything you could have done to avoid such a confrontation?" The context of why individuals were assaultive, what it meant to them, why they thought they had no other options, or why they chose violence first, not last, is vital information to the investigating Security Professional.

- "What do you do when someone really makes you angry?" "What kind of thing might someone say that would make you mad?" Among other things, this gives you advanced warning of what the individual's triggers are. Predatory intimidators sometimes seize this opportunity to try to say something vaguely menacing, like, "Oh, you don't want to know."

- "If you got mad at someone here, what would you do?" "How would you handle it?" "If you did get mad, how could I help you calm down?"

Each question is a gateway to further questions. Furthermore, the context of the situations in which a person became aggressive is all-important.

NOTE: These are just a few examples to help understand the scope and nature of the questions you need to ask. By asking open-ended questions which require more than a simple yes or no answer on the individual's part, the Security Professional can gather quite a bit of critical information. These types of questions can also be used to get the individual thinking about their patterns of behavior and their triggers.

Figure 2.5 Example: The Context of Warning Signs

Let us imagine two individuals, both of whom served time in prison for a life-threatening assault on another person.

- The first smirks and describes how he fractured the skull of a rival drug dealer. He airily says that he'd never do anything like that again, "because I'm not in the business anymore."

- The second describes, in a tone of outrage, how he went to a club with his wife, and while he went to pick up their drinks, returned to find a man mauling her sexually. He broke a glass and slashed the man's face, blinding him.

Which man is more dangerous? <u>We don't know</u>. We do know, however, that the context of their aggression is poles apart. Furthermore, they tell their stories in very different ways. One obviously savors the opportunity to recount his violence and probably savored the act as well. The other is horrified by what he did, but still feels justified in doing it. Not only are their triggers different, but it also suggests that they need quite different case plans and interventions were either of them to become enraged again.

Figure 2.6 Record Keeping as It Pertains to Violence and Risk

Clear and concise case notes are essential to the safety of fellow Security Professionals who may have to deal with the individual in your absence. In fact, poor record keeping or illegible notes in the individual's file should be considered professional malpractice. Critical information should be highlighted, or written in red ink, so that anyone opening the file is immediately aware of the risk factors involved.

Handwriting is not an issue in companies with electronic databases. However, critical information should be noted on the face page of the individual's electronic file, either through the use of a color-coding system or a visible "Alerts" tab.

The authors also recommend strongly that, outside of emergent situations, Security Professionals should take a moment to review the individual's case file before any contact with a person of concern, to remind themselves of previously noted information.

Do Not Let the Abnormal Become Normal

We cannot underscore how important it is to check out your concerns and intuitions with fellow Security Professionals, and sometimes with professionals outside your office. Security Professionals can easily become complacent when dealing with people they have become used to.

You should also consult when you *should* be concerned and are not. Some Security Professionals become so familiar with pathology that the abnormal becomes normal. The professional no longer reacts in a natural way, tolerating or not noticing covert aggression, or boundary trespass.

Figure 2.7 Example: When the Abnormal Becomes Normal

In one case, the Security Professional was asked to work with HR on a Security Assisted Termination, generally a higher risk personnel matter. The Security Professional was briefed on the reasons for the termination, including threats of violence towards co-workers, a history with law enforcement, and various performance concerns. He was asked to be outside the room and be available to react if needed. The Security Professional positioned himself in view of the door believing the matter to be proceeding without issue, called his wife on his cell phone to discuss an upcoming vacation. As they spoke, the employee being terminated ran out of the room in the direction of the Security Professional, and attacked him, believing that he was calling law enforcement. The Security Professional had his back to the door when attacked and sustained significant injuries.

CHAPTER 3

Safety Planning and Risk Reduction:
Practical Issues

No matter how skilled you may become at verbal de-escalation, you will sometimes have to deal with potentially violent individuals who may be unable or more likely, unwilling to stop themselves from acting violently, no matter what you might say or do. Whenever possible, Security Professionals should enlist the help of others rather than trying to solve dangerous situations on their own. It is not enough to be *willing* to help, however. Everyone must know *how* to help. You cannot create an effective safety plan on the spot. You must know what to do, collectively, if things do go wrong. When you are focused as an individual and coordinated as a team, you will be far more effective in managing the aggressive person.

Agencies that have a well-coordinated and well-practiced safety plan feel different as well because potential aggressors:
- See fewer opportunities to attack.
- Find fewer pretexts to justify an attack in their mind.
- See little chance of success in carrying out an attack.

Physical Site Safety

Your office is an extension of yourself, and although Security Professionals and staff should be comfortable, safety should not be sacrificed for convenience. A well-designed office will enhance security, while leaving an aggressor with fewer opportunities to act violently. Ideally, your personal office (or the dedicated interview room) should have a minimum of furniture and clutter. You should also position yourself closest to the door in case you need to exit quickly.

Establishing a secure office site may be compromised due to architectural design limitations, as well as the financial constraints of your company. For example, the installation of modern security and video surveillance equipment can be prohibitively expensive. However, there are many inexpensive ways of enhancing office site security, requiring only that Security Professionals and staff be alert to safety issues and communicate with one another. Listed below are just a few of the issues to consider regarding physical site security:
- Control ingress and egress to the office proper. A secure reception area should be established to control the flow of individuals into the office. Ideally, the door leading from the reception area into the office itself should remain locked at all times. Someone, either an employee, or in high security facilities, a Security Professional should escort each individual into and out of the office. In any event, never allow an individual to wander unescorted through the office.

- Security doors must remain locked if they are to be effective. Propping a security door open, or leaving the door unlocked, defeats its intended purpose.

- Particularly in larger agencies, interview rooms should be established and used to conduct all interviews. Such rooms can remain free from any extraneous clutter, office equipment, and furniture, leaving the room free of many potential weapons. Furthermore, Security Professionals can then feel free to place personal items or family pictures in their offices, which are not accessible to the interviewees.

- Any object on your desk or in your office can become a weapon.

   a. Pens, pencils, staplers, paper punches, and other office equipment can be used as weapons if a situation is escalating. Create a "sterile weapon environment" by keeping desks free of such items, particularly in an interview room.

   b. Are picture frames or corkboards secured to the walls? Any item that can be removed from the walls or picked up easily is a potential weapon. *NOTE: One of the authors was once knocked out by a wooden frame "frisbeed" between his eyes at close range.*

   c. Loose chair parts and light furniture can be used as weapons as well. Make sure that all necessary office furniture and equipment is in good condition and in proper working order. When designing an office, or acquiring new furniture, safety must be considered in addition to comfort and aesthetics.

- Personal photographs of family members and loved ones should not be able to be viewed by individuals; with current cell-phone technology, they can be imaged and used inappropriately. Not only will they attract the interest of the predatory individual, such photographs may exacerbate the envy of the "failure in life," who seeing the picture of your good fortune, wonders why you get to be so "lucky" and they are not. *One of the authors had to intervene in a case where such an individual began planning to burn down the house of his therapist, (who offered sessions in a home office) because "I want to see how much you'll still be smiling if your wife and daughters burn to death in front of your eyes."*

- Outside your personal office space, give consideration to all hallways, stairwells, staff and public elevators, parking and storage areas, and the reception area. Are there adequate sight lines to see who is entering the reception area? Is the lighting adequate in hallways, stairwells, and parking areas?

- If your department authorizes the use of weapons of any kind, make sure that they are in a locked cabinet or drawer when not in use.

- If possible, install panic buttons at the front desk and in each office or interview room. Drills should be conducted regularly to ensure that these panic buttons actually work, and that designated staff, respond when an emergency button is pressed. Other companies offer "key fob" type panic alarms, which are portable and can be kept on the person.

Communication for Emergencies

- **Develop an emergency communication plan.** Emergency numbers, including 9-1-1 (or your country's equivalent emergency dispatch number), poison control, child protective services, and the mental health professionals who, in your state or province, are responsible to place severely mentally ill people in a hospital, should be programmed into the office phone system or posted near each telephone in the security office.

- **Use a land line, whenever possible, to call for emergency assistance.** In North America, and in many other countries, your address will automatically be available to emergency call takers, letting them know your location even when you cannot speak freely. Security Professionals should also enter all emergency contact information into their cell phones, including numbers for local police departments, treatment centers, and their home office.

- Some agencies install emergency call buttons that trigger an audible or silent alarm, even including a light over the doorway of the room where the crisis is occurring. However, installing the buttons is not enough. Your agency should have regular drills to be sure that they actually work, and that the designated people actually respond when an emergency button is pressed.

- Because Security Professionals may find themselves in a situation where they need to summon help without alerting the individual that they are doing so, you should develop and implement emergency code words or phrases that will activate emergency procedures, including a show-of-force within the office, and a call to law enforcement, if necessary. This code phrase can be used over the public address system to summon aid as required, as well as over your office phone, in conversation with a fellow Security Professional, or over the public address system. A code word should be selected that can be placed in context to the situation being discussed without arousing suspicion. There must be consistent training in using code words or phrases so that staffs' reaction to them will be as immediate as they would were they to hear a siren. Attrition of Security Professionals requires both updating those on your current roster and training new hires.

Figure 3.1 Code Words

Whenever the agreed-upon code word or phrase is voiced, no matter what the *apparent* context of the call, the recipient knows that the designated safety response plan must be initiated.

For example:
- "I'm in the 2nd conference room. Would **Mr. HOLMES** get me our information on hiring practices concerning convicted felons" In this case, the use of the name **HOLMES,** by prearrangement means, "I need help right now."
- "I need an immediate consult with **Mr. HOLMES** concerning whether we are required to call the union as soon as a report of possible theft is filed."
- "Could **Mr. HOLMES** please come here with the records I was talking about? I'm in conference room B."
- (Over the PA system) Called **MR. HOLMES** to the lobby of building four.

- Some agencies use a second code to simply call one person down to check out the situation or offer support. Rather than using a fictitious name in this circumstance, we recommend a *code word* to alert the person that the situation is heated and it may be necessary that they stand by, ready to assist in de-escalation or in initiating a show-of-force. In *this* circumstance, you do not have an emergency yet. There is, therefore, no need to obscure your intentions from the person. Instead, you could call the front desk or a supervisor and say, "Mr. DeVore is troubled by our recent phone call to his insurance company. Would you send Ms. Bargetta to this office to '*lend a hand*' in explaining things to him." In this case, the somewhat stilted "lend a hand" is used, rather than the more common "help" and this word is designated, agency-wide, as the code that the situation demands immediate attention.

Figure 3.2 Explicit Announcements in Emergencies

There are other situations in which you must inform everyone in your facility, without ambiguity, that they are in an emergency situation. In these cases, speak explicitly. For example: "A man with a gun, wearing a red jacket and brown pants is in the building. He was last seen on the second floor. Staff must initiate emergency procedures now!"

- Develop and implement the use of critical incident reports, which are to be completed following the resolution of the emergency or critical incident. The authors recommend that Security Professionals fill out a critical incident report anytime they feel that their safety has been threatened or jeopardized, *even when it is hard to define what was of concern.* For example, grooming behavior by an individual to set you up for a possible assault or blackmail can be an investment of considerable time. It is sometimes only revealed when a Security Professional has noted subtle behaviors that, taken as a whole, are revealed as showing a pattern when lined up in a series of reports.
- Supervisors should compile a list of emergency contact numbers for each of their Security Professionals in the event of an emergency. Supervisors should keep a copy of the emergency contact list at home as well as in the office.

With proper planning and attention to detail, many potential emergencies can be curtailed before they develop into a harmful situation. Of course, even the best laid plans will not prevent an emergency from arising, which is why regular practice of the safety plan is a requirement for the safety of all concerned. Regular practice will also highlight areas of the response plan that need to be modified and improved upon, *before* a true emergency occurs. Security Professionals and staff who have developed a safety mindset will foster a safer and more cohesive office culture, one where safety is paramount.

On the Phone With People Who Are in Crisis

The major differences between speaking with someone on the phone, as opposed to face-to-face, are in the primary mode of perception and the distance separating the Security Professional and the individual.

Although you are not able to assess the body language or facial expressions, nor often, do you even know if the person has a weapon, your hearing, without the distraction of other senses, becomes sensitized to pick up changes in tone and pace that might suggest that the person is becoming angered or enraged.

The below are questions that might be relevant in specific situations. Ask for a description of the problem: then ask further questions to understand the context.

In the event of a true emergency, the Security Professional should remain on the line with the individual, if possible, while another Security Professional calls 9-1-1 to request a police response to the residence. Should a police response be necessary, the Security Professional must relay as much relevant information to the responding law enforcement officer as possible, including, obviously, the individual's address, age, immediate mental state, level of risk, and the possibility of weapons being involved, and the nature of the crisis.

The following are questions that might be useful in obtaining as much relevant information as quickly as possible:

- Ask for a detailed description of the problem, and then ask further questions to understand the context.
- Ask direct questions to ascertain if there is any threat of violence or suicide.
- Ask if the individual has access to weapons, and what type, particularly if a police response is necessary.
- If there is any sense of chaos, violence or danger, ask if anyone has been hurt. If so, ask how. Get specific.
- If you have any sense that the individual is being circumspect or unresponsive because a dangerous person is nearby, say, "If you are in danger right now and don't want someone else to hear what you are saying, just say 'yes' or 'no' in response to my questions." This may be most common in a domestic violence situation. If you think that will sound strange, you can answer like you are talking to a friend. For example, you can say, "Yes, I do hope your dad's cold get's better," or "No, I don't think my cousin is going to get the job." What I will listen for is just the "Yes," or the "No" in the sentence.
- In some situations (different from the last item, of course), ask to speak to others in the residence to get a better picture of what is going on.

Be Aware Who Is in Your Agency

Outsiders such as visitors must not have the freedom to enter your agency and move around at will, without anyone being aware of where they are and who they are. Given that you will have many people entering and leaving your company on a daily basis, many whom are unfamiliar, it is imperative that no one "disappears" while on agency property. It is typically the responsibility of security to control access, or respond to a person who has not complied. Access control is the literal front line of the organization's defense.

Preemptive Planning With the Subject of Concern or Their Associates

Certain policies will unavoidably upset people. It is often valuable to have such policies explained CLEARLY in written form, which you should review in detail with the person and have them sign to signify agreement. Rules regarding sobriety, sexual harassment, and weapons on-site, etc. should be explained clearly, and offered on a written form that new employees are required to sign. If the individual violates any of these policies, the consequences should be absolutely clear, unambiguous, and universal. If enforcement of such rules is made "judgment calls" at the whim of various staff, it is a guarantee that manipulative individuals will soon succeed in setting various members of your team odds at each other. This practice will also make your organization a prime target for wrongful termination claims and lawsuits based on inconsistent application and enforcement of these rules.

Planning for Potentially Volatile Meetings

Even the most secure office site cannot prevent an individual from becoming agitated or aggressive. There are many situations where the individual must be informed of something that is potentially upsetting, that is, being told to leave a location, a termination or reduction in pay or status, or being investigated for theft, to name only a few. Therefore, Security Professionals and staff must also have a workable safety response plan prior to the meeting, allowing for an appropriate response with a minimum of confusion and delay.

Each Security Professional and staff member must be fully aware of their designated role in the overall safety plan, and possess the skills and training necessary to carry out their assigned duties. Inadequate staffing or poor planning for the situation you might be facing is a guaranteed formula to kindle people who are already on the edge. Individual security, professional limitations, or liabilities must be taken into account when preparing a safety plan and duties and responsibilities should be assigned accordingly. For instance, some Security Professionals may be better suited to being the designated "Communications Officer," responsible for establishing and maintaining effective communications with emergency responders or other agencies. In fact, having one Security Professional assigned to communications will lessen confusion and allow other team members to focus on their assigned tasks. Other Security Professionals may be much better suited toward the tactical and physical aspects of the response plan, such as the detention of aggressive individuals, or the establishment of physical site security pending the arrival of emergency responders.

Regardless of individual assignments, ongoing communication among Security Professionals and other employees must be considered one of the most vital aspects of office safety. Security Professionals have a responsibility to inform both their team and other employees of your company (the latter as needed to ensure safety) that a confrontation may occur when a particular individual reports to the office, or that a termination will be taking place. Of course, not all potential emergencies can be foretold, but many can be anticipated and an appropriate response can be planned accordingly.

A Security Professional or other member of your organization who anticipates an aggressive encounter should never "surprise" their co-workers with a last minute request for assistance *after* the individual has already been admitted into the office proper. Notifying other Security Professionals and staff as to the potential for an emergency situation takes but a moment, and can be accomplished while the individual remains in the reception area or before they arrive. Failure to do so is a guaranteed formula for escalating an otherwise manageable encounter into a critical event. Therefore:

- Alert staff to the possibility of an emergency and have intervention procedures in place.
- Work with Human Resources (HR) to set up the room both in the interests of safety and to best influence their behavior in the way that you desire. This includes making sure that there is an escape route and that there are people (Security) in earshot. HR might decide to choose a room with warm lighting or soft chairs, or on the contrary, you may choose to select a room that sets a formal tone, where you speak across a table, as if in a business meeting.
- Strategize how best to communicate the disturbing news to the person, based on HR and your collective knowledge of the individual. Be prepared to call law enforcement for assistance. If there is any concern that the employee may become violent, notify your local law enforcement agency *before* the meeting starts, so that a unit can either be in position or on patrol nearby, available in the event of an emergency.
- Consider who should be present in the room. The assigned Security Professional will follow the lead of HR or the manager, or direct the other Security Professionals in regard to the situation.
- If this is a potentially higher risk person, the manager or HR should not be in an undue hurry to conduct a termination or suspension. Engage the proper people to discuss the history of the person and prepare a proper risk assessment and plan for addressing the situation.
- Alert all relevant staff for the possibility of an emergency in any potentially high-risk situation and have intervention procedures already set up. In many situations have someone outside the room ready to initiate necessary emergency procedures.
- Consider the position of people in the room. Should the person be closest to the door to allow him/her to leave the room, or should Security be closest to the door to prevent the person from leaving? Either of these offers a set of risks that your contingency plan must address.
- If they will be escorted to their desk and then off the property, or directly off grounds, then the team should be assembled and advised of the reasons for the action, the individual's propensity for resistance, and who will be doing what in the room.

Depending on the location of your agency, that is rural versus urban, local police departments may not be able to quickly respond to requests for non-emergency assistance, In the event of a true emergency, staff must not hesitate to call 9-1–1.

Figure 3.3 Example: Things Can Go Wrong If Security Is Not Notified in Time

An employee made a number of threats towards his manager and HR. We were notified of all of this about one hour before his scheduled termination meeting that was to occur in his manager's office. We quickly met with HR to set up a safety plan for the termination and were going to the site, when the manager came running from around the side of the building yelling that the employee, 6'5" and approximately 400 pounds had a knife, and the HR manager was trapped with him.

We initiated conversation through the door and he wound up cutting his wrists in front of us. Police arrived, and he was taken into custody without further incident. (NOTE: The police plan was that if he did not surrender, they would stage paramedics, and wait until he passed out from loss of blood, and then render medical aid while securing him in restraints). Because things had been sprung on us, we were not prepared. Thankfully, no one was killed. **Proper planning protects lives!**

How To Enter a Room to Ascertain If There Is a Problem and How To Extricate Employees of the Company

The following list is given to help you in your planning for handling a difficult and possibly dangerous situation:

1. Let us imagine that you hear loud or threatening voices coming from an office, cubicle, or conference room.
2. If such behaviors are occurring, encourage the manager or HR to exit the room.
3. Security should then make themselves visible in an effort to mitigate the problem.
4. Security should not attempt to physically prevent the aggressive employee from leaving; the person should be escorted from the premises.
5. If the person threatens violence, police should be called.

The Five Ws: WHAT Kind of Information Do You Need When an Emergency Is Happening?

There is some information that is absolutely required when trying to assess threat level in any emergency. Therefore, the reporter of any crisis should find out:

1. **Where?** Get the location of where the incident is happening, and get the informant to tell you again! Absolutely nothing can be accomplished if emergency responders cannot reach the correct scene.
2. **What?** Always ensure that you know what is going on, and do not assume that the first thing the person tells you is the real story! History teaches us difficult lessons in some cases. For example, in dealing with witnesses, information tends to vary as the level of stress or urgency increases. Descriptions of people, activities, weapons, and the type of violence may be inconsistent, leading responders to a conclusion not necessarily accurate. It is important to listen to information being presented, at the same time understanding the circumstances under which it is being presented. *For example,*

one of the authors, in responding to a threat case by an employee, encountered multiple employees running towards him, screaming that the person was armed with a knife. The person had an unopened pocket-knife, and was holding it in his hand. To be sure, Security Professionals need to be aware that circumstances may be under reported as well. It is a function of awareness and maintaining composure.

3. **Who?** Be sure to find out everyone who is involved: those presenting a threat, those who are injured or victims, and others on the scene. As obvious and basic a statement as this may be, the irrational or confusing verbiage of mentally ill, confused, or agitated individuals can cause the person taking information to miss essential data.

4. **When?** When did the crisis happen: recently, currently, or is it about to happen? What level of urgency is present, drives decisions and actions.

5. **Weapons.** Concerning emergency responders' safety we must do everything necessary and possible to keep our police officers, firefighters, and EMTs safe. Questions about weapons and their locations, a history of violence, past or current threats to responders, drug or alcohol use, and any other potential dangers must be answered as fully as humanly possible.

Staying Calm by Being Prepared for the Worst

Do not shut your eyes to signs of danger. The calm of the professional is very different from the calm of the clueless person. You must be conscious of what the aggressor is doing and the likely meaning and implications of that. While you are trying to calm or soothe them, or while you are controlling the crisis remain conscious of the following:

- Where are your escape routes? Is something blocking your way out?
- Are there any obstacles, sharp corners or other hazards that you need to avoid?
- Are there any weapons around that can be used against you, or in the worst case, that you can pick up in your own defense?
- Is the person's aggressiveness escalating? If so, what is the proximate cause of their escalation and what mode of aggression are they moving into?
- Do they have allies, confederates who are waiting for you to get off-guard at which point they will join in the attack?
- What are your non-verbal behaviors? Are you getting mad too? If so, it is best to disengage or you will merely get very angry together and the situation could become explosive.
- Where is your "team?" Is other staff organizing to help you?

Calling the Police

Police should be called when anyone is at physical risk or when the aggressive individual is so disruptive that their behavior cannot be modulated and they are disrupting the activities of your facility. It is the Security Professional's responsibility to give as complete information as possible, including a description of the aggressor, their current location, whether they have weapons, and their current behavior and potential risk. Whenever possible, inform emergency responders of exactly what help you are requesting. You must understand that the police, as emergency responders in cases of potential danger, will take over to establish safety based on *their* assessment of risk at that moment.

Figure 3.4 Crisis Intervention Team/Training

One of the most exciting innovations in law enforcement in both America and Great Britain is the Crisis Intervention Training/Team (CIT) model, in which law enforcement officers get 40 or more hours of training on dealing with mentally ill individuals. In many law enforcement agencies, somewhere between 20-40 percent of the officers are CIT trained.

- If your local law enforcement agency has a CIT team, ensure that all members of your security team are familiar with its existence. If your local police do not have such a team, do some research, and lobby with the police agency to get such training made available for its officers.

- If there is a CIT team, always ask for a CIT officer when calling emergency dispatch in crisis situations with apparently mentally ill subjects. You are not guaranteed a response from a CIT officer: this depends on their availability at the time of the call. Nonetheless, always ask.

CHAPTER 4

Show-of-Force

A show-of-force is a mark of solidarity and protection. It establishes to the aggressive individual that they do not have the freedom to victimize anybody who is present at your agency. In essence, the participants in a show-of-force bear moral witness as well as standing ready to act protectively to assist the potential victim of violence or other aggression. <u>NOTE</u>: The Show-of-force is a procedure for ***unarmed***, aggressive individuals exclusively.[4]

Basic Criteria for Show-of-force

The maximum number of people involved in a show-of-force should be seven. When fewer than this number is available, the team must adapt so that they can best address some or all of the functions enumerated below. Tactics may vary if you have a uniformed security guard squad, who may or may not carry weapons or if the show-of-force will be manned by Security Professionals and perhaps other employees of your worksite. Below are some basic criteria for a show-of-force:

- One **Lead**, who is attempting to de-escalate the aggressive or agitated individual. This can be a Security Professional or other employee of the company.
- Up to four individuals who constitute the show-of-force, standing close, usually behind the Lead. One member of this team is the **Organizer**, who either calls the team together or guides them into position. The Organizer, too, can be a Security Professional, as may all members of the show-of-force. However, in some companies, some or all of these people may be (trained-in-show-of-force procedures) employees. In other situations, the Organizer and/or the rest of the team are uniformed security guards.
- **Perimeter Security Professional** who is responsible for the "environment." This can include clearing bystanders out of the area, moving furniture, and other hazards out of the way if, by chance, the other members have to restrain the aggressive person. The Organizer should assign one person to be "responsible for the environment."
- **Communications Officer**, who calls for emergency assistance. Here, too, this person could be a Security Professional, other employee, or security guard depending on your company's resources and protocols.
  a. In lower risk situations, this person stands close to a phone to call your standard emergency number (9-1-1 in the U.S. or equivalent number in your country) if the situation continues to escalate.
  b. In higher risk situations, this person calls 9-1-1 immediately, gives an address and exact location where the problem is occurring, as full a description as possible as to the circumstances—what the perpetrator looks like, who is involved in the situation, and if there are any weapons.

c. Larger numbers of people are not helpful. In fact, the likelihood of intervention to help a victim goes down as the number goes up beyond four or five. When too many people are in a crowd, there is a diffusion of responsibility: everyone looks to the others around them to know what to do. If you are in a group of ten people, and none of them are moving to intervene, it is very likely that you will not move either. This "crowd inertia" is the cause of many infamous incidents where a person is assaulted or even murdered with a myriad of onlookers standing by, none of them moving to help.

Your organization must also be keenly aware of its policies regarding application of force. Many corporate cultures forbid physical contact by security with any employee or visitor, requiring an "observe and report" operation, and calling the police when necessary. Of course, Security Professionals are allowed to defend themselves or others when attacked, but it is essential that Security Professionals know policy and local laws applicable to these circumstances.

Your organization must establish and train for whatever protocols are in place. At the time of an encounter, there is no time to create a sound plan under trying conditions. For example, in a corporate environment, the preparation and implementation of a "Security Assisted Termination Protocol," working with Legal, HR, and management, provides a consistent and defensible program. In addition, it provides provision for Security to conduct a pre-termination risk assessment and prepare accordingly. Unfortunately, in all too many cases, Security is given little to no notification of a termination, which occurs within minutes. This amplifies the need for an established procedure that all Security Professionals "switch on" and can follow comfortably.

Procedures for a Show-of-force

A Show-of-Force is a presentation of tactical strength in order to indicate to the potentially violent subject that you are a trained, coordinated team, prepared to act to establish a safe situation both for the potential victim of aggression and for your agency as a whole.

1. The situation starts when the Lead calls for help, or the Organizer, alerted that there is a problem, gathers the show-of-force team.
2. The Organizer is either the first person to become aware of the need for the show-of-force or the person delegated to lead. No matter what the person's position is within the agency, the Organizer's orders must be obeyed (unless, of course, they are dangerous or unethical).
3. The Team goes to the place of confrontation and lines up. Ideally, they are behind or to the side of their fellow worker. The team must not block the exit unless you and they are in a deliberately locked area (a locked unit in a hospital, for example), or the aggressor will present serious risk to others on the other side of the door. When not required to block the subject's departure, it is ideal for your team to angle themselves in such a way that they create an avenue indicating the exit. As noted earlier, we would not allow an aggressor to exit the office if you have arrived at when they are a danger to others. If they are allowed to leave, it is only because you have handled the situation and determined that it is reasonably safe to let them go, or that no charges will be filed, violations scheduled, etc.

4. Do not circle around the aggressor. They will feel surrounded and under attack. Furthermore, they will stop focusing on the Lead and what she/he is saying. When you encircle the aggressor, you are indicating that you have given up on a peaceful resolution.

5. Each member stands with the arms in front, one hand holding the *wrist* of their other arm. One foot should be in front, with the back foot angled somewhat out in a so-called "blade stance." Do not stand with your feet in a "T" or "L" stance: the back foot is off to the side, with about two fists between the heels on the east-west axis.

6. Your faces should be blank with your eyes staring distantly, as if you are wearing masks. The members of the show-of-force (other than the Lead, of course) look at the silhouette of the person, not into their eyes.

    a. Do NOT stand square: although appearing strong, it is weak. The smallest shove will unbalance you.

    b. Do not clasp your hands. In your nervousness or anxiety, you may begin to wring your hands. Remember: clasp one wrist with the other hand.

    c. Do not put your hands in your pockets (clueless), behind your back (clueless or hiding something) or cross your arms (confrontational).

    d. Do not let your hands hang at your sides. Again, if nervous or tense, you will begin to use your hands in unconscious movements to soothe or discharge tension.

7. The members of the show-of-force team present a united front, demonstrating that their fellow worker is not alone and that they *witness* what is going on. They must not respond verbally to the assailant, merely witness. **No matter how provocative the assailant is, no matter what ugly things he/she says, the participants in the show-of-force must not verbally respond, or even change facial expression.** If a participant does respond, that splits your strength and puts the perpetrator of aggression in firm control.

8. The Lead continues verbal de-escalation tactics.

    a. If the aggressor demands to know why "these people" are there, why they are listening in or violating his/her privacy, say calmly: "They are just here to keep things safe." Do not debate the aggressor about this. Redirect them to solving the problem at hand.

    b. As described above, if the aggressor attempts to split solidarity by abuse, verbal attacks, or threatening statements and gestures towards the show-of-force participants, the Lead must redirect the aggressor to communicate only with the Lead, continuing to try to de-escalate them. The Lead might say, using their name, "Kenneth, you are talking to me."

    c. Remember, direct eye contact on the part of the Lead, blank, almost mask-like faces on the part of the show-of-force. By standing in unison, you appear organized and trained. This is why everyone should clasp a wrist with the other hand and stand with the same blade-stance.

9. Whenever possible, the Lead keeps the lead. In other words, whoever is trying to de-escalate the person should continue to do so. There are, however, exceptions when someone needs to step in and take over:

    a. The Organizer should step in, tactfully, if the Lead is emotionally overwhelmed. This would most likely be the supervisor of the office or the senior Security Professional on scene.

b. If the Lead begins to act in an aggressive or unprofessional manner and is too involved to be aware of it, the person present who has the most authority (be it institutional or the respect of the embattled Lead) should step in tactfully. <u>This requires training and trust</u>. There must be an institution-wide agreement that such intervention will be respected. *Effective training of all staff will make this the most rare of occasions.* If you do not want someone stepping in this manner, you must ensure that you have participated in and understood centering and de-escalation procedures fully.

c. The Lead should hand-over the role in certain circumstances voluntarily. The best "trade-off" of responsibility is that initiated by the Lead rather than when the Organizer sees a situation falling apart and *must* take over. When should the Lead pass the interactive role to another?

 i. When the Lead is aware that the individual has a special rapport with one person in the vicinity. One must be careful here, however. If one hands the Lead role over to the aggressor's "favorite" person automatically, your staff can be enmeshed in an individual's manipulative game-playing. For a "hand over" to occur, the overall situation and everyone's safety must *demand* it. It is not enough that the aggressive individual simply likes someone else better.

 ii. The Lead should hand over the responsibility to de-escalate the aggressive individual when the Lead is aware that they are becoming angry or otherwise becoming so flooded or overwhelmed that effective interaction with the aggressive person is no longer possible.

 iii. If the aggressor is focused <u>absolutely</u> on one person as the source of their grievance, and the entire situation is centered on their ramping up to assault them, it is sometimes a good idea to remove that targeted person from the scene.

 iv. In the event that another party intervenes, the Lead MUST step back and hand over the Lead role. If there is a disagreement with the intervention, the Lead must bring it up in a post-crisis staffing after the incident is over. Particularly if the Lead is angry, he/she will be the last person to acknowledge their lost temper. By definition, anger justifies itself. **No matter what the Lead's perspective, the agency requirement must be that if someone "steps in," the Lead "steps back."**

What happens next?

A confrontation necessitating a Show-of-Force can result in a variety of outcomes.

- On many occasions, the individual will leave: sometimes quietly, sometimes yelling threats or cursing. This does not always happen.
- In some milieu, the team will shift to physical restraint tactics. These tactics require hands-on training and will not be outlined here.
- **If the individual attacks the Lead or anyone else, of course, you should assist your co-worker. You have a moral responsibility to help protect them.**
- When police arrive, one person, usually the Lead or the Organizer, will brief police on what is happening. Be sure to inform the police clearly what it is you wish to accomplish, be it a trespass warning, an arrest, simple assistance in calming someone down, getting the person to the hospital, reporting a crime, etc. To reiterate, you must understand that police *will* take over from this point.

When NOT To Enact a Show-of-force

If the aggressor is brandishing a weapon, in particular, a gun, knife, or other lethal instrument, staff should <u>not</u> execute a show-of-force. A gun or a knife conveys an almost "godlike" status to the wielder. With a single gesture, they can take life.

The standard protocol with an armed aggressor is to clear the building or go into lock-down status (doors-locked and barricaded). The choice of what to do is driven by your ability to escape. ***Call the police***, and give an accurate, detailed description of the subject, the address, the subject's current location, and what weapons the subject has. Also alert emergency dispatch if any of your team have weapons, what they are, and include a description of those team members.

A show-of-force to an armed individual simply offers up your staff as hostages. To make matters worse, the more hostages the more dangerous it is for everyone. Most hostage takers injure or kill their victims because of heightened anxiety or other stressors. Given that a large group of people is harder to control, the hostage taker may, panic-stricken viciously hurt or murder one of the hostages to control the others.

As odd as this may sound, escape or lock-down is the right way to make the hostage safer. The armed individual, feeling in control, is less likely to attack his/her single hostage, than they would if they had a group of hostages.

The purpose of security at this point is to follow the ICE (Isolate, Contain, and Evacuate) convention:

- **Isolate.** Isolate the situation to as small an area as possible, allow police to focus on a reduced area to manage.
- **Contain.** Try to contain the incident to a single building or location; the smaller the area, the easier it is for police to deploy and contain it.
- **Evacuate.** Security's responsibility is evacuation of as many people from the location as possible. It is important that Security Professionals be aware of locations and risks as evacuation is occurring. Security Professionals should not place themselves at higher risk where avoidable. Instruct people evacuating where they should assemble, and remember that with a person using a weapon, distance is preferable.

Be aware that other employees or bystanders may attempt to intervene, trying to be helpful. Isolating and containing means what it says: once out, no one should be allowed in. The police will be there quickly and will both appreciate the fact that you have isolated the event and the fact that you have not allowed it to become more complicated by letting others into the scene.

If trustworthy employees are available, Security may utilize them to help control the perimeter established to protect the scene. <u>They must be given very specific directions as to what to do, and clear instruction on what is not allowed</u>. Most people will help in the ways asked of them.

SECTION II

Honing Intuition

CHAPTER 5

Training Your Intuition
to Pick Up Danger

Intuition is that small voice to which professionals must listen. Such "gut feelings" are sometimes vague, but they are often the *first* signs that a dangerous situation is developing.

- Security Professionals should not minimize their gut feelings and intuitions when exchanging information. Do not begin by stating "I know it's nothing, but…." In doing so, the Security Professional may lead others to minimize the situation as well.

- Security Professionals should not be hesitant because they do not have "hard evidence" to support their concern(s).

- Veteran Security Professionals or senior staff members, who *claim* to have the most experience, may sometimes belittle other professionals or support staffs' intuitions of danger. The old biker adage springs to mind here; "If you have not been in an accident yet, you will be. And if you have, you will be again." Even the most senior Security Professional has not experienced every possible contingency.

- Differences among Security Professionals and staff must be discussed respectfully, particularly in regard to questions of safety. A security team may be an environment in which humor, occasionally rough humor, is part of the day-to-day routine. However, this should never contaminate safety issues. In many circumstances, each person has only part of the picture. If one person's idea or intuition is discounted or dismissed out of hand, he/she may cease to speak up, and vital information regarding everyone's security will be lost.

Figure 5.1 Author's Example: Lifesaving Intuition

I once visited a home, and something inside me, very powerfully, ordered me not to knock on the door and to retreat to my car. I returned to the office, and wrote in the homeowner's new chart (she had been referred by her concerned landlord) in huge red letters "Something is wrong. Do not go to this house without police back-up." As unprofessional as my supervisor deemed this note, it had to remain in the chart, as state law required that no chart note be destroyed. Thankfully, a co-worker heeded my "irrational" advice, and several days later, she and the police found a floridly psychotic woman behind the door. She simply opened the door and handed the lead police officer a loaded handgun.

As we later found out, in a previous psychotic episode, she had been attacked by two men intent on raping and murdering her. She held them off with a gun and was eventually rescued by police. Now, some years later and again in a psychotic, paranoid state, she was waiting with her gun, having seen me approach the house. It is probable that only my <u>not</u> knocking on the door saved my life. When my co-worker went to the house with her rescuers—that is how the woman viewed police, she willingly turned over the weapon. What did I perceive? Was it a stirring of the curtains, a soft click of the bolt of an automatic weapon being pulled back, or was it ESP? To be honest, I don't care. What matters is that I, and anyone I work with, respect such intuitive commands.

LESSON: If it does not look or feel safe for any reason, even vague intuition, DO NOT attempt to make a contact alone. Retreat, regroup, and go back with others.

Honing Your Skills: How to Assess your Personal Workspace

A sense of spatial awareness, of potential escape routes, likely weapons, and access to help should become a natural part of the Security Professional's personal and professional life. This routine attentiveness is often referred to as "having street smarts;" however, the truth is that some folks are naturally street smart, and others are not. This applies equally to Security Professionals and individuals. The next two chapters offer a method to teach Security Professionals to pick up danger on an intuitive level, if that is not something that comes naturally to you. You somehow need to gain insight into the thinking patterns of an aggressive individual when he enters your territory or when you enter his.

Awareness of escape routes, potential weapons, and access to getting help should be as natural to you as to a deer or elk that surveys a valley for predators before entering open space. Considerations in a work-environment must go beyond practical questions such as what objects you will place on your desk and where you decide to put your chair. Use a tactic known as "shape-shifting" to get insight into the intentions and planning of a potentially aggressive individual by entering the room in his state of mind.

- Enter a room with a predator's mind and a predator's movements: slowly, gracefully, with calculation. Imagine that you are going to hurt the next person who comes in that room. How would you cut off their escape routes? What could you use as a weapon? Where would you position yourself to attack? Where could your victim best escape?
- The point of this exercise is that when you move like someone, you get insight into their way of thinking from the inside out. Moving in the same manner as a predator or other aggressor (you can use any of the aggressive styles described later in this book) enhances your ability see the world through their eyes. If you are in the habit of noting potential danger (items that can be thrown, sharp objects, etc.), you will have a far greater likelihood of avoiding harm when it is offered.
- Do this on a regular basis. Consider it a refresher course on the mind of a predator. Done over time, you will start to develop the ability to automatically scan any room to see if there is any-

thing there which makes it a place of danger, as well as switching your mind on to picking up predatory or other dangerous behaviors on the part of individuals.

Figure 5.2 Author's Example: Scanning Surroundings Saves Lives

I entered the apartment of an elderly woman, reportedly demented. She began screaming at me to get out, but my job as a mental health assessor required me to be there. The apartment was not messy, but it was filled with all sorts of small objects, the collection of about 80 years of living. My eyes picked up something sticking out of a beaded curtain across the room. I walked quickly over, past the woman, and found two large butcher knives jammed into the window frame. I pulled them out and put them on top of a cabinet, telling the woman I'd return them when I left.

As it turned out, she was acutely psychotic, and believed that she was being harassed by Satan. She decided that Satan would come in the front door, so she planned to back up to the curtain, grab her knives and disembowel the "Lord of Darkness." My habit of scanning, trained through the above exercise, very likely saved me and an accompanying social worker from a very difficult situation.

CHAPTER 6

The Texture of Relationship:
Intuition in Action

Communicating with hostile or mentally ill individuals is often difficult, particularly when they are becoming agitated. Suppression of all anger should not be your goal. Security Professionals must develop the ability to differentiate between true aggression, with the very real possibility of physical attack, as opposed to allowing the individual to get something off their chest: expressing their frustration with the company, their personal difficulties, concerns about retirement, transfer or outplacement, and the like, all while remaining ready to respond to a physical confrontation.

While there is no sure fire method of predicting future behaviors (such as an impending attack), the information gleaned from your threat assessment (Chapter 2) plus an awareness of "tells" that the individual is exhibiting in the moment, will enable the Security Professional to reasonably predict the likelihood of the individual escalating to physical aggression. The manifest behaviors of aggressive individuals will be discussed in detail in the latter sections of this book: this chapter will focus on developing the ability to *sense* when a potential aggressor is beginning to escalate.

Comfort Zones and Physical Spacing

Agitated people lose the ability to accurately listen to what you are saying, much less maintain a coherent train of thought in their own right. Instead, they will be tracking other aspects of communication: your muscular tension, the amount of physical space between you, the positioning of your hands, and the quality of your voice. <u>You should be doing the same!</u>

As the individual becomes more agitated, the Security Professional must take care to remain calm and prepare mentally for the possibility of a physical confrontation, while simultaneously maintaining focus on verbally de-escalating the situation. **Most importantly, do not feed the anger!** This is a trap that many Security Professionals fall into during a confrontation. It only makes the situation worse. <u>Most people cannot sustain their anger for more than a couple of minutes, so if you can keep your composure you can maintain control.</u>

Although the basic emotions are physically expressed in pretty definitive ways, irrespective of culture,[5] non-verbal behaviors can be idiosyncratic: not only do people often have their own ways of physically expressing their emotions, but they also have their own ways of interpreting (or misinterpreting) yours. It is not enough, therefore, to learn a list of the typical behaviors that aggressive people are likely to display. Security Professionals must also hone their intuition to detect subtle warning signs that a dangerous situation is developing. The leading edge, so to speak, of intuition, is a sense of personal space. This is not just a matter of feet and inches. Simply asserting that you keep an arm's length and a half, or two arms length apart between you and a subject is not enough. How much space would you want if the person has a blade, or is twice your size, and half your age? How about if they are wearing a strong cologne, or simply smell bad?

Our attitude can also affect our sense of space. For example, the more relaxed you are in the company of someone you trust, the less personal space you require, something that manipulative aggressors try to take advantage of. When you are uncertain or suspicious of someone, you instinctively move to get more distance from them. If you are having a bad day, you need more space to tolerate anyone's proximity.

Figure 6.1 Two Cautions Concerning Personal Space
1. DO NOT knowingly step inside someone's personal space, unless doing so helps you establish a clear tactical advantage.
2. DO NOT accommodate anyone by allowing them to stand too close to you.

You MUST be aware of the physical sensations of someone in your "zone." When you set such a limit as "Sir, I very much wish to hear what you have to say, but you are standing too close to me. Move back five feet and then we will continue to talk." The reply you get will be great threat assessment information. You are dealing with very different individuals when one, told to step back, responds with profuse apologies compared to someone who smirks and says, "What's the matter, are you nervous around men?"

This is especially true for uniformed Security Professionals as people who take these actions may have a specific intent in mind and are challenging the Security Professional to see what their reaction might be.

The Brain Wants to Survive

There are parts of the brain that are solely concerned with survival. These parts of the brain do not care about being polite, politically correct, or intellectualizing why someone is the way they are. These parts of the brain do not use words. They perceive by recognizing significant patterns, and signal their recognition through physical sensations and reactions. The survival section of the brain is fast, about half a second faster than the thinking brain. About to step on a squiggly shape on the ground, the adrenaline hits and you jerk back your foot even before the rest of your brain thinks, "SNAKE!"

Interpersonal space has a kind of "texture" that we perceive through both physical and emotional reactions. One trains intuition through becoming more aware of the signals your body sends to you. Paradoxically, many of us get "skilled" at tuning out those signals, treating them as a kind of unwanted "noise." Being mindful of the space between you and others can give you an early warning system that a situation is becoming potentially explosive.

Thus, if someone is aggressive, psychotic, excited, depressed, menacing, hateful, or is trying to con you—any "strong" interaction—the survival brain recognizes a pattern in what they are doing, and reacts. For example, when in proximity to the scared person, perhaps you feel warmth in your chest, but with the con-man, your lips compress and neck tightens. With psychotic people, you feel a sensation of cold in your stomach and your hands and jaw clench with aggressive people. There are no rules to these physical reactions: they are individual to you. Another individual would experience different physical reactions to the same person.

Some of your physical reactions may be unpleasant or unflattering to your own self-image. For example, let us imagine that you get somewhat sick to your stomach when facing an aggressive person, or experience a subtle, but real sense of revulsion when dealing with someone who is depressed. You do **not** need to change this reaction. When you are a person of integrity, your feelings and emotions convey information, but they do not *demand* that you act. For example, you are talking with an individual and you notice that previously mentioned sense of revulsion. Although he is smiling, perhaps talking fast, you know that this physical sensation happens to you very often when dealing with depressed and despairing individuals. So you shift the conversation to assess if he is depressed, because a sense of hopelessness and helplessness, the hallmarks of that state of mind, can lead to either suicidal or homicidal thoughts.

If you continue to hone your awareness in this matter, you will develop a form of conscious intuition called **MINDFULNESS**. Mindfulness is the ability to be consciously aware of what is going on in your interactions with another person.

Figure 6.2 Honing Intuition

It is very easy to train yourself to become more mindful. Carry a small notebook in your pocket. If you encounter an individual who interacts with you in a significant way (aggressive, manipulative, depressed, etc.), note down (later) how your body reacts.

IMPORTANT NOTE: We should be far more concerned with physical sensations than what we normally refer to as "feelings," our description of emotional states. For example, you have a sensation of high energy, with tension in your stomach. Some would call this "anxiety," while others would call this "anticipation." If you think that a sense of anxiety does not "fit" the situation you are in, you will tend to ignore the physical sensation. If, on the other hand, you merely associate a physical sensation with a situation, for example, "Every time someone tries to con me, I get a little smile and tension in my neck." You will notice your physical reactions without biasing them based on what you *think* you should feel.

Where these reactions really come in handy is when someone is trying to hide their intentions: smiling, for example, while trying to get close to you to stab you. Let's say, in this case, it is a woman whom you helped when her baby choked on food in the corporate lunchroom. Your "thinking mind" tells you, "She wouldn't want to hurt me! I saved her baby's life!" But your eyes are tightening and you are getting the same tension in your lower back that you have had on every occasion when someone has assaulted you in the past. Don't talk yourself out of it! Danger – and a very sharp point – is about to hit you right in the gut. ***By taking notes on sensations, you are training yourself to consciously recognize the patterns that your survival brain notices on a subconscious level.*** Instead of assuming: "I was having a lucky day. Something told me not to knock on that door," you say, "I had that feeling in my hands I always get right before a fight. I knew something was going to happen, so I went around the back, looked in the window and saw him standing behind the door with a glass paperweight."

Figure 6.3 Author's Example: What happens when you do not respect your intuition?

An individual once thanked me profusely at the end of my encounter with him. Instead of the warm pride I get when I've helped someone (and I HAD helped him), I had a very strong reaction that I always have when someone overtly threatens me. I mentally brushed it aside, thinking, I'm being an idiot. The man just complimented me." Sometime later, he poisoned me. I am only alive today because he chose to degrade me by contaminating my food rather than putting something lethal in it. I learned in the most ugly way possible to always pay attention to what my body "tells" me.

As we wrote above, the body is linked to the most primitive areas of the brain structures that serve to protect us from danger through pattern recognition rather than verbal cognitions. To treat our bodily reactions with disrespect is to disavow that which has kept humanity alive for eons.

SECTION III

Centering

CHAPTER 7

Introduction to Centering

Some security work presents higher risk than others. Interacting with people who may be mentally ill, drug dependent, victims of traumatic events, struggling with developmental disabilities, brain injuries, and personality disorders, poverty and a lack of education, or simply bad luck can be an honorable calling. You may occasionally be in daily contact with the most unfortunate members of society, as well as the most virulently anti-social individuals.

Such work can also be terribly demanding. Being frightened, confused, or intimidated by an individual can be debilitating and can easily lead to poor decision-making. Even more troubling is the realization that your reactions to the individual sometimes make things worse. Internalizing feelings of frustration can lead to burnout, a state of being which could be summed up in the phrase, "I don't want to see any more of this." Burnout can cause you to not pay attention, at moments when awareness is most necessary.

Nonetheless, Security Professionals can find such work rewarding, and even thrive in the midst of it. The strategies in the following chapters of this section revolve around maintaining self-control. This is also about mentoring other Security Professionals. Mastering methods of self-control is a way for you to role model proper behavior to others. This is the ability to adapt to circumstances in a powerful, fluid, and purposeful way. Not only will this make you more able to roll with the seemingly never-ending problems that aggressive and mentally ill individuals present, on both a personal and systems level, but also it will make you more effective in crisis situations.

Figure 7.1 Centering: It Is All About Tactics

Given that this section includes tactical breathing methods and an awareness of triggers that an aggressor could use to set you off-balance, we have been concerned that some Security Professionals might interpret this as "touchy-feely" stuff. It's not. Consider the Security Professional that approaches the office of one of the managers, hearing loud voices and a hand slamming on a desk. The secretary informs the Security Professional that an employee with a long-standing grievance has marched into the office without an appointment. The Security Professional uses breathing methods to stay absolutely calm so that he/she can accomplish the task. Or consider an individual screaming at the receptionist at the front desk and you are running down the hall to protect her, all the while using a tactical breathing method so that you are ready for anything (and breathing smoothly!) when you arrive on the scene.

Pretty much all of the tactics in this book are dependent on being centered. You can say all the right things, but if you are not "lined up right," they will be of no use.

So we will keep it here. Remember, given that the aggressor, be they mentally ill or not, is potentially attacking you, the more control you have over "you," the more certain you will do the right thing to create peace in the situation, and the more certain your victory in the event that it becomes physical.

CHAPTER 8

The Power of Gravity

"*No matter what, I have all the time I need*" is the basic rule of crisis intervention. Think back to the days when you learned to drive. Remember how it seemed impossible to look toward the horizon while noting in your periphery what might run into you on the street, while using the same foot for the brake and the accelerator, while shifting in proper sequence, while wishing your passenger would *STOP TALKING AND DISTRACTING you,* so that you could concentrate! But now that you are an experienced driver, you can do all these activities at once, and you feel as if you have all the time in the world to carry them out.

When you are facing a person in crisis, *they* believe that there is no time and no hope to solve the problem. If you agree, you are part of the crisis. You must have an attitude that you have all the time you need to find an answer to the problem, no matter what. Whether the other person agrees or not is not the question. The answer must start within you.

This is not merely a cliché to help you stave off anxiety. With this attitude, you become a person of "gravity." You embody the force that draws the universe into form. Considered this way, can you see how powerful a quiet confident stance can be, and how profoundly you can affect the other person?

CHAPTER 9

A Fair Witness:
Peer Support Is a Survival Tactic

There may be nothing worse than feeling helpless or shamed after experiencing a physical or emotional attack. This is especially so in security work, because if an individual is verbally aggressive or even physically violent toward us, our own professional pride is violated as well. One often feels terribly alone when under assault, even with others present. This sense of isolation gets far worse if there is no one with whom we can discuss what happened to us. Who can Security Professionals talk to that will understand and sympathize with their experiences? Some of the things that most powerfully affect Security Professionals are so ugly that they are reluctant to discuss them in detail with their spouses or other family members. To do so would be inviting violence or obscenity into their home, and Security Professionals do not wish to pass the burden of grief or horror on to a loved-one.

When you find yourself in such circumstances, you need **fair witnesses**, people, often fellow Security Professionals, who know you, who respect you, and who are willing to hear you out. Such peer support can include strategizing sessions, (debriefings) or tactical reviews, but we must underscore that there are times that these are the last things you need. Part of the culture of a well-run security team is an ongoing, informal level of peer support: when one or another Security Professional runs into difficulty, he/she knows that they can approach another Security Professional, or sometimes supervisor, to talk through the incident.

To some of our readers, this chapter may seem far from a discussion on safety, but when we talk about someone "getting our back," it does not only mean that they are with us while going through the door. If we do not have an assurance that someone will be there after we come back out, it's a lot harder to go through the doorway in the first place.

Critical Incident Response Teams for High-Intensity Work Environments

Some companies that work in high intensity environments would do well to formalize the fair witness process to prepare for "critical incidents." This term designates an extraordinary event that forces a Security Professional to face vulnerability and mortality during the course of their official duties. These incidents typically occur without warning, and jeopardize one's physical safety or emotional well-being. Incidents such as being victimized in an assault or engaging an individual in a lethal force encounter can overwhelm the Security Professional's stress capacity. A prompt and structured departmental response by a Critical Incident Response Team (CIRT) can reduce the negative consequences of such incidents and help restore the affected Security Professional's physical and mental health.

CIRT members (CIR: Critical Incident Responders) are fellow Security Professionals who are trained to respond to critical events within the agency, and provide the affected Security Professional with emotional support and assistance. In the event of an emergency, CIR report to the scene as soon as possible where they will assess the Security Professional's physical and mental condition, request that emergency medical services and police be dispatched to the scene if necessary, or serve as a liaison to law enforcement and other first responders already present. The CIR will also accompany the affected Security Professional to the hospital if necessary and attend to any number of related duties, such as contacting the Security Professional's family.

Following the incident, CIR will consult regularly with the affected Security Professional's immediate supervisor and recommend services (counseling, for example) for the individual as deemed necessary and appropriate. They will also assist with any necessary paperwork that must be completed by the affected Security Professional. Typically, the CIR will contact the affected Security Professional once a week for at least one month following the incident, and remain in contact with them until they are confident that the affected Security Professional's physical and emotional needs have been addressed.

Figure 9 The Debate Concerning Documentation in CIRT

Some CIRT protocols recommend submitting a critical incident report to the administrative unit for the purpose of collecting information necessary to provide short and long-term assistance to the affected Security Professional, as well as documenting activities, services, and progress.

A potential problem can be that although this report is not intended to be used as an investigative tool, it can be. As an official record, it may also be subpoenaed in a lawsuit or other legal proceeding. Therefore, many CIRT protocols recommend that nothing should be put in writing. This helps the affected Security Professional feel like he/she can talk more freely. Written records should be confined to formal after-action reviews.

On the other hand, a written report by the CIR can function for the Security Professional, making a case for counseling, medical leave, or other services without those in headquarters feeling like they must interview the professional as well. Agencies should weigh both options and come to a decision regarding this point.

CHAPTER 10

It Is Not Personal
Unless You Make It So

Security Professionals must take care to not personalize any disagreements or altercations with individuals no matter what the provocation. Responding to an individual, perhaps mentally ill, on a personal or emotional level will cloud a Security Professional's judgment, while distracting him/her from legitimate safety concerns.

We believe ourselves justified when counter-attacking, because they "hurt us first." What we forget is that a defensive reaction or move towards revenge is also a manifestation of an attempt to assert dominance over the other. When people hurt your feelings because of what they say or do, remember that <u>it is an act of valor not to respond in kind</u>.

At any rate, although their attacks on you might *seem* personal, that is only true if you make them so. If the attack is untrue, what is there to be upset about? And if what the individual said is valid, then you are reacting in anger when someone tells you the truth. You knew it anyway, so what are you upset about?
- They call you fat? Well, you knew that already, didn't you?
- They called you a Nazi? Well, you aren't, so why are you taking it personally?

Security Professionals must also remember that personal feelings of revenge, of "getting even," are unacceptable in the true professional, and your actions must be the result of unbiased decision-making, based on the facts at hand. Individuals cannot be sanctioned simply because of a personal vendetta or hurt feelings, and recommendations to your company at any sanctioning proceedings must be relevant to the individual's actual behaviors.

Some people use obscenity and verbal violation to get you focused on what they are saying rather than what they are doing. Others are just spewing nasty verbalizations and suddenly realize that you, upset at what they just said, have lost focus and are open to attack. Still others suddenly perceive in your response to what they said that you have lost your composure and they "attack you first," because they believe you are about to react.

Others challenge you by trying to offend you or by making you explain yourself. Provocative challenges are for the purpose of getting leverage on you.

No One Will Own Me

The verbal aggressor is trying to "push your buttons," often in an attempt to elicit an unprofessional or off-centered reaction. As previously described, the brain is organized to respond to danger through pattern-recognition. A large object moving rapidly towards us, a sudden pain, or a violent grab initiates a cascade of responses—fight/flight/ freeze/faint—that are geared to keep us alive in the worst of circumstances. At lower levels of danger, particularly that presented by another human being, we are provoked into posturing—dominance/submission displays—that serve to maintain or enhance our position in a social structure.

The curse of being human, however, is that these survival responses are precipitated by any noxious stimuli, particularly those that shock or surprise us. When someone unexpectedly violates our sense of right and wrong or verbally assaults us, we often respond by automatically shifting into those aforementioned primitive responses, even when survival is not truly an issue. ***When our buttons are pushed, we react as if we are threatened with bodily harm.*** When this happens, we end up losing our dignity and our integrity, a reaction that ill-serves the Security Professional at establishing effective control of the aggressive subject.

Bracketing: Naming Your Hot Buttons

Anything that puts you off-balance puts you at risk. Therefore, it is important that you are aware of what your buttons are. Beyond that, use a technique called ***bracketing*** to make it harder if not impossible for others to even get to your buttons. Bracketing is a technique that entails facing your vulnerabilities head on, so that no one can use them against you. It takes guts to examine yourself and say, "Here are my weak spots." Doing so however, will give you greater strength. Not doing so will make you more vulnerable to attack.

You might think that a fair witness could be of great assistance in helping you to stay truthful and strong. However, talking about such difficult issues with another person often results in them, reframing the "bad" as "not so bad," or giving you an excuse to explain why you are the way you are. To really identify your vulnerabilities, Security Professionals must face the worst without the refuge of a comforting friend or witness.

Here's a worksheet that can help you name and bracket your own hot buttons. (You can make a photocopy to work on it separate from the book). Some example statements may include:

- I can't stand it when someone attacks or demeans < >, because that's something I love and treasure.
- I feel outraged when someone demeans < > because it is something I believe to be unquestionably right and good.
- People get me defensive when they say or point out < >, because, to tell the truth, I hate it in myself. (or, it is a flaw . . .).
- When people say or do < >, I lose it because it's as if they are taking control of me, or disrespecting me.
- They better not say < >. That's the one word I won't take from anyone.

Statement	Why Does this Get to Me?
EXAMPLE: When people say or do < >, I lose it because it's as if they are taking control of me, or disrespecting me.	

Taking Inventory

Not surprisingly, we are most likely to lose our temper (our flexibility and strength) when we are blind-sided. Sudden emotional shock elicits the same responses in the nervous system as a physical attack. For example, if someone you trust suddenly insulted your race, religion or gender, it is very likely that you will shift into a response using those parts of your brain—the limbic system—that expresses raw emotions. The limbic system is not concerned about the truth, about negotiation, or how to make peace. Instead, it views the world as one at war with the other person trying to destroy one's position of strength.

To avoid this, you must do the equivalent of checking your kit before going out into the field. **Every morning, upon waking, and maybe even a few times during the day, simply run an inventory, as if flipping through a set of cards, and call to mind each of your emotional triggers.** By bringing them to consciousness, you prepare yourself for the possibility that someone may try to set you off that day. Some people might find this sort of inventory depressing, but this is no more valid than complaining about being required to check your mirrors before backing out of your driveway. When an aggressor tries to push one of your buttons, you are not surprised or caught off guard. You expect it without being anxious about it. If you take inventory, you center yourself for another day, ready for the worst without it tearing you down.

Figure 10 The Power of Bracketing

One of our Security Professionals, who had taken this training, is of Samoan ancestry. He encountered an extremely irate customer, who came into the building, demanding to speak to the CEO. As our Security Professional attempted to help him and calm him down, the man began berating the Security Professional, calling him a variety of names, a number of which were slurs on his ancestry. The Security Professional, who had practiced bracketing to specifically deal with his protective pride regarding his heritage kept his cool, and was able to calm the man down, and actually provide the help he was seeking (without him getting to see the CEO, of course).

CHAPTER 11

Circular Breathing:
Be the Eye in the Center of the Hurricane

Aggression and violence can smash through a previously peaceful day with the suddenness and force of a hurricane. Chaos does not only take over the day; it may take you over too. However, when you can respond by stepping coolly into the worst of situations, you embody the eye of the hurricane, with all the chaos coalescing and revolving around you. The root of this skill lies in breath control. Using a method called "circular breathing," where you breathe slowly, with focused attention, you regain control of your physical self. When you control your body, you control your life. Then you are in a position to take control of the crisis as well as the person causing it.

Figure 11.1 Author's Experience

Lest there be any confusion: This is NOT a "time-out" where you take a few deep breaths and then return to the subject, refreshed. That is ridiculous. You can be moving very fast while breathing very slowly. You are training your body and mind to go into this breathing as a response to danger and stress, a trained response that should be instantaneous.

As someone who has practice the following technique for over 30 years, I can assert that it has become automatic. Unlike my younger days when the adrenalin would hit and I would start breathing fast and high in the chest, now my breathing usually slows down in emergency situations.

You are practicing to develop a "pseudo-instinct"—a trained response so bone-deep that you do not even have to think about it, anymore than you have to tell yourself to yank your hand from a hot stove.

Two Variations

Circular breathing is derived from East Asian martial traditions and was used to keep warriors calm on the battlefield. There are two variations. Try both, alternating between them, until you know which one works best for you. From that point on, exclusively practice the one you prefer. ***If you train regularly, it will kick in automatically, rather than being something you must think about.*** In essence, your breath itself becomes your center: not your body posture, not the situation in which you find yourself, or whatever is going on between you and the aggressor.

Circular Breathing Method #1: Initial Practice Method

- Sit comfortably, feet on the floor, hands in your lap.
- Sit relaxed, but upright. Do not slump or twist your posture.
- Keep your eyes open. (As you practice, so you will do. If you practice with your eyes closed, your newly trained nervous system will send an impulse to close your eyes in emergency situations. If you want to use a breathing method for closed-eye guided imagery or relaxation to get *away* from your problems, so to speak, use another method altogether).
- Breathe in through the nose.
- Imagine the air traveling in a line down the front of your body to a point 2 inches below the navel.
- Momentarily pause, letting the breath remain in a dynamic equilibrium.
- As you exhale, imagine the air looping around your lower body, between your legs and up through the base of your spine.
- Continue to exhale, imagine the air going up your spine and around your head and then out of your nose.

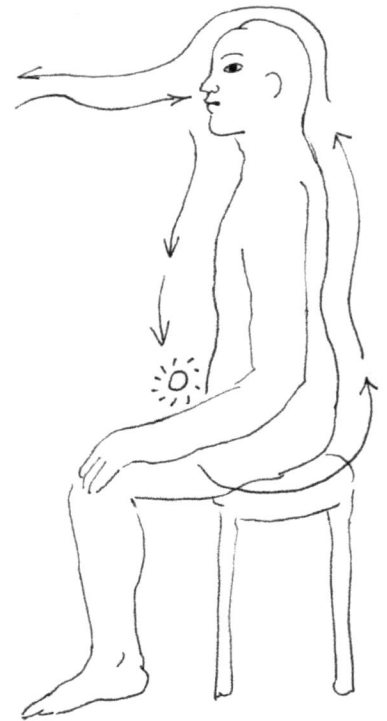

Circular Breathing Method #2: Initial Practice Method

- Sit comfortably, feet on the floor, hands in your lap.
- Sit relaxed, but upright. Do not slump or twist your posture.
- Keep your eyes open. (As you practice, so you will do. If you practice with your eyes closed, your newly trained nervous system will send an impulse to close your eyes in emergency situations. If you want to use a breathing method for closed-eye guided imagery or relaxation – to get *away* from your problems, so to speak – use another method altogether).
- Breathe in through the nose.
- Imagine the air going up around your head, looping down the back, falling down each vertebra, continuing down past the base of the spine to the perineum, and looping again, this time up the front of the body to a point 2 inches below the navel.
- Momentarily pause, letting the breath remain in a dynamic equilibrium.
- As you exhale, imagine the air ascending up the centerline of your body and out your nose.

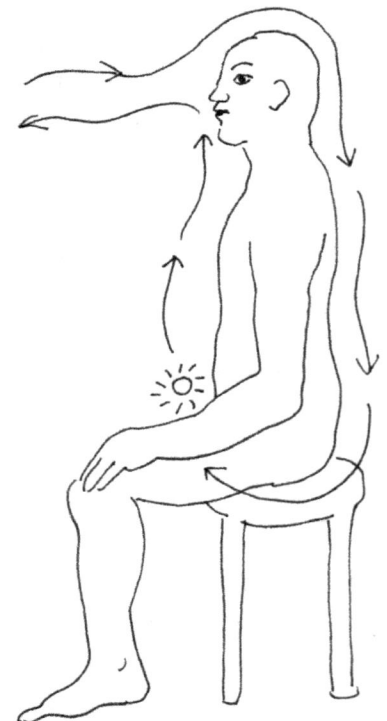

How to Practice Circular Breathing

Some people find that imagining their breath has light or color is helpful. Others take a finger or object to trace a line down and around the centerline of the body to help focus their attention. Again, choose which of the variations works best for you.

When you first practice, do so while seated and balanced. Once you develop some skill, try circular breathing standing, leaning, or even while driving. Most people find that after a short period of time they do not need to visualize the circulation of the breath. You literally will feel it, a ring of energy running through your body. You begin to feel balanced and ready for anything.

Once you are comfortable with your chosen pattern of breathing, experiment with it in slightly stressful circumstances, like being caught in traffic, dealing with an angry individual demanding to pass security without a security check, or sitting through a meeting as a supervisor drones on about new paperwork requirements. When you can better manage yourself in these slightly aggravating or anxiety-provoking situations, you will naturally shift into this mode of breathing when a crisis hits. There will no longer be a need to tell yourself to "do" circular breathing. It will become reflexive, automatic, replacing old patterns of breathing that actually increased anxiety or anger within you.

Remember, this is a skill to be used during emergencies, not for relaxation or meditative purposes. Instead, you are trying to enhance that ability to do whatever is needed: to fight, to dodge, to leave, to think gracefully and intelligently, whatever is required for the situation at hand.

When should you use circular breathing?

The way you organize physically affects your thinking. For example, if you assume the posture and breathing of a depressed person (slumped body, shallow breathing, sighing), and maintain it awhile, you will actually start to feel depressed. Similarly, if you clench your fists, and start glaring around you with a lot of tension in your body, you will start to feel angry. (You have probably observed a number of individuals working themselves up from anger through rage into an attack in just this way.) Similarly circular breathing creates its own mindset, one adaptable and ready for anything, equally prepared for an easy conversation and for a fight, yet fixed on neither.

This method of breathing is very helpful when you are anticipating a potentially dangerous situation, anything from walking down a hallway to check out loud voices from an office to seeing potential danger in a lane between two buildings and moving in that direction to check out what is going on. This breathing activates the entire nervous system in a way that enhances both creativity and the ability to survive.

Even in the middle of a confrontation, particularly a verbal one, there are many times when this breathing will have a very powerful effect. Not only do we get more stressed or upset in the presence of an upset person, but we also become more peaceful in the presence of a calm one. People tend to template their mood to the most powerful individual close by. We are sure that you know Security Professionals who, when they walk onto a scene, often calm it down before they have said a word. You have probably seen the opposite as well, where a certain Security Professional comes on scene and it immediately gets worse. Using this breathing method is a vital tool in making you the former type, a man or woman of quiet power.

Use this method of breathing after the crisis as well. You will need to regroup to go on with the rest of your shift. Circular breathing will bring you back to a calm and relaxed state, prepared to handle the next crisis, should one occur.

If you bring feelings from a crisis situation back home, you carry violence back to your family. Therefore, before entering your home, sit quietly in your car or even in the yard, and practice this breathing for a moment or two. The only thing that should come home is you, not the crises you weathered.

Circular Breathing to Ward Off or Even Heal From Trauma

Figure 11.2 Protecting Yourself from PTSD (Post Traumatic Stress Disorder)

Although the material in this section may seem a little too "therapy" oriented for some, it is invaluable if you ever find yourself having difficulty dealing with a traumatic reaction and, for one reason or another, help is either not available, or you cannot or should not avail yourself of the help that is offered. Keep this in reserve for those times when you need it.

Post-traumatic stress is not defined by how horrible the event sounds in description, but is defined by the victim's response to the event. PTSD is not exactly a problem of memory. It is a problem because the event has not fully *become* a memory; the event is still primarily experienced as if it is happening right now. When an event is fully a memory, it is experienced as something in the past, over and done with. Another way to think of it is a scar: it may not be pretty, and it certainly is a signpost that something significant happened, but it no longer hurts. A trauma, on the other hand, is an open-wound. It is an *experience*. It is not in the past, and in fact may be affecting every moment of the person's life, or emerge suddenly, when evoked by something that elicits a sense that the event is happening again.

In PTSD, the person's nervous system is set to react as if there is an emergency whenever the trauma is recalled. This can be anything from an explicit memory to a small reminder; for example, although he does not consciously know why, a soldier gets anxious every time someone coughs, because one of his squad coughed right before an IED went off. Because trauma affects the brain at the deepest levels associated with survival, logical interventions (anything from reassurance to cognitive therapy) offer only equivocal success in helping people emerge from trauma. Image-associated breathing techniques, on the other hand, which affect the brain as a whole, can assist people in realizing that the event is over and no longer a part of present experience.

- Let us imagine that something very upsetting has happened to you. Perhaps you even recall an old trauma that still plagues your mind.
- Whenever you think about it (or it forcibly intrudes into your consciousness), your body tenses or twists in various ways. Your breathing pattern often changes.
- If this is your situation, go someplace where you will not be disturbed for a while. Make the mental image of that trauma as vivid as you can tolerate. This takes some courage, because most of us simultaneously avoid as we remember. Rather, if only for a moment or two, meet it head on and re-experience it. If you physically organize *as if* something is happening, the brain believes that it truly is. Therefore, notice, in fine detail how you physically and emotionally react. As difficult as this may be, it is important to establish for yourself what your baseline response is to the trauma. You must clearly experience what it "does" to us.
- Now take a couple of deep sighs. Sighing breaks up patterns of muscular tension and respiration. This is like rebooting your computer when the program is corrupt.
- Mentally say to the ugly experience: "Hush. You move right over there to my right (or left). I'll get to you in a minute." For some people, it is even helpful to make a physical gesture, "guiding" or "pushing" the experience off to the side. You cannot force yourself to stop thinking about an experience if it has psychological power. Instead, move it aside, as if you are guiding a wounded person to a waiting room while you organize yourself to properly deal with it.
- Now initiate your preferred method of circular breathing.
- As the memory creeps back in (and it will), just breathe and center yourself, again placing the memory off to the side." Once again say, "Hush, I'll get to you in a minute." You can't fight it, so don't try. Just ease it aside until you are ready.
- When your breathing is smooth and your body is centered, you will be relaxed like an athlete, ready to move but with no wasted effort.
- Now, deliberately bring that ugly memory or trauma into your thoughts and imagination. Now, as you find yourself reacting, continue circular breathing, trying to bring yourself back to physical balance as you focus on the traumatic memory.
- Bit by bit, in either one session or a few, you will notice that you are increasingly able to hold the image with a relaxed body and a balanced posture. You are now able to re-experience the memory without the same painful, tense, or distorted response you used in the past. You are, metaphorically speaking, turning the open wound into scar tissue.

Think of how you hold babies so that they are safe: you do not drop or squeeze them so tightly that they are frightened or uncomfortable. To be strong in the face of trauma is very similar in that you internally hold the memory with all the grace and strength with which you hold babies so that they are safe, whether asleep or struggling to see over your shoulder. You are not wiping the slate of memory clean. Rather, you are placing it in a proper context—something that happened to you, but does not define you.

Figure 11.3 Value of Circular Breathing Imagery: Doing for Yourself

What is particularly valuable to many Security Professionals is that it allows one to take power back on one's own. There is no doubt that counseling, sometimes, is invaluable. However, it is sometimes hard to find a good counselor who understands a Security Professional's situation. Furthermore, ongoing litigation, in which confidentiality can be threatened by subpoena or court order, can sometimes force Security Professionals to forego counseling that they might really need. This particular breathing method offers an option when counseling is either not an option, or something that the Security Professional does not want.

Furthermore, if one can, on a daily basis, "inoculate" oneself against stressful, even potentially traumatic experiences, life will continue to be enjoyable, or will become enjoyable once again, even as you continue to work in a highly stressful environment. The goal is not trying to restore some kind of mythic "innocence," that one had "pre-trauma." The goal is to relegate the experience to its proper place—something ugly that happened sometime in the past.

CHAPTER 12

The Joy and Intoxication
of Righteous Anger

Most people consider anger to be a harmful emotion, one that upsets the angry person as well as the recipient. This is not true for everyone. There is a subset of people, including some Security Professionals, who do not mind fighting whatsoever, particularly when they believe their cause is just. These individuals go off-center in an interesting way, becoming calm, even happy, when someone offends them. As a boxer once stated in regards to an opponent, "When he gets hurt, he wants the round to be over. When I get hurt, I get happy."

Such people, when functioning in a professional capacity, have an especially difficult task. They must recognize that when they feel *good*, they are in danger of becoming part of the problem. Instead of imposing calm, they escalate the situation, not minding it in the least.

Circular breathing (Chapter 11), for those who are anxious, stressed, or frightened provides a real sense of peace and relief. However, if confrontation feels good to you, such calming breathing, dynamic though it may be, seems like the last thing you would like to do. You think, "Center myself? Hell, no. I'm right where I want to be."

If this description fits, your task is to recognize the special joy that comes with righteous anger, and act to center yourself to a calm state of mind, even though in the heat of the moment, it feels like a loss rather than a gain.

The righteously angry Security Professional may be known for this type of reaction. He/she is the one most likely to not recognize this, and not believe they need to do any breathing or calming. If this is you, recognize it. This is not about becoming some sort of Zen sage, never angered, never off-balance. Of course, you will be angry. In many situations you should be angry. It may even keep you alive. The problem is when anger justifies anything from treating aggravating or troublesome people with contempt to actions that are either immoral or illegal on the extreme edge.

Figure 12 Some Security Professionals Make Things Worse

There are times when you are responding to an angry individual, and you see several Security Professionals coming to back you up and at the sight of one of them, you think, "Oh, Lord, this is not going to go well!" He is exactly where he want to be; angry yet safe because there are other Security Professionals around to protect them if things go wrong. They act indignant and self-righteous, escalating the situation the moment they hit the scene. Other Security Professionals, without any intention to provoke a confrontation, walk into the situation with a particular attitude that ticks everyone off, individuals and Security Professionals included.

Those who willfully provoke such confrontation do not belong on your team. They need to be removed, as their attitude is both unprofessional and dangerous. However, many of the aforementioned individuals, subject to righteous anger, can be valuable Security Professionals, if they are able to see the strength and power in self-control.

Protecting Your Family From What You Otherwise Would Bring Home

Another type of righteous anger is that evoked when someone does something so clearly evil that one feels annihilation of the perpetrator is the only justifiable response. Returning to the subject of the last chapter, this is a particularly important example of how such breathing can protect your family. Both of us authors have had the experience of feeling utterly contaminated by being in the presence of the perpetrators of child abuse or sexual assault. Having done our job well, so that, for example, we have gotten a confession, evidence to make a case, or ensure that an abusive parent never has access to the child again, we each have left the room feeling a failure because we did not take his throat between our hands and squeeze the life out of him for what he did.

Both of us made sure that we never brought this feeling home. We'd sit in our cars, running the breath around our body, maybe going to a quiet place in the house or yard and working through the images in our brain so that when we walked into the presence of our wives and children, the only thing each of us ever brought home was ourselves. No child molester or other evil doer will ever walk into the house with us.

SECTION IV

Unusual, Intense, and Eccentric Styles
of Communication

CHAPTER 13

Overview

What is a mental illness anyway? Is it any odd or eccentric behavior, or should we confine the term for more serious disturbances of behavior and thought. It sometimes seems that we lump together mental phenomenon that are as disparate as the distinction between a common cold and lung cancer. Yes, both may make breathing difficult, but they are very different disorders.

Of course, Security Professionals should not feel it incumbent upon themselves to diagnose what a person may be suffering from, even in the most general way. We emphasize again that this book focuses on behavior, not on illness. It is not your job to figure out why a person behaves the way they do, or even what diagnosis they might have. However, if someone behaves in a way that makes it difficult to communicate with them, or even more problematically, enacts disruptive behaviors, then the Security Professional should be prepared with several skills:

- The ability to recognize the behavior as showing a pattern.
- Knowledge of best practice communication strategies to respond to a person who is displaying the pattern, whatever the cause of the behavior may be.

Not everyone who needs to be calmed or de-escalated is aggressive. However, those who display unusual or eccentric patterns of behavior are more difficult to communicate with, and when the ability of people to communicate breaks down, the risk of aggression increases.

CHAPTER 14

Rigid Personality (Asperger's Syndrome and Similar Disorders)

People with Asperger's Syndrome are frequently socially withdrawn, often very intelligent individuals, sometimes outcasts, who may live their lives mostly in an online environment. If you work in corporate America, particularly in the high-tech field, you should be aware that you will be seeing more and more such individuals; we now live in a world where their unique talents are at a premium.

Despite what can be formidable intellectual abilities, often sectored in one area of knowledge, individuals with Asperger's Syndrome often have tremendous difficulty in negotiating social interactions. They find other people to be incomprehensible, confusing, or threatening, and to make matters worse for them, they find it very difficult to know, from facial expressions, body posture, and vocal tone, what other people are feeling or thinking.

Other individuals, particularly some people with schizophrenia, often show a similar combination of "cluelessness" and rigidity in communicating with others. Although one might assume that people with schizophrenia will not be found in a corporate environment, this is not necessarily so. Advances in medication and other treatments have enabled many such people to function as productive, sometimes very valuable members of society, their illness only manifested in some eccentricities of behavior, and for many, only when they discontinue their medications. What typifies all such people is a rigidity of character, behavior and attitude.

Such rigid personalities become fixated on their own preoccupations, and may imagine that everyone else shares them too. They can also be very literal (concrete) and can get "stuck" on certain thoughts and behaviors (obsessive). Others are simply not interested in or aware of other people's feelings, which can lead them to be very blunt or brutally honest.

Figure 14.1 Examples: Socially Clueless Statements by a Person Displaying Rigid Personality Traits
- "What is the bump on your face? It's quite ugly. You know, it could be a melanoma, which could cause your face to simply rot away, or it could infect your brain and then you'd die. I've seen photos of tumors that have actually eaten right through the person's cheek and you can see their teeth and tongue out the side of their face."
- "You've gained a lot of weight in the last year. I don't mind, but many men don't think that is attractive."

There is no malevolent intent here. Other people's feelings—unimaginable and incomprehensible—are simply not a relevant bit of data to the person.

Such a person often does not appear to be mentally ill. Rather, they are stiff and socially awkward people, who are always a little out-of-sync. Their voice may be too loud, and they may sound odd. Their eye contact may be "off," or non-existent, and they are sometimes physically uncoordinated. They are frequently insensitive to body spacing and do not pay attention to the effect that their actions or appearance might have on others.. Because they find people unpredictable and unreadable, they frequently experience high anxiety, and use self-soothing movements, like flapping their hands, rhythmically tapping an object or body part to help distract them from what stresses them out.

If you are attempting to intervene in a crisis situation with such an individual, stating, or reiterating, the rules is the first method of intervention. Consider this: if you had difficulty figuring out what someone wants you to do, and the Security Professional's body language, tone of voice, and facial expression are incomprehensible, the rules, clearly stated, would be very reassuring. If you, instead, attempt to validate their feelings, this will often result in the individual becoming increasingly confused or upset. Rather, state each rule in a matter-of-fact way, as if simply providing information. Follow this up with a logical sequence of steps to resolve their problem. You must be as concrete and literal as they are. State the obvious.

- In a matter of fact tone, explain the rules. She says, "Why should I lower my voice? I am angry!" Your reply should be, "Because it is the rule here to speak about grievances with a quiet voice." "That's a stupid rule," she replies. "Nonetheless," you return, "it is the rule."
- Give them a logical alternative way to follow-up on their grievance.
- Even more than with other individuals, try to avoid physical contact. Many folks with rigid personality traits detest touch and can react violently. Only touch them if you are taking physical control of them (defensive tactics).
- If they are doing a physically, repetitive movement, such as flapping their hands, understand that it is for the purpose of calming themselves down. Nonetheless, if the movement (hand flapping near the waist or chest) could resemble a move towards a weapon, order them to stop, by telling them that it is "against the rules to wave your hands while standing near a Security Professional." When they ask why, simply repeat that it is against the rules. When they ask if it's alright while speaking on the phone, say that it is alright in that circumstance, but not face-to-face. Understand that their incessant questions are an attempt to try to figure out just what they can and cannot do. It is not game-playing. They feel the need to cover all possibilities. However, after a too many questions, you should "take over" and give a general policy that, hopefully, will cover all variations.

Figure 14.2 Example: De-escalation of a Person With Rigid Personality Traits

Grigori Surikov. "I can't use my key card. I have no other recourse, but to kick down the door."

Security Professional. "Mr. Surikov, all you have to do is wait. I've called to Building 4 for a master key."

Grigori Surikov. "Listen, you rental cop. I do not have time for this. I have a very important program that I am running and it is imperative that I check its progress. I'm going to kick it down."

Security Professional. (The professional has had past experiences with Mr. Surikov. She and the other security staff already know that trying to be "understanding," or "getting on the same page" with this eccentric man simply does not work. The rules do. "Mr. Surikov, the rules in this corporation forbid the destruction of company property. You must not kick down the door."

Grigori Surikov. "So you are content to see the destruction of two weeks of work. Is that it? Are you too stupid to understand that this is an emergency?"

Security Professional. "Sir, the rules of this company are that destruction of property is forbidden."

Grigori Surikov. "Oh, so how about if a terrorist crashed his plane into this building. Are you telling me that I'm not allowed to kick down a door to escape?"

Security Professional. "Exceptions are made for life-threatening emergencies. *(Quickly holding up a hand)* "Only life-threatening emergencies. Ah good, there is Thomas with the key now!"

NOTE: Do not expect to be thanked for your help.

Figure 14.3 Review: Dealing With Rigid Personality

You will recognize the person with a rigid personality because they get stuck on subjects that seem rather odd in the circumstances. They seem unaware of their effect on others. Their emotions, if they are even displaying any, are not those you would expect when someone calls with the complaint they have.

- State the rules in a matter-of-fact way, as if simply providing information.
- Follow this up with a logical sequence of steps to solve their problem.
- Discussion about their feelings will be counter-production. Tactical paraphrasing (Chapter 48) or other ordinary tactics to deal with an angry person tend to make things worse.
- No body contact unless it is part of defensive tactics or physical control.
- Do not get deflected from your task. Like a parody of a lawyer, they may bring up possible exceptions to your order. "Step through" the objections and simply state that they are required to follow the rule.
- NOTE: This type of person is relatively uncommon, unless you are working at a software or other technical site. Use this type of strategy only when it is clear that you are trying to interact with an individual who is rigid, stiff, concrete, and socially out of sync. Think of Data on "Star Trek" and perhaps include in your imagination, what Data would look like while mad: either coldly logical, or if that did not work, frustrated and out of control. In the latter case, as always, control based on the mode of rage (Section X) they are displaying.

CHAPTER 15

Tell It Like It Is:
Communication With Concrete Thinkers

Concrete thinkers have a lot of difficulty, or even a complete inability, to understand metaphors, slang, or imagery. Instead, they take everything you say literally. You will probably not be surprised to learn that many individuals with rigid personality traits (Chapter 14) also show concrete thinking. Sometimes, however, concrete thinkers can be more severely mentally ill or cognitively impaired.

When communicating with concrete thinkers, Security Professionals should use short, clear sentences, using simple, yet specific words that are easy to understand. Remember, they will understand what you say in a very literal manner. Such people can comply with the specific, but not even understand the general principal. Speak in a firm manner, and refrain from showing too much emotion. If you become angry or frustrated, the individual will react to your emotions, not your instructions.

Figure 15.1 Example: Dealing With a Concrete Thinker
A Security Professional has intervened with an employee in custodial services who deeply slashed his arm. Hysterical when you arrived, he is now relatively calm, sitting in a chair with a towel wrapped around his arm, as you wait with him for an ambulance.

Security Professional. "Okay. So you don't have to worry anymore."

Concrete person. "I wasn't worried. I was upset."

Security Professional. "Oh, okay, you were upset. Anyway, the ambulance is coming, and will be here shortly. I want you to sit tight."

Concrete person. "How do I sit tight? Should I wrap myself in a blanket?"

Security Professional. *(Sigh)* "No, you don't have to wrap yourself up. I meant you should sit quietly."

Concrete person. "You mean I shouldn't talk?"

Security Professional. *(Aghhhhhh)* "No, you can talk! I want you to talk! It's a figure of speech!"

We think you get the idea. Let us take this last example: What might be a better way to accomplish the task? Imagine this just from the Security Professionals side.

- "The ambulance is coming."
- "Sit in the chair right here."
- "Yes, sit where you are right now and keep talking to me. No, you don't have to wait by the door."
- "Yes, I can hear them too. No, sit in the chair until they come in the lobby."

Figure 15.2 Review

You will recognize *concrete thinkers* because they take what you say literally:

- Use clear, short sentences, with a firm, calm voice.
- Give directions using simple words that are easy to understand.
- Show a minimum of emotion. Do not get irritated when the individual does not immediately get what you want them to do. Simply clarify what you meant, using direct language. View yourself as translating reality for someone from another place. You are trying to make it easy for both of you by speaking in a way that there are no misunderstandings.

CHAPTER 16

Information Processing and Retention:
Consolidating Gains

Some people have problems in taking in and understanding information. This is particularly true when they are stressed. Otherwise normal folks, when being interviewed or even interrogated regarding worksite theft, for example, may have tremendous difficulty in tracking what you are saying. It is humiliating to not be able to understand what people are saying. When asking questions to have something further explained, people often feel forced to reveal how "stupid" they are. Instead, what they do is "fake normal." People around them may do confusing or overwhelming things, but they do not show their fear. Other people may anger them, but they smile and pretend everything is all right. Conversations and ideas may be too complex, too fast, or irrelevant to what is going on inside them, but they have learned to pick up the rhythm of other people's speech, nod at the right moments, smile or laugh when needed, and agree with the tag lines that invite such agreement.[6]

Therefore, never assume that a person, particularly one who shows any behaviors that suggest that they might be mentally ill, understands what you have told them just because they nod their head at the right moment. You need to verify what they have understood. The following will help with this verification:

- **The least effective method is to repeat yourself, using other words.** If they have either tuned you out, or did not understand you the first time, they may fake understanding again.

- **Have the person repeat your instructions.** However, some people echo what you say, which does not prove that they actually understand or will follow through.

- **Another method is open sentences.** An example of an open sentence would be: "So, Diane, if I've got it right, I will call your lawyer tomorrow and explain the problem. And you will…." Of course, you expect (hope) that the individual will complete the sentence.

- **Write down the most important points.** Many individuals do not assimilate a lot of information that they hear, no matter how hard they listen. The Security Professional may find that writing the most important points of your conversation or agreement down on the back of their business card or a 3 x 5 card, if there is more information, is quite helpful. Remind the individual to check the card if they have any difficulty remembering what they are supposed to do. (We are aware that there would be many circumstances where this strategy would be out of the question, but both of us have used it on occasion.)

Figure 16 Review: Consolidation of Gains—Verifying Understanding

- The least effective way is to repeat yourself, hoping that their replies and head-nods really mean that they understand you.
- Have the individual repeat back your instructions
- Use open sentences and questions, allowing the individual to fill in the blanks.
- When reasonable, write down the most important points of understanding on a card as a point of reference.

CHAPTER 17

Coping With Stubborn Refusals

There are many occasions when, despite having treated a person with clarity and respect, they refuse to comply with your requests, fill out required paperwork, appear at HR, or any one of a number of other issues, despite the possibility of sanctions. Of course, if you have been bossing them around, patronizing them, or treating them with disrespect, it will not be surprising if they resist you. All people, mentally ill or not, have pride, and no one likes another person talking down to them or controlling their life.

Once you are clear that it is not your approach that is creating the problem, what, if anything, can Security Professionals do to elicit compliance? You will find the following steps helpful in getting compliance:

- **Focus on the task.** Security Professionals should never take an individual's non-compliance personally. This just adds additional problems to your relationship with them.
- **Clarify the message.** Security Professionals must be clear on what the individual is required to. Do not bring up previous examples of their non-compliance, such as "the last time this happened," or "you always," or "remember when you...." Stay very specific.
- **Control the interview.** Stay on topic and do not allow the person to divert your attention to unrelated issues.
- **Use a strong and calm voice.** Keep your tone of voice strong, but not demanding or aggressive.
- **De-personalize your role.** Remind the individual that as the Security Professional you are merely enforcing the rules of the company or instructions from HR.
- **State the consequences.** Security Professionals should be very clear in explaining to the individual the consequences and possible sanctions that may be imposed for non-compliance. This should be provided as information, rather than threat, the same way you inform a child on a cold winter day, "If you stick your tongue on that metal pole, you are going to get stuck."
- **Place the power in the individual's hands.** Without handing over one iota of your authority, allow the individual to be the decision-maker, and clarify their role in complying, or not complying. Perhaps say something along the lines of "It looks like you've got something to decide. You are absolutely correct. You don't have to do it. We can just escort you off the property, and you can discuss matters with your union. Or, we can sit here like gentlemen and try to figure out a solution." Don't threaten the individual with anything that you cannot back up by action. Simply state the facts of the consequences for non-compliance.
- **Detach yourself, giving the individual *one moment*, so to speak, to decide to comply or face the consequences.** That pause is to make "space" for an attitude change but in these circumstances, the person will either make it right then or not at all. You can consider this a "soft ultimatum."

CHAPTER 18

Coping With Repetitive Demands, Questions, and Obsessions

Sometimes troublesome individuals will make repetitive demands for information that you have already answered or explained in <u>exhaustive detail</u>. They seem to get "stuck" on an obsessive thought or idea. No matter how many times you answer their question, they have to ask it again. This is often a sign of Obsessive-Compulsive Disorder (OCD), which is frequently missed because individuals become skilled in covering up such a humiliating problem. Such people experience unbearable anxiety when they do not give in to the obsession or compulsion. The Security Professional may be the first to really notice OCD behaviors when an individual gets stuck on things and cannot "let go" even when he/she is acting against his/her own best interests. If such an individual is an employee, they should get a referral to a company EAP program.

Other individuals obsess as part of a disorder like schizophrenia, developmental disability, or other serious impairments of cognition. Their repetitive questions or obsessing on a single point may be due to information processing errors. Use the strategies presented about in Chapter 16.

Sometimes individuals repeat a question *intending* to be irritating or challenging. In a bland tone of voice, simply say, "You already know the answer to that," or otherwise calmly point out that they already have the information, and move on. By disengaging, you are saying, "I'm not participating in the game." If they persist, let them know that continued game playing will only make their own life more difficult.

CHAPTER 19

The Need for Reassurance

Some people are quite anxious by nature or circumstances. For others, intolerable anxiety is either their primary illness or one of the most troublesome symptoms of their mental disorder. Anxiety is living as if something of which you are afraid might happen, **is happening right now,** or living with feelings of imminent doom. For example, you are part of an investigating team, and you perceive that one of the women you are interviewing is suffering from terrible anxiety. Perhaps she has been traumatized, either due to something that happened on your worksite or sometime in the past. You are at a loss on how to communicate with her because the longer you speak with her, the more distressed she becomes.

You must draw a graceful line. Do not coddle the person. If you treat them like they are too weak or frail for this world, they will probably believe you. They may think that something awful is going to happen and that is why you are talking in such careful tones. At the same time, do not affect a cheerful tone of voice, as if nothing is wrong. Instead, make you voice matter-of-fact. Take their anxiety into account, but speak with an expectation that they are strong enough to manage what they must do.

Figure 19 Do Not Promise that People Will Be Taken Care Of

Security Professionals must never make promises to people—including victims—that they will be taken care of. This implies that the Security Professional now has a <u>duty of care</u>. Security Professionals must not make promises or statements that would imply any such outcome.

CHAPTER 20

Dealing With Mood Swings

Individuals with mood swings (whose behavior is sometimes referred to as labile) can be verbally abusive, provocative, complaining, passive-aggressive, blaming, apologetic, ingratiating, and friendly all in the space of an hour, or less. They can be very difficult to communicate with, much less de-escalate, because just as we make progress with their current mood, they shift into another. They often try to get control of us even when they have no control over themselves.

Coping With Mood Swings

Rather than respond to the individual's specific mood with body language or words that manifest your own anger or frustration, the Security Professional has to remain balanced and emotionally non-reactive. *You influence them by being exactly what they are not.* The more you are unaffected by their emotional storms, the more likely the individual will calm down (Section III).

Figure 20 Review

Individuals with mood swings shift emotions rapidly with no particular relationship to the situation they are in. When interviewing or de-escalating these individuals remember:

- Do not mirror the individual's emotional state or lose control of your own emotions.
- Control them through controlling your own emotions. Remain powerfully calm.
- Speak in a firm, yet calm and controlled manner.
- Because they display any emotion you can imagine, use the de-escalation tactics, described throughout the book, as needed.

CHAPTER 21

They Are Not Moving:
What to do?

You have surely been in situations where you tell a person to do something and they stare at you vacantly, voice a million questions, express misgivings or anxiety, or drift off into a monologue about something completely different. Other individuals seem to lack motivation; they just won't do what you think is good for them. We are particularly referring to the individual whose disability impedes their ability to accomplish the things they are required to do. A word of caution here: some individuals, and even their family members or therapists, will use their mental illness, their physical illness, or their substance abuse as an excuse for their failure to comply with even the most basic rules and regulations. Infirmity becomes their "fallback" position for their non–compliance with company policy and worksite rules so that they never accept any personal responsibility.

The Security Professional must assess the individual's actual abilities, and use discretion when determining what constitutes an acceptable level of compliance, or at least an honest attempt at compliance on their part. In the event that the individual is incapable of complying due to a disability, the Security Professional should bring this to HR's attention.

If the individual is non-compliant despite their ability to do so, once again HR should be notified. In this case, the Security Professional gives clear evidence why the individual's non-compliance is by choice, not due to illness. It is up to HR at that point to decide what to do about this.

Finally, Security Professionals should take note of just how they attempt to motivate the individual. Do you like the sound of your voice? Are you overly threatening? Or conversely, are you pleading with them? Security Professionals must retain their dignity when trying to motivate individuals. Give directions in a firm tone of voice, do not cajole, or sound like a "cheerleader" in an attempt to try to get them to comply. People are far more likely to be compliant for Security Professionals whom they respect.

Figure 21 They Are Not Moving—What to do?

1. Do not do for them what they can do for themselves.
2. Do not require them to do things that they are incapable of doing.
3. If they are truly non-compliant due to a disability, refer to HR for follow-up to secure them the help that they need.
4. If they are truly non-compliant as a matter of choice or manipulation, refer to HR for appropriate action and follow-up.
5. Act with dignity. Do not try to "cheerlead" them into compliance, berate them, complain, or any one of a number of actions that compromise your integrity in the interests of getting them moving.

CHAPTER 22

Grievances: Should a Security Professional Ever Apologize?

Some individuals store up grievances, allowing feelings of persecution and perceived personal slights to affect their entire worldview. Frequent complaints about old history can become a significant source of conflict, not to mention being extremely aggravating to the harried Security Professional who must continually return the individual's attention to the immediate issues and future concerns. With mentally ill individuals, these feelings can be more problematic, because their memories may be distorted or even delusional.

Security Professionals must refrain from reacting emotionally to the individual's inability to move beyond the past, even as you try to redirect their attention to the present situation. Above all, do not personalize the individual's complaints or their feelings of prior injustices. The following will be helpful in dealing with such individuals:

- **Acknowledge their concerns.** Quite often individuals merely need to express their frustrations or feelings of helplessness regarding their case, and they view the Security Professional as the only available outlet to do so. As long as they do so in an appropriate manner, there is no problem, is there? Do not agree or disagree with them, or otherwise reinforce their feelings of persecution, just recognize their complaints and then move forward, in a "once and done" manner. <u>If they raise the issue again in subsequent meetings, emphasize that you have heard these complaints – you can quickly paraphrase what they are upset about to prove it – and refocus them on the issue of current concern.</u>

- **Apologize.** When an individual complains, yet again, about something directly concerning you, think about it very carefully. Perhaps, in this instance, you were wrong. If so, apologize sincerely and fully. In some situations, this is enough. However, the authors cannot stress strongly enough that Security Professionals should be wary of apologizing to an individual as a means of moving them off of a specific subject or grievance. Such an apology may lead the individual to believe they are now in control of the relationship, and that the Security Professional will act cautiously so as not to upset them in the future. The best thing for the Security Professional to do is to act ethically and professionally at all times. By staying calm and in control you are much less likely to say or do anything for which you would need to apologize.

- **What if an apology is not enough?** You might say to the individual, "You are still upset about this. You want to talk about it again, don't you?" Notice that you don't ask the individual: you merely state what you understand. This gives them the opportunity to correct or adjust your understanding, so that if their complaint turns out to be legitimate, you are able to effectively put it to rest.

- **Complaints as their own reward.** Certain individuals are never satisfied, because the complaint becomes a "rewarding" activity in itself. Others bear a pervasive resentment toward you, an institution, or even life itself. For them, complaints are merely a way to express hostility or an attempt to control the interview by getting you to talk about things on their agenda. In these cases, simply take the issue off the table, forever. Remind them that you have already addressed this complaint, so that there is nothing more to discuss. If necessary, terminate the interview if the individual persists in discussing the past.

Figure 22.1 Example: An Apology in Service of Peace

A Security Professional responds to an extremely upset customer, who claimed he had sustained injuries due to company products: the customer is demanding to speak to the Legal Department, and threatens to go upstairs to the executive suite. The Security Professional accidently calls the wrong number, and hands the customer the phone. With no satisfaction, the customer gets even more infuriated. The Security Professional apologizes several times, without abasing himself, and takes responsibility to try to get the right people on the phone, something he eventually accomplishes. Because of the Security Professional's calm demeanor and sincerity, the customer calms and thanks the Security Professional for his reaction to the anger.

Figure 22.2 Review: Should a Security Professional apologize?

- If they have a general grievance towards their situation, acknowledge their complaints in a "one-and-done" manner, as long as you neither apologize for things that are not your fault or responsibility and you do not compromise your authority. In future exchanges, redirect them to the issue of current concern.
- If you have wronged the individual, if it does not put you in danger, and if it enables you to assume tactical strength, then you should apologize.
- If the individual is stuck on the issue, say, "You are still upset about that," or something similar, giving them an opportunity to clarify why it is still a problem for them.
- If the individual is using the grievance or complaint to get control of the exchange, distract you, and/or simply complain for the sake of complaining, shut it down. Call them on their game and do not allow it to continue.

CHAPTER 23

If There Is a Problem Here, That Is Your Fault:
Useful Tactics for Dealing With Symptoms
of Paranoia and Persecution

Figure 23.1 Paranoid Character Traits

This chapter focuses on tactics specific to paranoia. We are here discussing an attitude, with the following characteristics: a sense of being persecuted, blame of others for any problem, and a hair-trigger sensitivity to being vulnerable. This is a character trait. The delusional paranoid individual (Chapter 31) has this attitude complicated by fixed false beliefs and even hallucinations.

Dealing with a paranoid individual can be exceedingly difficult. The person's motto of life could be summed up in a phrase: "If there is a problem here, that is your fault." The paranoid world is one of winning and losing: the paranoid tries to dominate the other people in his/her life and are terrified or enraged at being forced to submit. Such people can precipitate a number of problems on a worksite, provoked by their consistent attitude of blame, resentment and defiance of authority, hypersensitivity to criticism, fear of vulnerability, denial of responsibility for any problems that might occur, feeling that others are out to get them, and even an expectation of being betrayed by people they trust.

Stimulant users, notably those addicted to methamphetamine and cocaine, display these behaviors frequently. It is also a very common "solution" that those with a criminal attitude arrive at to excuse any failure. For others, it is simply a core trait of their character. Paranoid people are, underneath, terrified that they will be made vulnerable, but they are aggressive toward that of which they are afraid. One helpful image of the paranoid person is an angry porcupine, all quills, with a soft underbelly, hunched over, ready to strike in hair-trigger reaction.

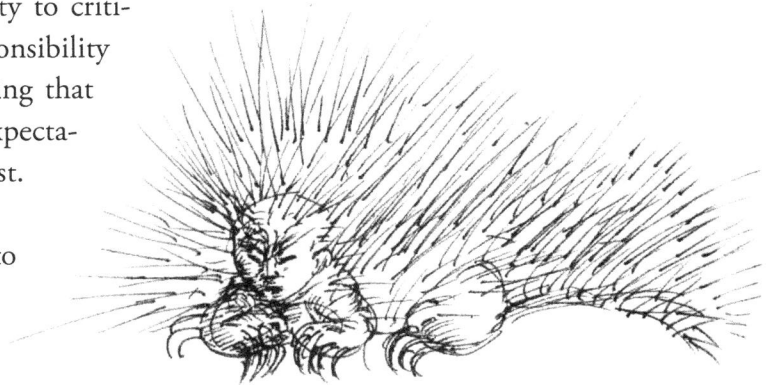

Paranoid people interpret relaxation as vulnerability. Therefore, they become more paranoid when you begin to establish rapport with them. (For this reason, paranoid people are particularly volatile within their families). Because friendship means letting your guard down, do not be surprised if paranoid individuals suddenly flare up with suspicion or accusations during times that are uneventful or even, within professional limits, friendly.

Being mistaken or wrong is another form of vulnerability. Rather than admitting wrongdoing or mistakes, paranoid individuals reflexively ***project*** negative feelings on the other person. If they feel hate, they believe, "You hate me." If they forgot to go to an appointment to discuss work related issues with HR, they will claim, "You set me up. You knew I couldn't get there on that day."

Paranoid people live like detectives, searching for evidence to prove what they already know is true. They have ***ideas of reference***, in which they believe that other conversations, glances, or actions are directed at them. They assume that others are conspiring about them, talking about them, laughing at them. Ironically, their reactions, in response to these paranoid ideas, frequently cause others to act in exactly the way the paranoid person expects.

Because of their aggressive or standoffish behavior, they can make other people uncomfortable or afraid. If they sense fear in you, they expect you to attack, and they "attack you back first," feeling fully justified because they *knew* "what you were about to do."

Try to Let Them Know What Is Going On

Because paranoid individuals are so suspicious, they will often question your actions and instructions. Although you would do this with any other individual, it is especially important with these individuals to clearly and explicitly explain general rules and regulations as well as any specific things that the employee is ordered to do to rectify problems at work.

However, you should not accept being quizzed incessantly. You are not required to explain every action. In fact, it might be a tactic to throw you off guard or to distract you.

Security Professionals should also clearly explain the potential consequences of violation of company policy and non–compliance with rules. In many circumstances, it is important to have the individual initial their understanding of each point and sign their name to a form attesting to their understanding.

Personal Space—Physical and Psychological—With the Paranoid Individual

Many paranoid individuals are preoccupied, even obsessed, with fears that they will be invaded, violated, or controlled in some fashion. Some of the following are, of course, relevant when dealing with anybody, but they are doubly important when the individual is paranoid.

- **Maintain the angle.** Whether standing or sitting, turn your body at a slight angle, so that physical "confrontation" is a choice rather than a requirement. If you directly face a paranoid individual, you *force* them to turn away if he/she does not want to face you.
- **Mindfulness.** Never let down your guard. You are in an avalanche zone, and anything could set off another slide.

- **Too friendly is as dangerous as a threat.** Try to be aware when things are getting too relaxed. If the paranoid person relaxes, they may suddenly startle, realizing that for a brief moment, they let their guard down. They may respond by exploding to make sure you do not "take them over."
- **Differentiate.** Paranoid individuals feel safest when you differentiate yourself from them. It is better to be somewhat emotionally distant rather than too warm and friendly.
- **Cover your triggers.** Paranoid people will try to provoke you. If you lose your temper, they will feel justified in whatever they do to you as well as it keying into their terror-based aggression. A slang expression for this is "fear biters." They bark and snarl and when you react, they attack as if you had gone after them first.

Figure 23.2 Example: Threat for the Purpose of Control

The paranoid character frequently manifests in families, either in parent-child relationships or in a domestic violence relationship. They will use threat and violence either to force the other person to comply with their wishes or in a rage state because the victim is acting in a way that diminishes their control.

The victim, a 24 year old married employee of the company recently cut off all contact with her father, an abusive, controlling man. The father has been living in an RV on the victim's grandfather's property. The grandfather recently died, having willed the property to the victim. She told her father that she was going to sell the property, which would necessitate his moving. He responded by calling her at work and telling her that he was going to come down there and get her. He owns a hand-gun and was a figure of interest in two arsons some years ago.

Is there a specific paranoid rage or violence?

There is no specific "paranoid rage." Instead, paranoia is an "engine" that drives rage in all its various forms. De-escalate the individual using tactics specific to the mode of rage they are exhibiting (Section X) rather than de-escalating "paranoia" itself. Paranoid individuals can exhibit traits of fear, frustration, intimidation, and manipulation. With their focus however, they are rarely disorganized. Even so, some disorganized people can experience an "omni-directional dread," a pervasive terror that is inescapable.

Figure 23.3 Review: Paranoia and Persecution

The paranoid individual has an attitude that anything wrong is another person's fault. Whether delusional or not, they see others as conspiring against them or persecuting them.

Depending on what will prove useful, use any of the standard tactics for delusional people when speaking with person whose delusions are paranoid. Beyond that:

- De-escalate based on the behavior, not the paranoia.
- Let them know what's going on.
- Speak in formal tones. Do not be too friendly.
- Be aware they may try to provoke you, so they can "hit you back first."
- Be aware of both physical and emotional spacing. Maintain a correct distance: neither too close nor too far.
- Differentiate: do not be too friendly, and if they are delusional, clearly separate yourself from their paranoid ideas without getting in an argument about them.
- Maintain calm: the paranoid individual is usually assaultive when they feel under attack, or when they perceive you as controlling them
- Remember: as they attack out of fear, they expect an attack *from* you when you display fear. They may, in these circumstances, pre-emptively attack you, because of what they are sure you are about to do to them.
- If you detain them, or otherwise control them, let them know what is going on and why. Paranoid individuals are most likely to become dangerous when they base their actions on their imagination rather than reality.

SECTION V

Recognizing the Strategies of Manipulative and Opportunistic Individuals

CHAPTER 24

Divide and Confuse:
Borderline Personality Disorder and Splitting

> **Figure 24.1 Borderline Traits and Suicide**
> Individuals with borderline traits frequently display suicidal and para-suicidal behaviors. These behaviors will be discussed in detail in Section VI.

Character disorders, also called personality disorders, are habitual patterns of behavior that sometimes cause an individual and almost always cause others associated with them considerable distress. Most types of personality disorder do not cause behaviors that significantly affect safety. One that does is the paranoid personality (Chapter 23). People with another character disorder, borderline personality, frequently figure in problems on a worksite. In essence, such a person believes that whatever feeling they are having right now is the only possible reality. For example, road rage is a borderline reaction: someone cuts a person off, it makes them mad and instead of cooling down, they chase after them and smash into their car. So is the most typical type of domestic violence. On the flip side, they meet someone attractive in a bar and within five seconds they know that it is the love of their life.

Any of us can be overcome by feelings that seem beyond our control and make emotional decisions that are not in our own best interests. Sometimes we are impulsive, and sometimes we get angry, even enraged. For us, however, such experiences are an aberration, while for the volatile individual, they are an everyday occurrence.

Those on the mild end of the spectrum will be quite emotional, over-reacting to things that others could take in stride, displaying frequent mood swings (Chapter 20). For those whose disorder is more severe, it is as if their nervous system, at least that part which regulates emotion, seemingly lacks any protective sheathing. Imagine trying to live your daily life with two layers of skin peeled off. On an emotional level, that is borderline existence. One's current emotions are inescapable. The borderline person lives with the intensity, but also with the lack of emotional resilience of a toddler. They experience the world and the people in it as good and bad, perfect and foul.

Because of this combination of character traits, volatile individuals frequently find themselves in various crises. Among them are genuine suicide attempts, para-suicidal acts (self-mutilating behaviors or repeat suicide "gestures" staged for discovery and attention, discussed in Chapter 39), impulsive acts of assault (particularly those involving family members or others close to them), and brief psychotic episodes.

Most relevant to Security Professionals is that fact that such individuals come into frequent conflict with co-workers and also bring family problems onto the worksite.

The Security Professional may discover that many of the people associated with the individual, (HR, family doctor, a counselor, the union, as well as the Security Professional), will disagree over the most appropriate course of action to deal with them even to the point of arguing about who is at fault for the individual's current crisis. In particular, those involved in a therapeutic relationship with the individual, often lean to contextualizing, explaining, or excusing the behavior, especially when the individual has a previous history of trauma or abuse. When the individuals associated with a borderline individual get tangled up in intense disputes about what is best for them, this type of conflict is called *splitting*.

Splitting does not happen in a vacuum. The individual, although not really conscious of what they are doing, is at the center of the conflict, presenting a different facet of their personality to each person with whom they interact. This "divide and confuse" strategy often sets HR, counselors, union reps, and the Security Professional against one another regarding the proper response to the individual's behavior, thereby keeping the "heat" off of them.

It is not surprising, really, that individuals will appear quite different to a therapist trying to build a supportive relationship, as opposed to a manager who is focused on them functioning at an optimum level on the worksite, a union rep who is attempting to advocate for a member, and to the Security Professional, who is most responsible for company safety. Needless to say, each of these individuals responds to the individual somewhat differently, and each may believe that they have the best idea on how to deal with them. Unfortunately, these varying opinions, and not coincidentally, a measure of professional pride, can lead to arguments about the best course of action.

Although splitting is usually regarded as the fault of the volatile individual, one that is at best manipulative and at worst sociopathic, this definition is too simplistic. Splitting is a process, not an act. Security Professionals and others on your team or agency can also be participants in splitting, and quite frankly, sometimes the actions of these professionals *create* the splitting process. ***Heightened emotions in one person cause those around them to react with heightened emotions: just not all the same ones.*** Whenever there is a possibility of splitting, the individual's case should be respectfully discussed among the team, sometimes with expert outside consultation to figure out how best to work productively together. Otherwise, an incredible amount of time and effort can be spent arguing about the status of one individual.

Whenever a team gets intensely at odds regarding a single individual, suggest the possibility of splitting and see if you can, by comparing observations, figure out if the individual's interactions with various

people have created the adversarial situation in which you find yourselves. Help your colleagues understand that splitting undermines your ability to work cooperatively to address the issues at hand.

Finally, volatile individuals are, not surprisingly, quite reactive to other people's emotional reactions. The attitude of the Security Professional should be similar to a perfect uncle or aunt, someone who wishes the individual well, yet undeviatingly enforces the rules. By maintaining a type of "warm emotional distance," you do not get emotionally worked up over things, and the individual finds less to react to as well.

Figure 24.2 Example of Splitting

Crystal, an employee at your firm has returned to her abusive husband on five occasions, and has herself violated several restraining orders that she took out on him. On two occasions, they got in altercations in the parking lot of your factory.

She shifts from rage at him to complaints about how the police were too brutal during his last arrest, to panic stricken calls to EAP begging for help, and no-shows to meetings with HR regarding corrective action to be taken about bringing the conflict from home onto the worksite.
- One Security Professional regards her as her husband's partner in crime, saying, "Honestly, there are times I want to hit her too. I think they are just two scorpions in a bottle."
- A second professional feels sorry for her. She reminds the Security Professional of her own daughter, someone who tries so hard to do things right and fails over and over again.
- The Human Resources professional regards her as a manipulative game player, who is using the system to try to get "reasonable accommodation," which she interprets as Crystal getting paid for not working.
- Her counselor sees her behavior as a manifestation of her own trauma as a child, and has accused the company of being insensitive to abuse victims.

Figure 24.3 Review: Dealing With Splitting
- Stay focused on whether or not there is really an emergent issue.
- Do not be reactive to the complaints or side issues the individual brings up.
- Pool resources to arrive at a common viewpoint and plan concerning the individual.
- Maintain a "warm emotional distance," like a solid uncle or aunt, in essence saying, "I wish you well, here are the rules, and I won't lose sleep if you don't comply … but I do wish you well."

CHAPTER 25

Bad Intentions: Recognizing the Strategies of Opportunistic and Manipulative Individuals

In order to satisfy their need for instant gratification, some individuals attempt to manipulate nearly everyone with whom they come into contact, including family members, strangers on the street, fellow employees, and yes, even Security Professionals. Some use manipulation as a means of furthering criminal actions. Some view us as opportunities to gain something they want or animated toys to play with for their own amusement. Others live for hate and destruction, but delight most in duping people so that they do not even know how "dirty they were done." Some manipulative people lie so well and often that no one can pin them down, using a "divide and disappear" strategy so that the more powerful beings in their life argue about them, instead of focusing directly on what they are really doing.

Manipulative Strategies

Manipulative strategies[7] can result from a variety of emotions and intentions, such as those born of revenge, malice, desperation, laziness, guilt, or as the result of drug and alcohol use. Security Professionals should also be wary of individuals who appear to be overly compliant. Some of the most dangerous individuals you will ever deal with will be the ones who appear to take required corrective actions, attend to any special conditions of HR's requirements, and in general appear to be agreeable low risk individuals. This seemingly compliant behavior may in fact be nothing more than an attempt to manipulate and control *your* behavior. Remember, they know how busy and overworked you are, and knowing that, they "make it easy on you." Their motives are hardly altruistic. After all, why would an already overworked Security Professional focus on a compliant individual, when there are so many other issues to deal with?

Often their dishonesty is the result of "lies of omission." For example, such an individual perceives your caution at entering the meeting room and he/she says:

- "You can come in. The walls are all glass. Everyone can see inside."
- "I guess you are a little uncomfortable meeting with me today, as I had trouble with the last Security Professional. You don't have to worry: that was personal. It had nothing to do with you."

Neither of these statements establishes, in the slightest, that he/she does not mean to assault you.

Another sign of coercion is a reassuring promise when none was asked for. For example, you are walking back to your car from a restaurant and an individual approaches you. "Mr. Carcetti, I know you might be concerned about me approaching you, you not being on the clock and all. That's why I came up, because if you saw me and I didn't say hello, you'd think I was up to something shady. Are those your kids?"

Manipulative people sometimes use stories, overloading you with too much information to keep your attention away from what they are doing, either in your presence, or more generally, in the worksite. They charm you so that you actually look forward to meeting with them, but remain unaware of what's really going on.

Manipulative individuals will also ask the Security Professional for personal information, such as marital status, children, in which part of town the Security Professional resides, and so forth. These questions seem to be innocent enough, just the normal back and forth of a pleasant conversation. What the manipulative individual is doing, however, is gathering information, something that they can use later in the relationship. Security Professionals should refrain from answering any personal questions any individual may ask, and redirect the conversation back toward your professional duties.

Figure 25.1 Guarding Personal Information

Security Professionals can also reduce the amount of personal information available to the individual by adhering to the office safety precautions outlined in Chapter 3 related to the display of personal photographs and other personal information in the office.

Manipulative individuals are also quite adept at behavioral observations, such as noting the body language of others. They are particularly interested in potential victims, those who are easily intimidated or frightened.

These individuals are also interested in those who put up any kind of a front, including an attempt to appear tough. All the manipulative person has to do is challenge the "front," and the blustering Security Professional begins reacting like a yo-yo on a string, trying to keep up appearances, to an individual who has already read them inside and out.

Manipulative individuals are also likely to blame others for both their failures and their behaviors. Nothing is ever their fault: they were simply in the wrong place at the wrong time; they did not know their friend left the marijuana in the company car; it is the Security Professional's fault that HR is coming down so heavily on them. If there are requirements that the person comply with EAP referrals to, for example, substance abuse treatment, the onus of verification should be placed on the individual, and they must be required to produce letters of participation in, or completion of treatment. At the very least, individuals must sign release of information forms, so that the Security Professional can verify they are actually going to treatment with a treatment provider as required. If an individual fails to sign a release of information, or presents repeated excuses as to why they have not yet signed one, chances are they are lying about their participation.

Another means of manipulation is that of flirtation and sexuality, which can manifest in any gender configuration, including same sex. All Security Professionals must address any flirtatious behaviors or sexual innuendo with the individual immediately. Firm limits must be set as to the professional nature of the relationship, and what constitutes acceptable conversation. If this issue is not addressed instantly, the manipulative person will view that as implied acceptance, which may lead to further advances or even attempted blackmail. It may also lead others to assume that something is going on between the individual and Security Professional. This is yet another reason that Security Professionals should not allow themselves to be isolated with an individual, regardless of gender.

Consider "splitting," (Chapter 24). The borderline type, a volatile individual, splits staff without really knowing what they are doing. They template to people based on their emotional reactions to them. The manipulative person splits consciously, trying to play one person off against the other.

Figure 25.2 Example: Playing One Security Professional Against Another

During an interview with an employee suspected of various thefts, the employee was initially interviewed by a Security Professional of a different race. On his own, the employee contacted a second Security Professional of the same race, and tried to play one professional off against the other, accusing the first of "not liking people like us. You know the way those people do things." The person was very gracious and convincing, and made what sounded like a reasonable argument for his statements, so much so that the second Security Professional found him plausible until a review of the evidence proved beyond a doubt that his was lying.

Manipulative individuals also view their relationships as transactions with an eye towards gaining an advantage or placing the other individual in their debt, perhaps by doing them a minor favor. The manipulative individual will sometimes deliberately make things difficult, only to then suddenly "give in," or become compliant. The likely purpose for their new-found compliance is to engender a sense of gratitude within the unwary Security Professional, or at least a lessening of frustration, toward the individual. Along with a sense of gratitude however, can come a lessening of supervision or investigation, which is the individual's original intent.

CHAPTER 26

Tactical and Safety Considerations Concerning the Psychopathic Individual

> ### Figure 26.1 Psychopathy and Manipulation
> There is considerable overlap in this chapter with the safety recommendations made throughout this book, particularly in the last chapter on manipulative behavior. In Section X, we will discuss what to do when facing someone presenting with Hot, Predatory, or Aggressive-Manipulative Rage, all modes that the psychopath can manifest when they become dangerously aggressive. Here, the authors are highlighting the most salient point's specific to psychopathic individuals. We believe that this information is so important to professional safety that it must be presented as a stand-alone chapter for easy reference.

The terms psychopath and sociopath, you can consider these terms interchangeable, evoke very strong reactions. Estimates are that they are 1-3 percent of any population, and perhaps 40 percent of the population in prison. In other words, a small percentage of people do most of the crimes in any society; although there is a sociological component to crime, the psychopath, to a remarkable degree, seems independent of such factors.

> ### Figure 26.2 Anti-social Personality
> There is a third common term you may run into: Anti-social Personality. This is a clinical term that is shorthand for describing someone as a rule-breaking, aggressive criminal personality. This is "part" of the psychopath's profile. However, even very dangerous criminals can have both a conscience and a capacity to care for and love others. The psychopath, an aggressive narcissist, lacks both conscience and an ability to care for others. In short, psychopaths are anti-social, but anti-social individuals are not necessarily psychopathic.

Over the years the entertainment media as well as sensationalized news accounts of horrendously violent killers and rapists have introduced an image of the malevolent criminal mastermind or the sadistic murdering predator into the public's consciousness. Without a doubt, violent psychopaths do exist, but far more often, they are rather mundane in appearance and affect, blending in with their surroundings without attracting any undue attention.

Although psychopathic individuals can be charming and ingratiating, they can also be violent, provocative, dishonest, arrogant, and quite willing to break the law. Some are remarkably talented, even brilliantly creative. However, the only thing they really care about is themself. Everything we have just discussed in regard to manipulative strategies in the last chapter is relevant to a discussion of psychopathic individuals. However, the psychopathic individual presents problems beyond what you will experience with the "ordinary" manipulative person, however dishonest the latter may be.

Just as a leopard or a cougar is known to attack whenever a vulnerable animal turns its back and exposes its neck, psychopathic individuals feed off vulnerability. Because of their manipulative charm, they can easily get under the defenses of others. They will gravitate to the most vulnerable people on your team. They study everyone with whom they come into contact, making note of any apparent weaknesses and developing new strategies of manipulation and control. For example: "Hmm, when Ms. Gibb's tilts her head and smiles while I'm talking, I find myself relaxing a little. I can use this the next time I'm trying to get close to that soft looking woman who works in accounting." Not only do they lack a sense of remorse at the harm inflicted upon their victims, they often take uncommon delight in it.

Do not assume, by the way, that we are merely talking about the criminal you may be investigating for theft or intimidation of other employees. This may be the lawyer who is working with the union or the executive assistant or vice-president who should be doing his/her job. This can even be a victim whom you believe you are protecting, who is, in fact, setting you or someone else up.

Because such individuals are easily bored, they deliberately agitate people on the worksite whenever possible, through gossip, initiation of conflict, or provocative actions. A few psychopaths are violent predators, but most are not. Many are fundamentally parasitic in their behaviors, and they revel in the instigation of emotional drama or conflict through the use of lies, rumors, or intimidation.

Psychopaths are impulsive in their actions and their sense of invincibility often leads them to ignore consequences. Such individuals owe their allegiance to no one, although they may form quasi-sentimental attachments that last until a stronger interest or desire pushes them away. This loyalty is on the level of, "Who do you think you are patting my dog without my permission."

Their impulsivity can also result in sudden and unexpected displays of violent behavior if they are frustrated in their desires. Many psychopaths are violent as a means of obtaining that which they desire: "just business," so to speak. For others, the act of violence itself is gratifying.

Although the psychopathic individual is a bit of a rarity among the overall individual population, Security Professionals will benefit from becoming familiar with the behaviors and characteristics of such individuals. The authors recommend strongly Paul Babiak and Robert Hare's illuminating work, *Snakes in Suits: When Psychopaths Go to Work* for a detailed discussion of this subgroup of individuals.[8]

Once you realize that an individual is behaving in the manner described here (and in more detail in Babiak and Hare's book), your goal must be the protection of the employees and the company. Security Professionals must enforce the rules of your company unfailingly, monitor such individuals closely, and work closely with HR to ensure safety for everyone. When supervising and interacting with the true psychopathic individual, Security Professionals need to remain conscious of the fact that these individuals are quite skilled in reading other people: how strong they are, their susceptibility to manipulation, and most significantly, what danger they represent to themselves. Therefore, your personal and professional integrity is paramount as you have a lot to lose if you succumb to the psychopathic individuals attempts to manipulate and control you, including your reputation, your career, and your personal wellbeing.

Figure 26.3 Example: A Predatory Individual Who Initiates Threats and Stalking After Being Reported for Sexual Harassment

An employee was terminated after several sexually inappropriate incidents. He professed interest in one female employee and he stated to her that "this is what I will do to you," staring in her eyes, all the while grinding his crotch into a filing cabinet. On another occasion, he began to explicitly comment on her body.

The female employee received several harassing phone calls, either silence or heavy breathing. She asked, "What do you want?"

He told her, "I want you." She threatened to call the police to which he replied, "Tell them I said 'hi.' My uncle works for that department." After a silence, he said, "It's not over. It will never be over and you brought it on yourself."

Tactical and Safety Considerations

The following will be helpful in your dealings with individuals who exhibit psychopathic traits:

- **You will be attacked through your best *and* your worst points**. The notion that the psychopathic individual will attack your weak points seems quite logical. If you are insecure about your personal appearance, for example, the psychopath will either make you feel more insecure, or in a more sophisticated tactic, reassure you that he/she, at least, find you quite attractive. What is harder to notice is when you are attacked through your best points. For example, if you appear to be physically fit, they will try to consult with you about your exercise regimen or ask where and when you workout. If you go to church, they will find a way to ask a very intelligent question about an aspect of the Bible you love so much. But they are asking you to gain some traction:

not to get your help. For such an individual, anything can be leverage. Remember, they do not even have to lie. The truth is an even better tool.

- **Notice when others start making excuses for the individual.** When conned or manipulated, people often find a way to rationalize what the psychopath is doing or has done. For example, after a frighteningly angry outburst in the legal department, in which he was escorted off the premises by security guards, a counselor says, "You have to understand. He was brought up that way. When you threatened him by telling him he had to leave the office, it was like a flashback to the way his father treated him." Do not permit others, either family members or treatment professionals, to sway your opinion or prevent you from attending to your professional duties.

- **Track any manipulation, document it well, and alert all other members of your team to the strategies they are using.** Consult and consult again. Do not discount the observations of other staff. Ensure everyone shares a common understanding of what and whom you are dealing with.

- **You may be intimidated.** The most obvious manifestation of intimidation is fear. <u>There is always a reason for fear.</u> If you are frightened of an individual, consult with your fellow Security Professionals or supervisors immediately. What is more difficult to recognize is an unconscious attempt to avoid being frightened by, colluding with, or giving into their demands. Ironically, the intimidated Security Professional may sometimes claim that they have a special rapport or working relationship with the individual, when in fact, all they are doing is giving the predatory individual what he/she wants.

- **Be aware of grooming behaviors.** The "grooming cycle" is a pattern of behavior designed to alleviate the intended victim's fears and apprehensions, while targeting them for attack. The individual will make their target feel a little off-balance, making them anxious, scared, or flattered. Then they lessen the pressure while making a request that the Security Professional would have granted anyway. The individual begins to "train" the Security Professional to experience a sense of relief when granting a request.

Figure 26.4 Example: Grooming

The individual stands too close to you (slightly, not enough to require you to issue a command that they back up). Then, simultaneous to moving back to a more comfortable distance, he asks for a glass of water. His goal is to cause you to associate granting a request with a release of tension. If successful, the individual will make requests that get closer and closer to a moral or ethical line. Once he can get you to do something *over* the line, however, slightly, you are now compromised: an object of blackmail or worse. Hard eye-contact, shifting to friendliness, is another common grooming tactic.

- **Guard all personal information.** As discussed previously, personal information can be used in a variety of ways. The psychopath can use such information to determine points of leverage against you. They can talk publicly about you, apparently displaying intimate knowledge of your affairs. In the worst case, such information can be used to track you down outside of your professional life or make you fear for the safety of your friends and family.

Figure 26.5 Example: The Danger of not Guarding Personal Information and the Reality of Publicly Available Information

A sociopathic person was being terminated for policy violations and had been made aware of an upcoming interview by security. When the Security Professionals arrived, he began naming their family members, home addresses, phone numbers, where the children went to school, and other personal information. This person very calmly provided this information to the Security Professionals, implying that if he were to be terminated they could expect a visit from him. It should be noted that he got the bulk of his information online.

- **Do not get beyond the horizon line.** *Do not meet psychopaths alone!* Do not close your office door when interviewing them. You are vulnerable to false accusations. You are also vulnerable to manipulation where with no one to monitor the interaction, you may not even perceive it happening; and of course, you are vulnerable to attack.
- **Calculated splitting.** As stated earlier, the psychopathic individual uses gossip, rumors, misdirection, and blatant lying to set all the stakeholders involved in their supervision and treatment against each other. Regular communication and consultation with the various members of the treatment team is the best way to detect, and confront splitting.

SECTION VI

Communication With Those With
Severe Mental Illness or Other Conditions
That Cause Severe Disability

CHAPTER 27

Overview

This section focuses on individuals you may rarely see: the profoundly mentally ill or those seriously affected by drugs, or other disorders of the brain. However, even if you only encounter someone like this once a year, or even once in a career, what an asset you will be to your company and your team if you know what to do and say when you are needed.

Such severe syndromes are not as rare as you might imagine. An individual may have a covert drug abuse problem and suddenly hit a "tipping point" and go completely over the edge. You may have an employee with bipolar disorder or schizophrenia and they discontinue their medications, and deteriorate to a terrible degree. An obsessive individual may become fixated on an employee or perhaps he/she is a customer and is upset at your billing practices or service and they present themselves at the front desk, incoherent and unwilling to leave. Our goal in this section is simple, whether you regularly encounter such individuals or not; we will become our best when we prepare for the worst.

Most encounters that you will have with mentally ill individuals are not emergencies. Nonetheless, the basic principles of communication presented here will serve you just as well with those who are manifesting a mild level of disorder as well as those who are on the extreme end of the spectrum.

Mental illness does not only refer to such disorders as schizophrenia, bipolar disorder, or depression. For example, intoxication can be considered a time limited, substance induced mental disorder ranging from profound psychosis to merely being a very irritating, intrusive person who will not follow social rules while under the influence. Subjects of the Security Professional's attention, otherwise normal, can display acute, "out of character" behaviors, due to problems or stressors in their lives. Thus, for the sake of this discussion, substance abuse, distinct neurological disorders, as well as atypical episodes brought on by stress or other factors can all function as mental illness. The cause may be relevant if making appropriate referrals for treatment: the Security Professional, however, should most emphatically focus on the behaviors, whatever the cause.

Setting the Record Straight

Popular media often makes a link between mental illness and criminality, but this is not accurate. Most mentally ill individuals are merely struggling human beings who, although they have a lot of difficulties in life, either in dealing with other people, or with the stresses of work and home, mean no one harm. Do not assume they are stupid or slow just because they speak or act in somewhat strange fashion. Be aware, be cautious, but speak clearly and with precision. Always remember who you are, whom you represent, and that the person you are interacting with deserves you to act as a professional.

Mentally ill people are at the greatest risk of becoming dangerous when they are treated poorly: disrespectfully, roughly, patronizingly, or threateningly: modes of behavior that no Security Professional should display. **Respect for such people is simple: we can choose to speak to the illness or speak to the *person* who is so ill.**

Not Just Technique

It is unavoidable that when you read something in sequence it will seem that the advice given in an item is **THE** procedure to do. However, all of the strategies described here overlap. Some are applicable in general, while others are specific to only one type of behavior/symptom. People are very complex and this, of course, includes people who have a mental illness. Just because you might be dealing with a paranoid individual, for example, does not mean that person is not also disorganized, delusional, or manic.

Figure 27 Focus on the Predominant Behavior

What you should assume when reading the different chapters in this section is that the chapter heading is the *predominant* behavior that the person is presenting.

CHAPTER 28

Struggling in a Fog:
Dealing With Symptoms of Disorganization

Figure 28.1 Disorganization: An Over-Arching Category

See Chapter 51 for a detailed discussion of de-escalation of disorganized individuals in a state of chaotic rage and Chapter 55 for information dealing with agitated developmentally disabled individuals.

Disorganization is an "over-arching" category. A disorganized person can be latent, concrete, have mood swings, paranoia, anxiety, extreme agitation, confusion, delusions and hallucinations, and information processing problems to name only a few behaviors that we discuss elsewhere in the book. This chapter is concerned with the overall phenomenon.

Understanding Disorganization

Disorganization is a general term used to describe what it is like when individuals cannot adequately organize their thinking, perceptions, behaviors, and/or emotions so that they can adequately function in the real world. This can include developmentally delayed people, profoundly psychotic people, those suffering from any kind of dementia or delirium, as well as those who are severely intoxicated (a chemically induced version of the same phenomenon).

Due to their cognitive limitations, developmentally disabled individuals are not skilled at problem-solving situations. Furthermore, they often lack the maturity to manage complex or frustrating situations.

Psychotic people also become disorganized when they really deteriorate. Oddly enough, their delusions may serve them as an organizing principle. For example, if you believe yourself to be surrounded by enemies or are on a mission to save the world, you have to concentrate because of your mission, as delusional as it may be. When one becomes disorganized even one's delusions break down into chaotic thoughts, which are often manifested in incoherent speech.

We may also be talking about someone overwhelmed by emotions. For example, imagine if one of your employees just got word that one of his children was killed in an automobile accident, or an employee is terminated, due to downsizing after 25 years on the job.

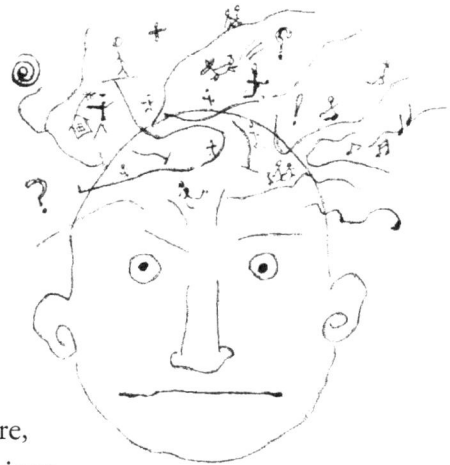

A final type of disorganization is manifested epilepsy, when the person, either during their seizure or afterwards, becomes profoundly disorganized.

Figure 28.2 Communication Difficulties

You will know you are dealing with a disorganized person because they are nearly incoherent or it is otherwise impossible to communicate with them. They may seem to shift from one emotion to another for no logical reason and it is very hard, if not impossible, to hold their attention.

Create Calm by Being Calm

The disorganized person pays far more attention to non-verbal communication. Therefore, keep the emotion out of your voice, and limit your physical gestures: self-control is particularly important when de-escalating disorganized individuals.

Small Bits at a Time

To better communicate with disorganized individuals, Security Professionals should divide instructions into small bits. Make sure that you are very specific in what you expect them to do. Your sentences should be short and each should only have one "packet" of information. There is no point in being irritable. That just makes things more difficult and confusing for the disorganized individual because they usually do not know why you are upset.

Let Me Repeat Myself

When we are not understood, our usual impulse is to elaborate: we use different words, expressive hand and facial gestures, and the emotional tone of our communication intensifies. ***With disorganized people, simply repeat the same statement or question word-for-word.*** When their disorganization is profound you may need to do these four, five, or even more times. The aim is not to browbeat them. You should not shout at them in hopes you will get through to them. Repetition is a touchstone of stability.

Figure 28.3 Repetition in the Service of Calming the Disorganized Person

If you change your vocal tone or get irritated, you will absolutely defeat the purpose of repetition. Rolling your eyes, making side-long glances of amusement to your back-up, sighing, raising your voice, pointing, standing close to them to get their attention, snapping your fingers, or suddenly clapping, to name only a few, undermine safety, whether you are repeating the same words or not.

By repeating yourself several times with a clear measured tone of voice, you can have the same effect on the disorganized person as you would were you to shine a light on a footpath in the fog. In this latter example, you have shown the lost person where to put their feet. By repeating yourself and telling the person exactly what you want them to do, you provide a verbal lifeline that they can focus on rather than the chaos that is otherwise overwhelming them.

Overstimulation

Loud noises, the presence of many people (particularly if more than one is talking), too much background noise, or even bright fluorescent lights will not only be distracting, but may further agitate the disorganized person. Consistent with both control and safety concerns, move the individual to a less stimulating environment, whenever it is possible. <u>It is particularly important with disorganized people that only one person speaks to them.</u>

Magical Thinking

"Magical thinking" is telling stories which you then believe. It is most common among small children, senile and demented adults, and developmentally delayed individuals. People displaying magical thinking do not show the same fixed quality of delusional people (Chapter 31), where a fundamental truth is suddenly revealed and then locked into place in the person's mind. Rather, the disorganized person verbalizes his fantasies, repeats them, and then believes them.

As far as Security Professionals are concerned, you will usually observe magical thinking in a developmentally disabled individual and is often presented as fable making: the kinds of stories told by very young people, either young in age or young in mind. Remember, you are interviewing the person for a reason. If they start "wandering off into fantasies, bring their attention back to the purpose of your interview. This is done in the same manner you do with a child whose attention is wandering: stay calm, stay firm.

Figure 28.4 Concerning False Admissions

Important: Research on false admissions to crimes reveals that a large number of such confessions are made by developmentally disabled individuals. This is relevant to the Security Professional, particular in investigations into theft or shoplifting. A developmentally disabled individual may admit to something when feeling emotionally pressured or if they are trying to impress or please you. You will get the most reliable information from developmentally disabled individuals when they are calm and feel safe.

Figure 28.5 Review: Disorganization

You will know you are dealing with a disorganized person when they are:

- Nearly incoherent, or otherwise impossible to communicate with.
- They seem to shift from one emotion to another with no logical reason.
- It is very hard, if not impossible to hold their attention.
- They are acting in a bizarre or chaotic manner.

You should:

- Give simple, specific instructions.
- Repeat your instructions rather than elaborate on them. Do not change your vocal tone.
- Only one person should be speaking to the disorganized person.
- Do not argue with magical thinking: redirect them to the reason for your contact as a Security Professional.
- Whenever possible, minimize environmental distractions: the TV in the background, other people talking, bright or flashing lights.

CHAPTER 29

Latency: Dropping Stones
Down a Well

> **Figure 29.1 Recognizing Latency**
>
> You will recognize latency when the person to whom you are speaking not only delays his/her answers for a long time, but when they do reply, their communication is somewhat odd and disjointed, not really responding to the questions asked. This is different from being silent or defying you. You get the sense that they are not "there," that it is about something going on inside of them, and not about you at all.

Latency is a behavior that is often a manifestation of disorganization, but because of both its significance and its confusing nature, we have chosen to discuss it as an entity of its own. It is a phenomenon in which people respond to communication in a very delayed manner. You ask a question and they talk to themselves quietly as they puzzle out what you might be saying. Perhaps instead, they do not even make eye-contact and engage in odd movements, often used as self-soothing behaviors. Some latent folks may simply stare away, a vacuous look on their face. When they finally reply, their reply is strange, perhaps nonsensical. Even when their response is coherent, it is usually very short, as if emerging with considerable difficulty from somewhere deep and far away.

Imagine your words to be like a stone dropping into a well. If things go as expected, you hear a splash as the stone hits the water at the bottom. Now, imagine the latent mind like an old well with bricks sticking out, and a tangle of tree roots halfway down. The stone hits the roots and bounces off a brick, then another and another. This time, you do not hear a splash; you hear nothing. So you start throwing more stones, one after another. You now have any number of stones bouncing around, colliding into each other, adding to your frustration and their confusion, without the first stone ever reaching the bottom of the well. All that is happened with the latent person is that they get more confused and overwhelmed. In other words, adding more words does not enhance communication with latent people.

Coping with Latency: Keep Things Simple

Although communicating with a latent person can be frustrating and often time consuming, the Security Professional should remain calm. Indeed, any frustration or anger you display will only further confuse them. Keep your sentences and instructions short yet direct, and minimize the use of qualifiers, such as "you might" "maybe" "kind of", etc., that you ordinarily put in your sentences. Security Professionals should also try to minimize the use of hand gestures or changing facial expressions. This does not mean you should speak robotically, but simplicity is best.

It is totally useless to try to "get through to them" by yelling at them. All this does is drive them further into the latent state, as they get more frightened, overwhelmed, or confused by the irate Security Professional yelling incomprehensible things at them.

Latent people usually do **not** need things explained in further detail; they just did not "get it" the first time. Say the same thing again, and yet again, as many times as is needed. This is like somehow throwing the same stone down the well over again, reinforcing the original. Rather than adding a new stone, you have added weight to the one already there. Now that stone can get through the roots and bricks and hit bottom.

Figure 29.2 Example: Non-emergent Dialogue Between a Security Professional and an Individual Displaying Latency

An individual is in front of the building, trying to tie himself to one of the railings with a piece of string.

- **Security Professional.** "Why are you tying yourself to the railing?" (*Thirty seconds pass with the latent man standing and staring at the ground, frozen.*)
- **Security Professional.** (*Asks again.*) "Why are you typing yourself to the railing?"
- **Mentally ill man.** (*He slowly raises his head, and his eyes vacant, slowly speaks.*) "Uh, rail roaded." He then resumes tying himself to the railing.
- **Security Professional.** "I can call for help so you can go to the hospital. I know there is someone there that is able to help you."
- **Mentally ill man.** (*Stops tying himself, his hands still holding the string in mid-knot. His lips move as if he is talking to himself. He raises his eyes, lowers them—raises them again. Finally, speak.*) "Don't take me steal me." (*He then resumes his activity without eye contact.*)

Note: The Security Professional's exemplary patience. This contact is not a failure. The professional has ascertained that the individual is so profoundly ill that he is unable to communicate even his identity. That the professional is calm probably keeps the individual from becoming fearful or combative in response.

Figure 29.3 Review
How best to speak to a latent individual:
- Keep your sentences short.
- Do not change your vocal tone.
- Repeat the instructions using the same words and the same tone of voice.
- Pause between sentences in order to give the individual time to process what you have said.

CHAPTER 30

Withdrawal From
Intoxicating Substances

First and foremost, alcohol and drug withdrawal is a medical emergency. There is no specific withdrawal anger or rage. Basing your interventions on their behaviors, as described throughout this book, use whatever tactics necessary to de-escalate and control them. The Security Professional should summons medical attention immediately, and then focus on keeping the individual calm while waiting for medical assistance.

Individuals in withdrawal are often in pain or feeling quite ill. They are also frightened or irritable, and very much focused on getting their needs met. This may include a high level of resistance to seeking medical attention. Of course, the individual often merely wants the Security Professional to let them go so they can go out and acquire more drugs. The signs of withdrawal can include:

- **Unstable coordination.** Try to get them to sit or lie down for their safety.
- **Restlessness and agitation.** Try to reduce any stimulating input.
- **Unpredictable and sudden actions.** Keep your movements calm and slow so that you do not elicit a startle reflex on their part, which can easily turn into an attack.
- **Slurred or incoherent speech.** Speak to them in a calm, quiet voice and make an extra effort to understand what they are saying. Provide short explanations.
- **Abnormally rigid muscles.** Note the abnormally rigid muscles in an individual in withdrawal.
- **Being argumentative and demanding.** Try to redirect them or de-escalate depending on the mode of anger or rage they exhibit.

Figure 30 Review: Calming of Individuals in Withdrawal

Be calm and firm. Redirect them when they get very demanding. Reassure them that help is on the way. You are simply trying to delay things until the ambulance and/or back-up arrives. To reiterate, this is a medical emergency. A person in withdrawal may die without help.

There is no specific withdrawal rage. They will display terrified, chaotic, hot, cold or predatory rage (Section X). Use the tactics that best fit the mode of rage they are in.

CHAPTER 31

Psychosis: Delusions and Hallucinations

Whatever the diagnosis (schizophrenia, bipolar disorder, trauma based, depression, or drug induced) the syndrome of psychosis is typified by delusions and/or hallucinations.

What is a Delusion?

A delusion is usually referred to as a belief that does not conform to reality. Actually, it is a lot more than that. The following will be helpful:

- People from different cultures have different beliefs. Shared cultural beliefs, however, are not delusional, even if you cannot conceive how others could see the world as they do.
- There is often nothing remarkable about the delusional belief, except that it is not true. For example, everyone knows the FBI follows people. The question in this case would be, "Is the FBI following this particular individual?"
- Lots of people have eccentric beliefs: unconventional religious rites, non-traditional dietary and health habits, aliens, crop circles, or telepathy. Some of these are possibly *your* beliefs: they are eccentric to us, but not to you. However, unusual ideas and beliefs are not delusional.

Being delusional is like being a member of a one-person cult. All the confusing thoughts the individual may have: all their worries, prayers, fantasies, or ideas suddenly coalesce into ***BELIEF***. Such beliefs are unshakable, inarguable, and unaltered by conflicting evidence.

Figure 31.1 Example: Delusional People Can Be Dangerous

A customer entered a cell-phone store and demanded two G1 phones because, he said he was President Barack Obama. He became increasingly agitated. One of the employees attempted to calm him down, and the customer became more agitated and stated to the employee, "I am going to get my gun and F***ing kill you. As the president, I am the commander-in-chief, and you will obey me." At that point building security was called. They escorted him outside and engaged him in a discussion, delaying him, while police were called. Police detained him and upon a search of his car found a loaded handgun.

Types of Delusions

The following are the types of delusions:

- **Grandiose.** People believe that they have been appointed on a special mission, that they have extraordinary or unusual powers or are special, remarkable beings.
- **Religious delusions.** Often linked with grandiose delusions, people may become preoccupied with religion, focusing all their attention on their beliefs, which may be self-made or associated with mainstream doctrines.
- **Jealous delusions.** The individual may believe, against all evidence, that their partners are unfaithful to them. Jealous delusions surpass the almost always irrational nature of ordinary jealousy. The jealous delusional individual concocts infidelity out of the slightest glance, a change in clothing, or a five-minute delay in returning home. Perpetrators of domestic violence, particularly those with a paranoid or borderline character structure (Chapters 23 and 24) often manifest this type of delusional psychosis in periods of stress.
- **Delusional stalking (erotomania).** Psychotic stalkers may believe that another person is in love with them, is married to them, or has been somehow designated as theirs, whether they know it or not. Special requirements for communicating with those who display erotomaniac stalking behaviors will be discussed below.
- **Persecutory delusions (paranoia).** Paranoid individuals may believe that people, institutions, or other powers have hostile intentions toward them; are committing evil actions against them; that others are sending energy toward them, thinking about them, talking about them, reading their minds; looking at them with malevolent intent or even poisoning them. In addition to general strategies for any paranoid person (Chapter 23) we must also include those relevant for psychosis when they are delusional as well.

What are hallucinations?

Hallucinations are perceptions through any of the five senses that do not conform to reality. Hallucinations are often, but not always, accompanied by delusions. It is possible to perceive a hallucination but be neither delusional nor psychotic.

Figure 31.2 Not All Hallucinations Are a Manifestation of Psychosis

A person may hallucinate, but realize that it is a disturbance of perception rather than reality. For example, people suffering from several days of jet-lag may complain of hearing voices. However, they are quite aware that the voices are caused by sleep-deprivation and pay them no more heed than people do when they have a song "stuck" in their head.

Types of Hallucinations

The following are types of hallucinations:

- **Auditory hallucinations.** There are two levels of halluci- nations perceived through hearing. The first level is ***auditory distortion***. One mishears what is said, something that is frequently part of persecutory delusions. For ex- ample, a paranoid person is sitting near someone in a res- taurant who says, "Do you want the chicken or the ribs?" They hear, "Let's get this chicken in the ribs." The second level is true ***auditory hallucinations***. Close your eyes when someone speaks to you. Do you still hear their voice? Of course you do. When people have an auditory hallucination, the voices are equally real. They are experienced not imagined. That is why you cannot simply say, "The voice isn't real." That makes as much sense to them as someone telling you that your foot is not real. ***Paranoid individuals often display a "listening attitude:"*** They enter a situation that evokes their paranoia and expect to be victim- ized, accused, talked about, or assaulted. Then they either mishear people based on what they expect to hear or in more severe cases, actually hear hallucinatory voices uttering just what they expected or feared.[9]

- **Visual hallucinations.** People may experience ***visual distortions***. The distorted visual image appears to move, melt, emerge toward you, or even speak. Think of a Salvador Dali painting in which the objects melt and flow. The second level is about true ***visual hallucinations,*** in which objects or beings appear that no one else can see.

- **Olfactory hallucinations.** This is sometimes a result or symptom of brain injury, as the part of the brain that detects odor(s) is at the front of the head, a frequent target of blows. If a previous- ly non-psychotic individual complains of hallucinatory smells, immediately get them checked medically. This is often an emergent situation that, if not addressed, can result in permanent brain damage. Other people, without head injuries and purely psychotic, can get focused on their own body smells, and believe, for example, that they are rotting away. Other times, people believe they can smell poison gas seeping through the walls.

- **Tactile hallucinations.** These are sensations felt within the body. The sensation of bugs crawling on the skin is a frequent side effect of such drugs as methamphetamine or cocaine. Tactile hal- lucinations can also be a side effect of the individual's psychiatric medication. A medical doctor should always check this symptom.

The Torment of Hallucinations

Hallucinations torment their victims in a variety of ways:

- For unknown reasons, hallucinated voices are almost always cruel. People can be ordered to do awful or degrading things. They may simply hear awful sounds and ugly demeaning words. Visual hallucinations can be as haunting as ghosts. Olfactory hallucinations are often foul and tactile hallucinations are almost always very unpleasant sensations.

- People try to tell others what they perceive, but their experience is denied over and over again. They can be teased or laughed at. Ironically, the people they tell often torment them in ways similar to the torment of the hallucinations.
- Psychotic people find that their worldview is called into question every day. They do not know what is real and what is not. Imagine perceiving your workmates whispering about you or that the handle of your coffee cup suddenly transforms and winds around your finger like a little snake. Imagine this is true of every object in your life. In such circumstances, the person finds it difficult to trust anything at all.

CHAPTER 32

Communication With an Individual Experiencing Delusions or Hallucinations

Disengage

It can be very draining to talk with a delusional individual. Like a cultist trying to convert you to their group, the individual may try to convince you that what they believe is real. They may insist that you accept their beliefs, or even more problematic, insist that you *do* believe, but simply will not admit it. They become focused on debating your resistance or furious that you deny what is, to them, absolutely true.

There is often no good reason to continue such a discussion. Delusions are not like some sort of backed-up fluid that you vent and drain away. The more the delusional individual talks about it, the more preoccupied he/she becomes, and more agitated as well. While delusional individuals may feel locked in their inner world and desperate to communicate what they are experiencing, discussion and argument seem to cement the delusions even further.

Security Professionals will face this situation when dealing with intruders or psychotic customers or clients (for example, at a utility company). Often the best thing to do is firmly and calmly escort them off the property, saying without heat that they are at the wrong place to discuss the subject of their concern, so it is time to go.

Figure 32.1 Rule #1: Disengage

There are many occasions when nothing at all can be accomplished by talking about delusions or hallucinations. There is no emergency and no need for investigation or information gathering. In such cases, disengage.

Islands of Sanity

Imagine being dropped overboard into the ocean. It is cold and rough among the waves, and there are all sorts of sea-life that demand your attention, everything from sharks to jellyfish. There seems to be no way to escape, and it is so overwhelming that you cannot take your mind off of it.

Even in the ocean, however, there are small islands. If you can only get to them, you can put your feet on solid ground. For psychotic people, too, there are "islands of sanity," areas of their lives where they are not delusional. They may be convinced, for example, that someone is poisoning their food and only canned goods are safe to eat, or that someone is beaming messages directly into their brain. But when you bring up the subject of football, and the two of you begin talking about how the Steelers demolished yet another opponent, the individual takes his mind off his delusions, and for a brief moment, has a moment of respite. If you steer conversations toward these islands of sanity, they may begin to see the Security Professional as the most stable person in their life, someone with whom they can have moments of clarity and peace.

The reader may think that such a relationship is an unlikely possibility. We ask you to again think of mentally ill customers or clients, in a large public defender's office, or a utility company. It may be the Security Professional's skill which enables him/her to smoothly, time and again, escort this individual, who may have a legal right to visit the premises, back onto the street with a minimum of fuss.

Figure 32.2 Rule #2: Move Toward the Islands of Sanity

Pay attention to subjects where the person is not delusional, so-called "islands of sanity," and whenever possible, direct your conversation there, rather than allowing it to focus on delusional subjects. Make links with other subjects that are also not tainted by delusions whenever you can. Think of yourself as expanding the size of the "land-mass:" making an area where it is predictable and safe. If the individual gets stuck within his/her delusions, you may find that changing the subject requires real finesse. Nonetheless, do so whenever you can, because talking about delusions makes it worse.

NOTE: These "islands of sanity" are not necessarily "nice" subjects. One of the authors worked with a very dangerous man for nine months and the only subjects that he was not floridly psychotic were bar fights and motorcycles. It was safer talking about the sound of a cue ball impacting on someone's skull than what he had for dinner or what his childhood was like.

Threat Assessment: When *should* you talk about the delusions or hallucinations?

Some of the most dangerously mentally ill individuals are those whom you see over and over again. Because they frequently decompensate, or go off their medications, it is necessary to do a brief threat assessment every time you see them.

Imagine you have a delusional individual who repeatedly enters your worksite, an area where the general public has a right to visit. She believes that she is the Archangel Michael. If you recall this biblical story, Michael, the righteous sword of the Lord, casts Satan out of Heaven. Some years ago, believing that she saw evidence of Satan's corruption among her neighbors, she acquired a sword and tried to break into their house. Thankfully, no one was hurt, but this made the news in the small town where your company is located. She was committed to an institution for almost six months. Now released, she is not "cured," but is stable enough to live in the community.

She drops by your worksite on a rather frequent basis. It is the Security Professional's responsibility to escort her off the property, once it is clear that she has no business there. In the process, however, it is incumbent upon that Security Professional to assess, as best as possible, if she is presenting a danger to those on the worksite and to the community at large. Therefore, whenever this woman begins to talk about God, angels, Satan, or anything similar, it would be a good idea to ask questions about that which she is preoccupied:

- "Mrs. Hampton, are you telling me that you think you have seen Satan? Where?"
- "Why do you think that this is Satan's work?"
- "Do you think you should do anything about this?"
- "What do you think you should do?"

If Mrs. Hampton's answers are bland and nonaggressive, change the subject to an "island of sanity" at the right moment. If her answers seem to manifest dangerous ideation, then immediate action may be required. For example, if she said, "Don't call me Mrs. Slut Whore-of-Babylon-Hampton! I'm Michael, the Lord's most beloved angel. Satan will have no place on this earth when I take my righteous sword in my strong right arm!" you would need to take action immediately.

Dangerous answers are an alarm call to get help, and the Security Professional should immediately alert both police and the designated mental health professionals. And one final thing to consider: a person who believes herself to be the mightiest angel in Heaven and on a mission from God is likely to object when you try to take her into secure custody. Be very alert to danger!

> **Figure 32.3 Rule #3: Talk About the Delusions to Assess Risk**
>
> Talk about the delusions as a means of threat assessment. Ask direct questions, particularly in regard to the person's intention to hurt himself/herself or others. When contacting such an individual bring up the issue of concern yourself if they do not do so on their own, just to see if she has become seriously delusional again. For example, "The last time we talked, you told me about the Angel Michael and Satan. Are you worried about the Devil today?" Remember, the distinction between this rule and the previous two is that in this case, you are assessing risk, not just indulging in a conversation about their preoccupations.

Do Not Agree—At Least Most of the Time

It might seem to be easiest to take the line of least resistance—simply agree with the delusions, or pretend that you, too, perceive the hallucinations rather than get caught in arguments with a mentally ill person about reality. There are a number of problems in doing so:

- When you agree with delusions and/or hallucinations, you will entrench them even more deeply into the individual's belief system.
- Agreement can also lead to the Security Professional being *incorporated* into their delusions and hallucinations. This can become dangerous if the individual decides that you are in collusion

with their perceived enemies, or they may perceive you as either scamming them or making fun of them. In almost all circumstances, do NOT agree with the delusions.

Figure 32.4 Rule #4: Do Not Agree Most of the Time

In almost all circumstances, do NOT agree with the delusions.

Do Not Disagree—At Least Most of the Time

Common sense seems to demand that you speak for reality. When an individual sees something that is not there, shouldn't you tell them so? If they have an irrational belief, why not argue them out of it, or at least, diplomatically point out where they are wrong. The problem with arguing with delusional or hallucinating people is that you are telling them that their perceptions are lying to them. If they had any trust in you before, it is unlikely that telling them that the world as they see it is not real will improve that rapport.

Sometimes, however, a delusional individual may ask or even plead with you, for disagreement because they do not want to believe what their delusions seem to tell them. At other times, a hallucinating person can make a tenuous distinction between real perceptions and hallucinations and will ask if you think something hallucinated is real. In these cases, *when you have been invited*, you may state that not only do you not perceive or believe the hallucination or delusion, but you also do not think it is real.

Figure 32.5 Rule #5 Do Not Disagree, at Least Most of the Time

Do not engage in arguments about whether the psychotic person's perceptions are real. However, if they <u>ask</u> you for a "reality check," then you can state that you do not believe that the delusional belief is correct or the hallucination is real. In this case, you are helping the person understand that what he or she perceives is not the "rule" of the world.

Important Exception to the "Do Not Disagree" Rule—Delusional Stalking

Stalking delusions[10] are dangerous because they involve another person as the victim. In addition, the individual is often possessed of an absolutely entitled sense of their right to approach or harass the victim, either in person, or as is becoming more common, through the use of electronic media such as text message, email, or social networking websites. Such unwelcomed advances may be criminal in nature (especially if the individual is already under supervision for a crime against the same victim), and the individual must be confronted about their behavior immediately.

You will usually be involved in stalking situations when an employee is the victim. The safety of the victim is the Security Professional's paramount concern, and you must act quickly in response to calls from the victim reporting harassing or threatening behavior. This includes accessing law enforcement as well as creating a safety plan on-site as well as assisting the victim in establishing safety when off company grounds.

When making direct contact with the delusional stalker, Security Professionals must calmly, but directly, inform the individual that the subject of their delusions is not destined for, in love with, or otherwise involved with them. Calmly and directly tell the stalker they have no right to the victim they stalk. Do what ever you can within your professional responsibilities to keep them far away from their victim. Establish a comprehensive safety plan.

If the individual threatens or hints at committing an act of violence against the subject of their delusions, the Security Professional must contact law enforcement immediately. Security Professionals should consult with their company's legal advisor to prepare for the possibility that a stalker will target one of your employees. Developing an understanding of all the legal ramifications in your state or country must be accomplished before a stalking incident occurs.

Figure 32.6 Rule #6 Exception: Disagree With the Delusion of Erotomania (Delusional Stalking)

Calmly and directly tell the delusional stalker they have no right to the victim they stalk. You task must center around whatever it takes to ensure the safety of the victim.

Differentiation: Distinguish Between Your World and Theirs

Delusional beliefs are nearly inescapable. When an individual experiencing psychotic symptoms attempts to talk about their delusions they are often brushed off, minimized, or even ridiculed. How, then, can Security Professionals respond in a respectful way to an individual's delusional thinking, while also trying to get the individual to recognize the distinction between the real world and theirs? ***Differentiate*** yourself from them.

To differentiate is to perceive or express a difference. The authors mean that the Security Professional should acknowledge the individual's perceptions and beliefs, while also informing them that although you do not share their perceptions, you are not arguing that theirs are invalid, unrealistic, or fantastical. You are, however, attempting to have the individual also concede that other viewpoints do exist. The following are some examples:
- "Sal, I only hear two voices in this room: yours and mine. I don't hear a woman's voice at all. What do you hear her say?"
- "Jamey, I know about the democrats and the republicans. I've never heard of the Illuminated Ones. I'm not arguing with you here. I'm just saying that I've never heard of them, so I'm not the person to talk about them."

Remember, the point here is not to convince the individual that their delusions are not real or even that they are wrong. Basically, differentiation helps you keep the lines of communication open. Think of two people from different cultures, trying to explain what it is like to live in their respective worlds, or even two beings from different planets. If the mentally ill individual finds they shut-down or discounted when they try to talk about their perceptions or beliefs, it is very unlikely that they will be compliant with the Security Professional when it is necessary to require them to do something.

In some circumstances, you can act in concert with their belief without endorsing it. For example, "I can't see the laser beams, but I know lasers don't pass through solid objects. Maybe you will feel safer sitting in that ambulance over there."[11]

Figure 32.7 Example: Acting in Concert With Beliefs Without Endorsing Them

Our Security Professionals were directed to an employee who actually believed he was a vampire (and looked it). There was a history, unknown to the Security Professionals, of paranoia on the part of this employee about a) sunlight; and b) that Security Professionals and HR were the enemy out to destroy him. When the employee, who had to be escorted out, expressed fear of the sunlight, Security Professionals maintained a differentiated stance, and without agreeing with his delusions, escorted him out of the building via the garages and not in the sunlight. The person expressed gratitude for the understanding.

Figure 32.8 Rule #7 Differentiate

Give the person the "right" to their own perceptions and beliefs. Inform them that while you do not perceive what they do, you are not arguing with them about what *they* see or believe.

In some cases, take their delusions into account without agreeing with them. Example: "I don't see any razor blades in the bushes around the premises here, but if I did, I wouldn't walk around here anyway. Seriously, if what you are seeing is true, what are you doing in the bushes instead of staying safely somewhere else?

Steam Valve: When the Pressure Is Too Great

Some people, either psychotic or manic (Chapter 33) are so full of things to say, think, or feel that they seem like they are going to explode from the pressure. Their speech can become pressured as well. Words burst out of them in a cascade.

Sometimes they make sense, but they totally dominate the "air time" in the room, talking over other people. Even if there is a task to be done, they cannot focus and they make it nearly impossible for you to focus as well. Other times, they make no sense whatsoever. Their words may sound like poetry as they link words by sound, not by meaning. They may jump from idea to idea, in what are called "loose associations," or "tangential thinking."

A Security Professional will usually encounter such an individual if they are an outsider coming onto the worksite. However, as noted previously, bipolar individuals may be very valued members of your company, highly functioning employees of whom no one has the slightest idea that they have any mental disorder. They may go off their medications for a variety of reasons: unpleasant side-effect, boredom (the manic state is like a high) or even doctor's orders (she is pregnant, and the medications are not good for the baby). You will be talking with the individual to keep them stable, until emergency personnel (police or EMT/paramedics) arrive to secure their safety.

Obviously however, you cannot partake in a one-sided conversation where the individual does all of the talking. The Security Professional must regain control of the interview. Sometimes you simply have to say, "You have talked enough for awhile. We need to move on to other matters." For some individuals this works quite well; it is honest, it is direct, and it sets a limit.

At other times, one needs to let out a little pressure like opening a valve in a steam pipe. Then you take over saying one portion of what you have to say. The steps for steam-valving are as follows:

- First, put out a hand, palm down, fingers curved at waist level to interrupt them. If they do not perceive it, put up both hands, using a little drama in your facial expression to get their attention and interrupt.
- You have let them speak for a little while about their preoccupations, and in the process, you have let out a little pressure, so to speak.
- Sum up what they said in a sentence or two. Put a little energy in your voice to prove that you are really "with" them. Then, ask or say something, getting either some compliance or a bit of information. "That is serious. Politics right now are terrible! You HAVE to tell me more about the left-wing conspiracy, but before you do, did your brother come home last night?"
- In return, let them return to their cascade of ideas, allowing a little more pressure to be released.
- Once again, firmly interrupt, and ask your next question or get agreement on the next item on your list.

Figure 32.9 Example: Steam Valve Technique

Subject. *(Flight of ideas)*

Security Professional. *(Interrupting)* "Madeline, you are really upset about health care. I want to hear more, but first, where is your office key? Okay, thank you."

Subject. *(More flight of ideas)*

Security Professional. *(Interrupting)* "So you think this will make us all sick, that if we all go to the same clinics, we'll all get the same bacteria, and this is the government's plan. I want to hear more about this, but first, did you remove anything from your office, or is everything still there?"

In essence, you sum up what they said to prove you were listening, and *then* ask your question or make your statement. Steam-valving is for the purpose of letting the individual say enough of what is pressuring him/her internally so that they do not fight you for the conversational floor.

This "steam valve" technique is useful with individuals whose speech is a cascade of words, ideas, often tangential or delusional. You listen, and then, tactfully but firmly, interrupt. Ask a question or interject a statement, get a response, and then let them return to their cascade of words. Listen a bit, and then interrupt again. Remember, you must show in your response/interruption that you have been listening to what they say.

Figure 32.10 Example: Use of the Steam Valve Technique With an Employee Undergoing a Psychotic Episode

Employee. "I was looking outside my window at the birdfeeder, and it was covered with goldfinches. The lemony yellow just burned my eyes so badly I closed the curtains. My eyes were burned by the fiery birds."

Security Professional. *(Interrupting firmly)* "Charles, I want to hear more about those birds. I haven't seen any goldfinches this year. But first, did you call your wife to pick you up?

Employee. "Yes, I did, behind the closed drapes, where the birds couldn't burn my eyes out. I called and talked to her—very loving she was. They have a sound that is piercing to the brain, and a single glance can burn your eyes to a crisp—the birds, not my wife."

Security Professional. "I can see you are worried about your eyes. That's why you have the sunglasses, huh? I want you to tell me how the sunglasses are working, but first, when will she get here?"

Employee. "Fifteen minutes, she said, but I don't know when, or what time. I'm burning among the birds, you see, with their lemony scalding flame."

As you can see, the Security Professional was able to get the information that the individual actually did call home. At this point, the Security Professional should call to confirm that she's on her way.

Figure 32.11 Rule #8 Steam-valving

This is useful with individuals whose speech is a cascade of words and ideas that are either all over the place (zigzag) or delusional. Listen and then interrupt. Sum up what they said, and tell them you want to hear more, but before they do, you have a question (or instruction) for them. Then let them return to their cascade of words. Listen a bit more, then interrupt again. Continue with multiple sequences of release of pressure, interruptions and questions, until you get the information you need.

Physical Space, Physical Contact, and the Use of the Eyes With Psychotic People

Concerns about eye contact and physical contact are incredibly important in regards to people with psychosis.

- Even more than in ordinary circumstances, be acutely aware when you are inadvertently "pressuring" the psychotic person by standing or sitting too close to them. Consider this *your* responsibility: do not expect the psychotic person to necessarily tell you. The first sign that you are too close—if you are not paying attention—may be an attack as the psychotic person believes they must protect themselves from your "invasion."

- Other psychotic individuals are not aware whatsoever of personal space, and stand or sit too close to you. Firmly, without aggression or heat, tell them to move back. "Monty, I really want to hear what you are saying. But you are standing too close to me. Step four big steps back and tell me more."

- For many psychotic folks, direct, sustained eye contact seems to pierce them to the brain. It is as if you can read their thoughts. Other mentally ill people can misinterpret direct eye contact as aggressive, threatening, or seductive. Therefore, if they are uncomfortable with being directly looked at (You will know it!), occasionally "touch base" by making brief eye contact, then ease your eyes away, and then back again. Of course, never take your eyes off of the individual so that you are unaware of any precursors to assault.

Figure 32.12 Rule #9 Body Spacing, Body Contact, and Eye Contact

Be aware of physical spacing—do not stand too close, and do not accept the person standing too close to you.

Most psychotic people are made anxious by too direct eye contact, experiencing it as either a threat or a challenge. Limit eye contact when it is not emergent so that you have to establish control through command presence, a situation where direct eye contact is a necessity.

CHAPTER 33

Welcome to the Rollercoaster:
Tactics for Dealing With Symptoms of Mania

Figure 33.1 Concerning Mania

Do not assume that people prone to mania will not be present on your worksite, either as customer/clients or as employees. Mania usually emerges from two sources: stimulant drug abuse and as the "up" phase of bipolar disorder. (Also known as manic depression.).

One of the hallmarks of stimulant abuse is that in its beginning stages the person can actually function *better* than normal. It is only after continued abuse that the hallmark signs of deterioration emerge, including hyperactivity, agitation, paranoia, even psychosis.

Similarly, those with bipolar disorder can function as very productive members of society. For many, the medications allow them to live absolutely uneventful and normal lives. Many others do not take medications, but they either show no signs of the illness most of the time, except for brief, albeit dramatic, episodes, or as often happens they have their first manic episode while on the worksite. In other words, no one, including themselves, knew that they were ill: their lives suddenly explode.

Mania is a state of high energy. Manic individuals need little sleep, and can be excited, grandiose, agitated, or irritable. They often have flights of fancy, which can be either creative or completely irrational. Their speech is often pressured: not only is it rapid, but there is a sense that there is more to say than they can get out.

They are usually extremely confident, even to the degree of believing themselves to be invulnerable. Manic individuals are often self centered. They feel wonderful, and their own needs and desires are the only things that matter. Their judgment can be extremely poor and impulsive, and they engage in behaviors that can put them or others at risk.

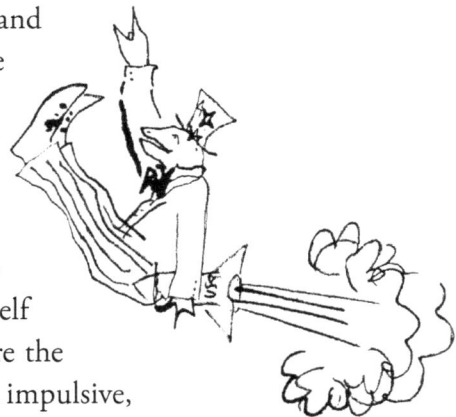

> **Figure 33.2 Beyond Mania Is Chaos**
>
> Aside from bipolar disorder and stimulant drug abuse, people with different brain malfunctions can have periods of agitation that may look very much like mania, but this kind of delirium is usually more extreme than the classic manic state. Such people are usually quite confused and disorganized. On the other hand, manic people can get so agitated, called manic excitement that they shift into a delirium state. All such individuals are de-escalated using the strategies described in Chapter 51 on Chaotic Rage.

Manic individuals are particularly vulnerable because they are most susceptible to making harmful decisions when they feel wonderful. Imagine the best spring day of your life. The sky is blue, birds are singing, and a gentle breeze keeps things just cool enough to be comfortable. You wake up and literally jump out of bed, happy to be alive. You have so much energy that it feels like there is champagne in your veins. You know you will make some new friends today, so you are going to go to the park, the club, and the bar—whatever—and just enjoy life. Imagine that feeling day-after-day, multiplied by ten or twentyfold. Can you see how easy it would be to begin to make unwise choices, how your confidence could lead you to, for example, hijack that freight train because you always wanted to be an engineer?[12]

When you feel this good, it seems like a good idea to feel *even better*! Thus, manic people very often want to party. Drugs and alcohol are very tempting, spending money to buy anything and everything one wants leads to credit cards run to the max, and often the energy turns sexual and the manic person gets involved with people who may be inappropriate for them or even dangerous. On the flip side, manic people—stimulant drug users or not—sometimes try to calm themselves with other drugs: barbiturates, heroin, and alcohol. Alcohol can have a "paradoxical effect" on some manic individuals, further exciting rather than sedating them.[13]

Manic people often talk in rapid cascades of words, a waterfall of ideas leaping from one area to another. Sometimes you can follow their thoughts, although they are speaking very rapidly, but at other times, they leap and zigzag, making connections that have little or no meaning to you.

In extreme manic states, people can become psychotic, with all the symptoms of grandiosity, persecutory, paranoid, and religious delusions that any other psychotic individual might.

Some manic people become very irritable. They can have a hair-trigger temper, and may also be provocative. Rather than merely being reactive, some will aggressively tease and taunt other people. It may seem to be in good fun, at first, but it goes way too far. Others may simply try to pick a fight. Because manic individuals can easily become angry or even violent, the authors recommend strongly that Security Professionals familiarize themselves with the latter sections in this book concerning the de-escalation of anger and rage.

Brittle Grandiosity

Manic people can act as if they do not have a care in the world. They spin ideas, one after another, and expect both agreement and admiration. They seem utterly self-confident. However, truly self-confident individuals are resilient; unfair criticisms seem to bounce off them. They can respond either with a gracious laugh or a dignified response. Think of manic grandiosity, however, as a fragile structure, like a tower made of spun sugar. It glitters, it glows, and it is huge! But tap the wrong strut or beam and the entire tower falls down in shards.

If you bluntly criticize individuals who are manic, they can experience your criticism as a personal attack, and from giddy happiness, they suddenly turn on you in rage. If you tease them about their somewhat irrational ideas, try to joke around with them, or laugh at something funny that they said, they easily misinterpret this, too, as an attack, thinking you are making fun of them. In other words, consider the manic flight of words to be a kind of hysteria. Even when they appear happy, it is as if they are on a giddy flight hanging onto a helium balloon. It certainly is thrilling: until they look down! Miscalculated teasing or criticism is experienced as if you are poking at the balloon with a needle

Figure 33.3 Author's Example: They may be acting like a comedian, but they are not trying to be funny!

One of the writers recalls a little guy who had lined up over five thousand "matchbox" cars on every projecting surface of the inside of his house. None were glued, but they were perfectly balanced, even on the molding on the walls! Because he had overdosed, we took him to the hospital. He was given charcoal, and as he sat on a gurney, belching black fluid down his chin into a pan, he was talking non-stop, chirping like a little bird, asking why, if this medicine was so bad, they had given it to a man like him? It was both a reasonable question and, under the particular circumstances, funny. One of the nurses began to laugh, and he threw the metal basin he was holding right at her head, and still spewing black vomit, grabbed her by the throat, screaming, "This isn't funny. Nothing's funny!"

Watch Out! Mania can be Infectious

Although manic individuals can present themselves as brilliant conversationalists, witty, sexy, provocative, entertaining, Security Professionals must be wary of being seduced by the their overt friendliness or entertaining demeanor. Do not allow an individual's apparent personality (He is such a nice guy, a lot of fun!), to cloud your professional judgment and responsibilities.

If you accept, or go along with, the manic individual's actions without contradiction and appropriate limit setting, he/she will assume you are in agreement with them. However, when you subsequently sanction them for those behaviors, they may suddenly turn on you in betrayed anger.

Do not get swept up in the individual's behavior, no matter how apparently innocuous or entertaining they appear. Manic individuals can be very manipulative, while appearing to be friendly and engaging, they are only doing so in an effort to control the relationship. Remember, the manic individual may be very provocative (think of the relationship of the Road Runner and the Coyote), trying to set you up for an over-reaction or making you look like a fool. As said earlier, they often sexualize interactions; you must be very cautious that they do not perceive sexual interest on your part based on your letting pass some innuendo or mild flirtatious comment.

There is an old expression: "He's a drag," referring to someone who slows the party down. That can be an effective approach with the manic person. In order to do this:

- Stay centered.
- Do not get swept away or swept up in their energy.
- Focus on slowing things down. Speak slower, and take things step-by-step.

Figure 33.4 Review: Dealing With a Person in a Manic State

You will recognize the manic person because they will display super high energy. They will often be talking very fast and their ideas will "zigzag" from one to another. They often act like comedians, with a rapid-fire delivery. Their behavior may also be either sexualized or hair-trigger aggressive. In either case, they will very likely be provocative.

- Remain calm and centered.
- Be conscious of their "brittle" state of mind, in spite of how confidently they behave. Grandiose does not mean strong!
- Do not bluntly criticize their actions.
- Do not tease or joke around. If you use any humor, it is for the purpose of slowing them down, not having fun.
- Do not join in what sounds like fun. It is not.
- They may try to provoke you (Think of the Road Runner and Coyote, or Bugs Bunny and Elmer Fudd.).
- They can be very volatile, exploding into rage with the slightest provocation. Be relaxed but ready for the worst.
- If the manic person is also psychotic (Chapter 32), those tactics will probably take precedence. In these situations, you basically have a hallucinating or delusional person who also happens to be moving and talking very fast.

CHAPTER 34

Communication With People
With Dementia (Elderly)

Effectively dealing with elderly people, particularly if they are also mentally disabled, is one of the most challenging situations a Security Professional might face.

Are there any verbal interventions that might possibly keep the situation under control at a lower level of force with an elderly, demented individual? Remember, older adults are not a monolithic category. They are people, just like us, simply older. Everything—every character type, every mode of aggression, every mental syndrome, and every de-escalation strategy—applies to the elderly as well as those of other age groups. Despite their age, elderly people do assault others. Their rage can emerge from dementia, medical conditions, pain, adverse drug reactions, mental illness, pure meanness or hate, or any number of stressors.

Many elderly people are prescribed a number of medications from a number of doctors. Not all the medical practitioners may be aware of one another, and the elderly individual, rather than being demented or mentally ill, may be suffering from a complication from drug interactions, or, due to age and confusion, taking the prescribed medications improperly. This may become a medical emergency.

Considerations Relevant to Both Human and Tactical Concerns With Elderly, Aggressive People

Be aware that elderly people may be resistant to help. This may be due to disorganization, confusion brought on by dementia, by a combination of severe depression and fear, or by pride ("At least I still have the strength to refuse someone.")

- Speak respectfully, befitting the age and seniority of the person. Too many people speak in a patronizing demeaning tone to elderly people, and even when cognitively impaired, they often know they are being talked to as if they are a child.
- Use their honorific and last name unless specifically invited to use their first name. If you wish to achieve a more informal relationship, ask "Would you prefer to be called Mrs. X or by your first name?" Let them *offer* the first name.
- When it is not an immediately emergent situation, take a little bit more time. Attempt to "nibble around the edges," talking about life, about family.
- Be prepared to get enormously frustrated at their leaden stubbornness, that "they simply won't do what is good for them." However, what appears as inertia may be a profound expression of fear. Remember that the most proximate change that many old people are concerned with is

death, and therefore, any situation provoking anxiety evokes the fear of death. ***You may think they are defiant: they may simply be scared out of their wits.***

- Do not talk around or about the person to others as if they are not there.

- Do not barrage them with choices, decisions, or too much information.

- Paranoia, (Chapter 23) whatever the cause, is one of the frequent triggers of rage in elderly people, particularly those with dementia or adverse drug reactions. As the person becomes suspicious, you can often change the subject, so that the object of their suspicion recedes from their awareness.

- The rage and violence that emerges with elderly people is frequently chaotic. Please refer to Chapter 28 on details regarding communication with Disorganized people and Chapter 51 on de-escalation of people in chaotic states.

- Be aware that the individual's behavior may very possibly be brought on by improper use of their prescribed medications, or interactions between different prescribed and over-the-counter medications. This may be a medical emergency.

SECTION VII

Suicide

CHAPTER 35

Why Should Suicide Be a Concern
of a Security Professional?

Security Professionals are not counselors. Therefore, one could legitimately state that suicide should be the responsibility of a mental health professional, not a Security Professional. However, there are several reasons that Security Professionals should be very concerned about suicidal people.

- Suicide is an act of profound aggression. The biggest difference between suicide and homicide is what direction the weapon is pointing. If security intends to adequately address safety issues, then Security Professionals need to be familiar with the signs of potential suicide.
- The person may present allusions to suicide in circumstances that the Security Professional must assess, whether at that moment, to call the police or organizational resources.
- An ability to assess, to some degree, if the suicidal threat is manipulative or false can be an invaluable skill.

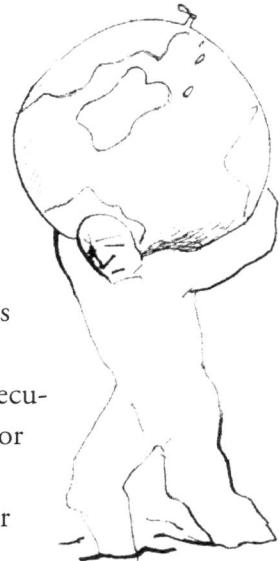

While the Security Professional may not diagnose the suicidal person, there may be circumstances where HR or managers approach Security with a problem employee and begin to describe a set of behaviors like those listed below. It is important that the Security Professional recognize these "red flags" so that an accurate initial assessment can be made to avoid possible escalation.

Why would you suspect that an individual is suicidal?

For those who are not suicidal, the act itself may be incomprehensible. Many people find it difficult to believe that life's problems could be such that suicide is even a consideration. For the suicidal individual however, it is a problem-solving answer to the seemingly unending pain, trauma, and frustrations of life. They feel trapped, unable to conceive of an end to their torment, or other possible solutions. However, problem-solving activity that it may be, suicide is also an act of violence resulting in the death of a human being. This is an important consideration because of the individual's expression of anger and desperation, and the fact that there is often a weapon involved. Therefore, Security Professionals should use extreme caution when interacting with a suicidal individual.

Warning Signs

Given that few people announce that they are suicidal, to what should you pay attention?

- **Significant negative changes in the subject's life.** Examples of these are: divorce or a romantic break-up, events such as conflict at the worksite, an incident that is humiliating, a large disappointment such as being fired, economic reverses, or the like.

- **Other warning signs that should elicit concern even when you do not have direct knowledge of such radical changes in their life.** A radical change in clothing or appearance, particularly styles that sets one apart from the society of which they are a member, hostility towards peers, workmates, or family, social withdrawal and isolation, the giving away of prized possessions, writings or drawings with morbid or despairing themes, a depressed demeanor, and allusions to a lack of a future or to the "pointlessness of it all," or reassuring statements when you know nothing has changed for the better, such as "you don't have to worry about me anymore. I'll be taking care of things. It's not an issue, anymore," etc.

- **The intangibles.** Sometimes, without knowing why, you have a sense of foreboding, or at other times, you think something which, on the surface, may seem "ridiculous," like, "I don't think that man will live out the year," or "I wonder if this is the last time I will see this person." Such thoughts are often—let us emphasize, _very_ often—an intuitive sense that something is very wrong. To be sure, approaching someone when your "evidence" is so vague requires some tact or delicacy, but approach you must.

CHAPTER 36

The Essentials of Intervention With Someone
You Believe Might Be Suicidal

Are you the right person to ask this person questions? The fact that you like people, and that they often like you in return, or are "good with people," does not grant you special skills for dealing with someone that may be suicidal or will lead to this person opening up to you. A better question to ask is "Do I *know* that this person respects me?" If you know that they do not, you are probably not the person to speak with them. To be sure, there are people who are isolated and alienated, and it is *only* through the asking of the questions of concern that respect between you will be born, but you must at least have a sense, knowing this person, that he/she does not hold you in either personal contempt or indifference. If you are not the person to speak with them about suicide, your task is to clearly organize what you have observed so that you can pass on your concerns to the appropriate professional. When speaking to an alleged suicidal person the following points will be helpful:

- **Meeting Location.** Try to speak where you will have no interruptions. At the same time, you do not want a place that is so private that you and the individual are isolated. Also consider if you should include a security guard, armed or unarmed, nearby, to help maintain a safe situation.

- **Demeanor.** Too much direct eye-contact, close physical proximity, or an overly-gentle, "concerned" voice may shut them down. Speak easily but not overly confidently. If you present yourself as too "together," they may experience this as an implicit judgment on them, their lack of ease contrasting so dramatically with your confident demeanor. Sit at an angle, with only an occasional glance toward the individual. Your occasional eye contact will then have significance, rather than being experienced as a constant, intrusive examination.

- **Meander.** With a wary individual you may wish to "wander around," so to speak, talking about this and that to build up rapport. As long as they are talking, they are not killing themselves. This gives you time and also helps to build trust.

- **Ask direct questions.** When you have a real concern that an individual is considering or planning suicide, you must be more direct. Do not tiptoe around the subject, as vague statements leave the person an "out." Instead of asking an individual, "are you thinking of hurting yourself?" ask "Are you thinking of killing yourself?" Such direct questions often come as a relief because they indicate that there is someone who is strong enough to listen to what is really going on inside them. If the individual is not suicidal, they will let you know. If they are outraged by your questions, explain why you are concerned. They should be able to give you a clear explanation why you do not need to be concerned. One final point, asking them if they have thoughts of suicide will *not* put the idea in their head if it was not there to begin with.

- **Speak in a calm matter-of-fact tone of voice.** If you sound nervous, you will appear unreliable. If you are joking or off-hand, the individual will feel that you are not taking them seriously. If you are overly concerned, overly warm, or sensitive, you will sound like a hovering counselor, that soft-voice, earth-tone wearing, gentle soul who cannot be trusted to stand up and fight, but seeks refuge only in being "nice." A calm, matter-of-fact tone shows that you are not panicked by the situation, and that you can handle anything they say. Remember it is *their* crisis, not yours. Your job is not to save them but rather to offer them a hand so they can help themselves.

- **Act as if you have all the time in the world.** If you act like there is little time, the person you're talking with will believe you, and they'll rush to a decision or conclusion. When you take time, you give time; the suicidal person begins to believe that there is enough time to figure out a better solution than suicide.

- **Do not give advice too soon.** Until you become more familiar with the situation, don't hand out advice. Even then, keep it to a minimum. For example, if you immediately say, "Think of your family," the individual might think, "Yeah, they'll be sorry. Their tears dropping on my grave are the best payback I can think of!" The interview process is a means to get them to reveal themselves, so they feel less isolated, and furthermore, so you know the right thing to say.

- **Never dare them to do it.** That kind of stupidity only works in the movies. The archetypal stupid sentence is, "Cutting? If you were serious, you would cut your wrists lengthwise, not crosswise." The idea here is to "scare the person straight." "It is obvious," the aggressive intervener thinks, "they are attention seeking and not serious," and they try to shock them with the reality of what they are doing. In all cases we can recall, such "interventions" are born out of frustration, irritation, burn-out, or plain dislike of the often repeatedly suicidal person. It is a statement for us, not them. One of the authors met a man who took such advice regarding multiple lengthwise cuts. His crippled arm looks like corduroy, due to seven elbow-to-wrist razor slashes to the bone.

- **Do not debate.** Some individuals use suicidal behavior as a way of attaining some personal power in a world over which they have little control. Debates about the meaning of life, religion, or the immorality of suicide will break rapport, particularly if you are "winning."

- **The most powerful intervention with suicidal individuals is that you are talking.** The suicidal person, almost invariably, feels completely isolated, cut off from life and from people. A sustained, respectful conversation conveys on an almost primal level that they are still worth something because you, who are worth something, finds them worthwhile to speak with. Communication itself heals.

CHAPTER 37

The Four Questions

The following are the standard questions for assessing suicide risk. As you can see, there is a progression in which greater specificity indicates greater danger. You are not in the role of a therapist, but even if you were, the basic questions would be the same. You are assessing if the individual is safe, and determining the need to contact a mental health professional or the police. As always, your tone should be calm, straightforward, and non-threatening. Do not use the following questions as a mere checklist. Instead, use them in the natural flow of the conversation while understanding that the individual may wander off on all sorts of tangents before being ready to answer the next question.

The Four Questions

Question one. "Are you planning to kill yourself?" If they answer "*no,*" follow up with questions and statements why you believe they might ("Your boyfriend called and stated that you told him that you were going out in a blaze of glory tonight. And then you said, 'Don't look for the body'"). If they cannot counter your suspicions satisfactorily, then you may need to call emergency response personnel to assure their safety despite their denials.

If the individual replies something along the lines of, "*I don't want to kill myself, but sometimes I pray that I won't get up in the morning,*" this could be termed passive or soft suicidal ideation. Do not minimize this, as the individual's pain is very real, although their lack of an immediate plan usually allows you to link them with a mental health intervention, such as an outreach worker, EAP, or an appointment with their doctor the next day.

If you have collateral evidence that they might be suicidal, and the individual refuses to answer, link up with proper personnel for an assessment. Start with HR or their manager, or Security Management as escalation paths.

If the individual answers "*yes,*" that is a clear sign of their thought processes and intent. Follow up this answer with more detailed questioning, or take immediate action to ensure the individual's safety.

Question two. "How would you do it?" Obviously, this question is asked in response to the individual answering "yes" to question one. If their response is "I don't know," then you should have time to address the issue by negotiating an agreement to seek or accept treatment after further supportive discussion. You have to find out if there are any impediments to seeking treatment, such as "I'm not going to see a counselor. All they do is look at you and repeat what you say."

If the individual says that they "could do it all sorts of ways," offers a long list of possibilities, or simply says, "I'm not telling you that," this is manipulation. This does not mean they will not make an attempt, but their response usually stems more from an "I'll show you!" attitude. At this point, you must make it clear to them that such suicidal threats are taken seriously.

If the individual specifies a particular method (poison, overdose, hanging or weapon—firearms or edged weapons), the level of risk has just increased exponentially. Sometimes, the suicidal individual will offer a plan and a back-up plan; for example, "I want to jump off a bridge, but I think I don't have the guts. So, if I can't, I'll just O.D." This is usually not a manipulative strategy because it denotes careful planning. You may wish to conduct a field visit to their residence or living quarters to search for these items.

Question three. Often suicidal individuals may have decided on a method, but it is one that they have not yet acquired or have access to. Be sure to ask follow-up questions to ascertain if they have access to the method they have named, such as, "You say you are going to overdose. What kind of pills do you have?" Or, "You want to shoot yourself? Do you own a gun? Do you have it with you now?"

Question four. "When will you do it?" This question helps you gauge immediacy, and to determine if the individual has established the plan to make others suffer, and if there is anyone else who is "timed" to suffer; for example, "on my mom's birthday." The more "positive" answers you get to these questions, the greater the risk of a lethal outcome.

Follow-up Questions

In most cases, particularly when interviewing a subject regarding suicidal risk, you will have fully accomplished all that you need to do. You know that the person is or is not suicidal, and how close to the act they are. In many cases, however, you may have to keep talking: they are struggling and trust you and want to talk more, or they are on a phone and you are trying to keep them talking to you.

As people continue to talk, they often pull back from the intent to kill themselves on their own, or they *will* be more amenable to de-escalation because they feel that "at last, someone is willing to listen." Simple communication brings people away from suicide, even without a solution to the problems that drove a person towards it.

1. "Have you tried to kill yourself before?"
2. "Have you ever tried to kill yourself another way?" Desperate people become very concrete and literal, only thinking of their chosen method. They may have made several attempts before, by other means.
3. Have you ever *felt* like killing yourself before?
4. What stopped you? Who stopped you? Be sure not to make them feel like they "failed" when they were not successful in a previous attempt. When they recall someone or something that stopped them, this may help them regain a sense of responsibility for the people who cares for them, or some other factor that kept them alive in the past.

5. "Has anybody in your family or someone you cared about ever tried to kill themselves?" Such people have "shown the way."

6. "Have you been drinking? Using any drugs?" *(Do not push this one if you have a sense that the person will be more worried about getting arrested or fired for use or possession than finding a solution to the situation.)*

7. "What has happened that things are so bad that suicide makes sense?" OR What happened TODAY that you decided to kill yourself?

8. "What else have you tried to do to get yourself out of this situation?" (Be careful—some people can take this as criticism, such as, "**Now I have to explain myself again. I don't know why having a lovely wife, a good job and sweet children isn't enough!!!!!!!**"

9. Other areas to talk about include if the individual has suffered any recent losses, is ill, or has little or no social/family support.

CHAPTER 38

The Art of Communication
With a Suicidal Person

Dialogue Is the Lifeline

Suicidal people feel profoundly alone. They believe that nothing can end their pain, but death. They are often depressed or very bitter and angry. These emotions isolate them. When one is isolated, one does not even feel half-alive, because to be human is to be in relationship with others. When you are able to begin a dialogue with the suicidal person, the power, beyond anything you say, is that you are speaking. By definition, the person is no longer alone. Someone is hearing them out. Someone grasps how terrible life is for them. As time passes, the very fact of talking with you makes them feel alive again, and this gives hope, even when the person's situation has otherwise not changed.

Do not wear your heart on your sleeve. Quite often the stories that suicidal individuals tell are poignant and painful. However, this can also be a very sophisticated type of manipulation, and individuals who dramatize their problems, only to later minimize them or discount those who tried to help, can enrage or frustrate us. The authors are not encouraging cynicism here, but as Security Professionals you cannot allow yourselves to become so emotionally involved that you feel betrayed, or simply burned out, if the individual rejects your efforts to help.

Do not make guarantees of how wonderful life will be. When the suicidal individual makes demands of you, do not give a guarantee of results, just honestly explain the difficulties that lie ahead. For example, "No, I'm not guaranteeing counseling will help, and you will have to work hard in therapy; it won't be easy. In fact, it might be the hardest thing you've ever done, but it's something you haven't tried." You might wonder how a "negative" message would be helpful. Remember this: the suicidal person, and very possibly friends and loved ones have already tried looking on the bright side, cheerleading, encouraging, complimenting and portraying a positive attitude. If you give them more of the same, you will blow them right out of the water. Instead, you recognize that they have probably tried all sorts of things to make things better, and they did not work. Therefore, if you are offering a strategy that they have not tried, it is far more respectful to recognize how difficult things may be. You are trying to link up with the courageous side of the person that realizes that to heal, they will have to fight, and this is never easy.

Identify the intended victims, beyond themselves. Try to ascertain whom the suicide is intended to hurt. You will also get a better sense if the individual is also homicidal, intent on taking others along. You can tell if others are intended to suffer by asking "who will find your body, or who will identify you?" Some individuals are shocked at the question, so preoccupied with their own pain that they did not even think that a loved one would find them upon returning home from work. Others describe that same scene with happiness, hoping that a specific family member will discover their body.

Do Not Try to Bolster Their Self-esteem

You may know that they have got a talent, that they are attractive, or have a wonderful family. If you point this out to them—"You have so many reasons to live!"—you will most likely break rapport entirely. It is very likely that they know these things themselves. They look in the mirror and they see the beautiful face, but inside, they feel corrupt and foul. They look at their mom and dad, who they painfully and deeply love, and think, "they would be so happy without me." They have a talent, and they know it, but even as they play the piano or paint or score thirty points in a game, they merely feel an aching misery.

Figure 38 Dialogue—Not Praise—Is the Answer

Once you have achieved a deeper level of rapport, it is quite sound to talk about what the person loves: their vocation, hopes and dreams, their family, or their talents. The goal here is to participate in reminding the person of the value of their life. However, they have to realize themselves as they talk about these things. It is not effective to tell them what is special about them. If that were all it took, they would not be suicidal in the first place.

Talk about their family. A natural follow-up of the last question is to begin speaking about their family, and what will be the implications of their suicide upon them. You must be careful here. The suicidal person may become enraged with you, perceiving this as a manipulative trick to make them feel guilty. However, once you get a sense that the suicidal person does care for his/her family, particularly children, such talk may be very powerful. For example, one Security Professional, talking on to an individual on a cell phone, holding a gun to his temple, asked him what he would say to his daughter were she the one on the phone to him holding the gun. The suicidal man said some powerful things in favor of life, and, the Security Professional was able to say that his daughter would want to say that to him as well.

Suicide Is Selfish

If you get a sense that they do love their children, partner, or friends, but are so preoccupied by their own pain that they do not realize the implications of what their suicide will do to them, one can ask, "What happens to your pain if you do kill yourself." Quite frequently, the suicidal person says that their pain will be over. The reply to that, in a regretful tone, is, "That's not really true. You just wrap your pain up in a package and hand it to your loved ones to carry. Is that something that you want for them?" This can sometimes shock the person to consider the implications of what they are doing. *Caution:* This type of intervention only comes after some long talking. Many suicidal people are so preoccupied with their own painful situation that they become too selfish to care about their family. Rather than a healthy shock, they will resent you for reminding them of what they are trying to extinguish.

Suicidal Threats

You will encounter people who dramatize their problems, only later to minimize or discount those who gathered to help them. Particularly with people who make repeated attempts or threats, this can enrage or frustrate us. It is ironic that contempt, irritation, or frustration is exactly what they expect from people, and that is what their behavior elicits. One of the occupational hazards of working with people who suffer is that not all those in pain are endearing; some are frankly quite unlikeable. Others do not even have the ability or resources to accept help when it is offered. It is the hallmark of a professional that you do not become burned out simply because some people either play games, or are playing on an entirely different field than you thought.

How to respond to internal questions that sidetrack you:

- "I don't know if I would want to live in such a miserable situation." It is not about you! The fact that they are talking with you means they still have some hope for another answer.
- "Why is it important that they live?" OR "I know I should care, but I don't." In cases like these, make death itself your enemy. Your attitude should be that you will do your best to speak for life. You are a voice from the land of the living to one trying to cross over into the land of the dead. ***Not on your watch!*** If they wanted to die, they should not have come in contact with you.

CHAPTER 39

Self-mutilation and Para-suicidal Actions

Many worksites must deal with employees who seem to be in, or seem to create constant crisis. One of the primary methods of this is repeated suicide attempts or threats, or self-mutilating behaviors—usually self-cutting—that are sometimes called, "para-suicidal" behaviors.

If you do have to intervene with such an individual (as distinguished from a person who is in a unique, one-time crisis), the most important hallmark of your interaction should be a correct, but distant demeanor. If you are overly sympathetic to the person in constant crisis, this emotional "reward" will fuel further incidents. It can also result in the subject getting attached to you. This can be very dangerous to the Security Professional for the following reasons:
- The individual gets overly attached to the "strong, but sympathetic" Security Professional, and begins to stalk them.
- When the individual's solicitations for extra attention are rejected (and this can include an escalation of suicidal and self-mutilating behaviors to garner that attention), they feel betrayed and begin to target the Security Professional with attacks ranging from physical and verbal assault to claims of sexual harassment, or other false accusations.

Security Professionals should NOT try to manage this type of behavior alone. Instead, you need to work with specialists—definitely including mental health professionals—to either modulate the individual's behavior, or to make a plan where they do not negatively impinge on the worksite.

SECTION VIII

Recognition of Patterns of Aggression

CHAPTER 40

The Cycle of Aggression

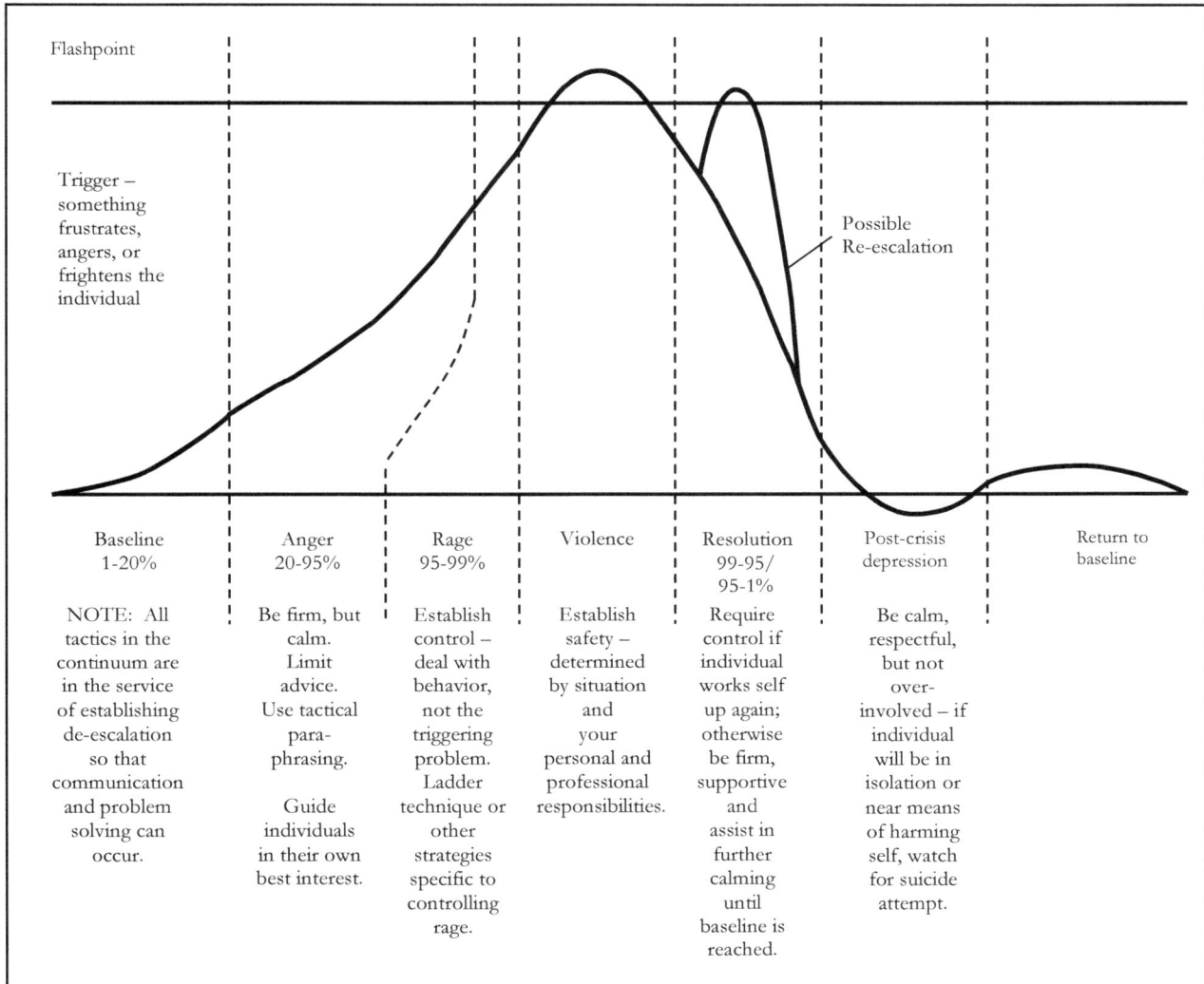

Flashpoint

Trigger – something frustrates, angers, or frightens the individual

Possible Re-escalation

Baseline 1-20%	Anger 20-95%	Rage 95-99%	Violence	Resolution 99-95/ 95-1%	Post-crisis depression	Return to baseline
NOTE: All tactics in the continuum are in the service of establishing de-escalation so that communication and problem solving can occur.	Be firm, but calm. Limit advice. Use tactical para-phrasing. Guide individuals in their own best interest.	Establish control – deal with behavior, not the triggering problem. Ladder technique or other strategies specific to controlling rage.	Establish safety – determined by situation and your personal and professional responsibilities.	Require control if individual works self up again; otherwise be firm, supportive and assist in further calming until baseline is reached.	Be calm, respectful, but not over-involved – if individual will be in isolation or near means of harming self, watch for suicide attempt.	

An outburst of aggression occurs in a cycle that starts with relative calm and ends with relative calm. The aggressive cycle often appears to start with an apparent ***triggering event***, though, in fact, the crisis may have been fulminating for some time. The reader may recognize the term "trigger," being familiar with it in terms of relapse in regard to substance abuse. The same concept applies with acts of violence. Just as many addicts have certain triggers that elicit the urge to use drugs, aggressive individuals have triggers that cue them to become violent.

Baseline: From 0-20

When we are calm, we are at *baseline,* which is represented as "0-20" on the accompanying chart. At baseline, we use the parts of the brain most responsible for our better human characteristics: thinking, creativity, and forming social relationships. The reason that the rating scale goes up to "20" is that we wish to underscore that one can have a little heat and energy, and still be fully rational.

Anger: From 20-95

A triggering event elicits a change in both thinking and feeling. This event can be something that threatens the individual's sense of safety; frustration at not being able to obtain what they desired; or simply a cue that they are now justified using a skill (aggression) with which they are confident. Once aggression is triggered, the individual first becomes irritable, then angry.

If baseline is presented as being "0-20" on the scale of aggression, with actual violence being "100," anger is represented by the numbers 20 through 95. Regardless of the numeric value of their anger, the individual is trying to communicate with you. However, because we perceive their attempts to communicate to be obnoxious, domineering, frightening, or just plain irrational, we often do not construe their actions as communication. The individual, on the other hand, experiences an increasing sense of frustration or desperation, and, not infrequently, a sense of helplessness at their inability to make themselves heard, further fueling their anger. There are several reasons such individuals grow angrier as the perceived or actual conflict continues:

- Certain individuals simply cannot accept anyone disagreeing with them, especially when they believe they are right.
- When you do not seem to grasp what they are saying, you are perceived as being disinterested, too obtuse to understand, or your lack of comprehension implicitly accuses *them* of stupidity or unreasonableness.
- When you do not agree or comply with an individual, you are frustrating them in achieving something they desire.
- Many individuals have a misconstrued and hypersensitive sense of "respect," especially those who have adopted the values of the street-gangster subculture. Resistance, disagreement, or perceived slights are often seen as being disrespect toward the individual, causing them to lash out in anger or violence in an effort to regain their "street cred."

Figure 40.1 Example: Incident of Disrespect

The Security Professional should not naively assume that this hyper-inflated "respect" is confined to residents of the inner city, or actual members of gangs. Many young men in the 21st century are acculturated by what they see on TV or in the movies. They may never have walked down a mean-street in the middle of the day, much less the night, but they have adopted the values of the "heroes" that they see on a television screen in the safety of their own home. (See the example below.)

A customer care representative (CCR) became involved in an argument with the team manager during a coaching session, the disagreement being around scheduling. The team manager copied the other employee's license plate number and had another employee determine the CCR's address. The team manager went to the address and waited outside for two hours. She later told the other employee that she had been disrespected, and the only reason the CCR was still walking around, was because she had not returned to her home that evening.

As an individual becomes more agitated, the areas of their brain that mediate basic emotions take over. At this point, equity, negotiation, or compromise becomes less and less attractive. In their frustration, angry individuals shift, increasingly, to attempting to dominate you, to *make* you see things their way, or for you to comply with them. Their domineering behavior is, as much as anything else, an attempt to "get through" to you.

Think of arguments you have had when, frustrated, you said such things as: "No, that's not what I'm saying! Do I have to explain it again?" Or "Let me put it another way!" Or "You just don't get it! What do I have to say to make you understand?" We become progressively more intense, often raising our voices (as if that will help the other person understand) because we want the other person to grasp what we are saying. This type of escalation is counter-productive, despite our intentions, because we tend to make less sense when we are angry.

For some individuals, anger is accompanied by physical arousal, which functions as a feedback loop, driving them toward further arousal. When our heart beats 10%-15% above baseline due to emotional excitement we no longer care about the truth. We care only about being "right" and proving the others "wrong." The disagreement has become a win or lose situation. We interrupt more frequently, cutting other people off, and we only pick out the flaws in their argument.

To de-escalate and control an angry individual, the Security Professional should attempt to *"line up"* with them. When you line up with the individual, you prove that you are not only focused on, but understand what they are saying, thereby proving that their concerns are important to you too. This in itself is powerfully disarming, not only calming them down, but also helping you to work together to actually solve the problem. Line-up strategies will be discussed in detail in the succeeding chapters.

Rage: From 95-99

As you can see on the chart, rage is represented as 95-99 on the aggression scale. How can you tell the difference between anger and rage? When someone is angry, you too, may become angry. You might also become concerned, upset, hurt, confused, or frustrated. Usually, however, you are not afraid. Why? Although angry people may *later* become violent if they are further agitated, that is not their aim. Instead, their intention is to communicate with you, albeit dramatically, loudly, or forcefully. At worst, they are trying to dominate or intimidate you into doing what they want. As abhorrent as this may be, it is still communication.

When individuals are enraged, however, they are, in effect, trying to "switch themselves on" to become violent. Many people slowly work themselves into a state of rage as a prelude to violence. Of course, others can lash out violently with seemingly no prior warning, verbal or otherwise. However, even non-communicative individuals will usually signal their anger or intentions through their body language and other non-verbal forms of communication. Security Professionals should be aware of these warning signs of impending aggression, as manifested on the intuitive level in Section II and based on observable behaviors, as discussed in the rest of this book.

Most of the time, anger does not result in violence. One reason for this is the various self-inhibitors that work to control behaviors and prevent us from acting out our baser instincts. Within a state of rage, an individual is *trying* to overcome those inhibiters, so that they can do what they actually desire—violence. Below are some of the prime inhibitors:
- **A fear of consequences.** The fear of counterattack, legal consequences, social disapproval, financial costs, and a host of other possible negative outcomes serve to inhibit one's resorting to violence to settle a dispute.
- **Morality.** Although some political and social ideologies may define another group as less than human and therefore fair game for violence, most individuals possess a core set of moral or religious principles that prevent them from harming others.
- **Self-image.** A man may see himself, for example, as the kind of person who does not hit women, make a public display of aggression, or lose control of himself. A woman may see herself as caring, nurturing, and empathetic to the plight of the less fortunate. A positive self-image, and fears of tarnishing that image, will often dissuade an individual from committing a violent act.
- **The relationship.** A feeling of responsibility toward the other person, for example friendship, love, family relations etc., will hold an individual back from violence.
- **Learned helplessness.** Some individuals, survivors of abuse for example, have tried to defend themselves in the past and have failed repeatedly. They may believe that fighting back is a futile effort, only leading to further pain and abuse. Their rage, however, is there: inside. There are phrases like, "a cornered rat," or "the worm turns," which describe a person who has suppressed their rage, sometimes for years, before acting out in violence and rage.

Rage therefore, is a set of behaviors, including both physical actions and verbalizations that serve to do away with one's self-inhibitors, so that nothing holds them back from violence. Individuals in a rage state are no longer trying to communicate; they are working themselves up to an attack.

What is the difference, then, between rage and violence? Anger is a rocket ship, all fueled up, with some fumes coming out, and the countdown initiated. Rage is right before lift-off. The rocket has not yet moved, but there are flames and steam billowing out, a terrible roar so loud the ground shakes. It is a roiling moment of explosive, tenuous equilibrium. Fuel could still be cut to the rocket engines so that it sits silent on the launching pad, but there are only a few moments to act, because the rocket is about to lift off. Lift-off is the equivalent of the initiation of **_violence_**.

What you _should_ experience in the face of rage is fear. This is not a bad thing. Fear tells us that we are in danger and that we must do something: NOW! Fear switches us on, so that our internal emergency response systems are activated. Fear demands attention, but it should not paralyze us into non-action, mentally or physically, in the face of anger and rage. A sense of powerlessness is not a given when one experiences fear; rather, it is a _conclusion_ that some people reach when they are afraid, limiting their ability to control the situation, or to defend themselves.

Once the Security Professional notices the onset of anger within an individual they would be well-served to begin preparing mentally for a potentially violent act and begin identifying an escape route, or if necessary, to ready themselves for actual physical confrontation, all while attempting to de-escalate the individual.

To work with the enraged person, you must establish **_control_**, especially if their behavior presents an immediate threat to you, themselves, or others. De-escalation and control tactics, whether they are verbal or physical, are geared to establish the conditions that make the aggressive individual no longer dangerous.

Figure 40.2 The Difference Between Anger and Rage

Imagine someone hands you a huge plastic container. Through its translucent sides, you can see a dark, hairy shape, a Goliath Bird-Eater, the world's biggest spider. It rustles around the container shifting in your hands like it's filled with mercury. Is it creepy? Sure it is. Is there any reason to be afraid? Not really. As long as the lid is on the container firmly, you are absolutely safe. This is the equivalent of anger. Internally you say, "I'd better keep the lid on this thing."

Now, imagine your "friend" takes the container back, and to your surprise and horror, takes off the lid. The spider emerges onto the floor right next to your leg. It raises its front legs in threat-display and opens and closes its ¾ inch fangs. There is something poisonous, hairy, and mean in the room, and it is not enclosed in any container! The spider is out of the box. This, metaphorically, is rage. However, the fear that now arises within you doesn't mean that you are helpless. You can step on the spider or jump up on a table. If you are ticked off enough, you can grab your "friend" by the neck and make him sit on it! A belief that you are helplessness near the spider is an interpretation, not a fact. Fear is simply the warning cry—the drums at the brink of battle—that demands that you _must_ act right now.

To deal with the enraged person, you must establish *control*, especially if their behavior presents an immediate threat to you, to themselves, or to others. Control tactics—be they verbal or physical—are geared to establish the conditions that make the aggressive person no longer dangerous. In essence, using our metaphor above, we say, "Put the spider back in the box. Now!"

Violence: 100 on the Scale

Violence does not begin when someone is hit or injured. Violence is also perpetrated simply through the fear of imminent danger and attack. Some of the legal terms for this are terroristic threats, harassment, stalking, and menacing. In short, a violent act occurs whenever there is good reason to believe that you or someone else is about to be hurt. In the face of such a situation, your guiding principle is to establish **safety**, and you must use effective means of protecting yourself and those around you. Very often, the best thing to do is to escape and get help. This is especially true when Security Professionals are alone.

Although actual physical self-defense tactics are well beyond the scope of this book, Security Professionals should also avail themselves of any defensive tactics and self-defense training that is available and appropriate to your professional responsibilities. As with any skill, self-defense techniques must be practiced regularly to ensure their viability in the event of an actual confrontation.

CHAPTER 41

Why Would an Individual
Become Aggressive?

Aggression is not an alien or unnatural emotion. Without a capacity for aggression, humanity would never have survived. Yet, much aggression is irrational, self-destructive, vicious, and/or cruel. Why would someone be swept by rage when it causes so much harm? Why would people be prepared to throw away a future, even a life, driven by emotions that they themselves might be horrified to have expressed even a few moments later? Security Professionals can better control an aggressive individual when they understand what has driven them to anger or rage.

Anger and rage can develop because the individual is **confused or disorganized**. They cannot understand what is going on around them or "inside" them, due to cognitive distortions or a chaotic situation (too much information for them to figure out). Among those who experience this confusion are those who are mentally ill, autistic, developmentally disabled, intoxicated, and those experiencing overwhelming emotions.

Some individuals feel **helpless, enclosed, trapped**, or beset with a myriad of seemingly unsolvable problems. This is often similar in effect to confusion or disorganization, but it is accompanied by a particular anguish. The individual usually perceives one person or entity as the agent of their situation, and they fight desperately to get free from their influence or oppression. Some Security Professionals evoke these when they pressure or intimidate a person.

The fear of attack elicited by an **actual or perceived invasion of personal space** is often a precursor to aggression. Each of us has a sense of personal space, a "bubble" within which an outsider is only permitted if invited (Chapter 6). In stressful or volatile situations, you will be perceived as an attacker if you encroach upon another's personal space, no matter your intentions.

An individual may resort to aggression if they **feel they are being wronged, or feel as if they are losing, or have lost, their sense of autonomy and power**. This is especially true of paranoid individuals who may believe that they are being oppressed by systems or powers beyond their control. You, as a Security Professional, may be designated as the representative of the controlling entity.

With mentally ill individuals, **hallucinations and delusions** can also play a significant role in the likelihood of aggression. The individual may feel compelled to act as the voices demand or in trying to make the hallucinations stop by any means, become violent. On other occasions, the voices, visions, smells, or sensations are simply distracting and irritating.

Anything that elicits profound emotion can cause an individual to become volatile or aggressive. ***Emotional stressors*** can include a recent loss through the death of someone close, dysfunctional family dynamics, romantic and other interpersonal relationships, job loss or threat of same, sanctions, divorce, infidelity, or feelings of insecurity.

The use of ***drugs and alcohol***, along with other organic stressors can also make an individual more likely to become aggressive. The drug and alcohol component to aggression is relatively self-explanatory, and one does not need an overactive imagination to realize just how desperate drug addicted and alcoholic individuals can become when in the throes of their addiction. By ***other organic stressors*** the authors are referring to a lack of sleep, a lack of regular exercise, and/or an insufficient or non-nutritious diet. Such deprivations can cause changes in perception, mood, and cognition, which can lead to an increase in irritability or hypersensitivity.

One of the biggest motivators of aggression is what occurs in families. Families often function as emotional traps; there is no escape from the people who, although loved, cause one the most pain. For Security Professionals, the most important thing to remember is that domestic violence frequently extends to the workplace.

People in ***romantic relationships*** often demand that the other person submit to their wishes. There are numerous grounds to fight, from money to sex to child care to infidelity. The rage is fueled by the same source: "You will 'love' me on my terms" even if the "relationship" is delusional, mere fantasy, or wishful thinking. As far as workplace violence goes, this includes both co-workers, and the relationships that employees have with outsiders.

For some, aggression, like its mirror-twin, suicide, is a "problem-solving" activity or a "what the hell" response when ***one has already given up.*** Related to this is a person's belief that he/she has no effect on the world. Violence ensures that you will make an impact. Depressed people, particularly males, often manifest this type of aggression.

Some people would not engage in aggression unless they had been ***set-up by others***. They are provoked by family members or friends who use the aggressor as an instrument of their vicarious desire to inflict harm. For example, a man's wife says to him, "I cannot believe you let your boss treat you like that. I thought you were a man, but I see I married a spineless little boy." Other people do this to *themselves* by "fronting," making a scene in front of others (friends, family, or coworkers) to increase their status in their "pack." Then, out in front, they are afraid to back down. Others carry the "audience" inside their imagination, demanding of themself that they conform to a macho self-image or a fantasy of themselves as a fearsome individual to whom others will submit.

One of the most powerful driving forces of aggression is ***a sense that one has been shamed or humiliated***. Shame is not a mild sense of social embarrassment; it is a sense of being exposed and victimized by others, with no hope of relief. Shame and humiliation are driving forces for revenge-based aggression, and are also prime motivators for attacks when the individual identifies you as someone who shamed or violated them in the past. This can also occur if they remember, correctly or incorrectly, when you do or say something that they believe to be similar to another individual who caused them harm. They may brood about past grievances, their anger slowly escalating until they explode into rage or violence.

Individuals may act aggressively out of a sense of ***protective rage***. This type of rage is not confined only to parents, but also as expressed by an individual who is trying to protect another individual from being victimized. The more one's identity is "merged" with that of the victim, the more aggressive the person will be in their defense.

Some individuals resort to aggression due to a sense of ***entitlement.*** They believe that if they desire something, they are entitled to it, and will use any means necessary to obtain that which they desire.

Others simply take **pleasure** in intimidating others and acting violently. For them, there is a joy in making others submit and a delight in causing pain. If you attempt to deny this ugly truth, you will convince yourself, in error, that you are safe or in control of the situation, and remain in the presence of a dangerous individual too long.

CHAPTER 42

What Does Escalation Look Like?

As an individual escalates in their aggressive behavior(s), they are priming their bodies to posture, to intimidate, to fight, or to flee. They can display a variety of different behaviors:

- **Physical and emotional withdrawal.** Some individuals will avoid eye contact, stop speaking, or respond only with short phrases or monosyllabic answers. Of course, some individuals are more naturally withdrawn and reserved; this does not mean that they are readying themselves for an aggressive outburst. Instead, here we are discussing a heretofore friendly and engaging individual who lapses into sullen hostility or refuses to engage in conversation.

- **Nervous, anxious, or frightened demeanor.** Such individuals usually lash out in defense. They are not looking for a fight; they are trying to protect themselves.

- **Overwhelmed or disorganized behavior.** Individuals who speak in repetitive loops, pacing and muttering incoherently to themselves, are displaying symptoms or either a chaotic mental state or perhaps intoxication. They can be unpredictable, and they may react to your attempts to communicate with sudden, unexpected aggression.

- **Hostility.** Any individual displaying open expressions of dislike or hatred should obviously put the Security Professional on guard.

- **Seduction.** Seduction is not reserved for just sexual expressions or desires. It is any attempt to make you collude with them; for example, "C'mon. It's just marijuana. You aren't going to report me for smoking one pipe? You mean to tell me you never smoked?" Such an individual is showing masked aggression. The danger here is that if the seduction fails, the person becomes frustrated, scared or enraged that you will not play along.

- **Mood swings.** (Chapter 20) These involve rapid shifts in mood and emotional affect, from boisterous to morose, then shifting to belligerence. Such individuals present a particular risk due to their unpredictability and their inability to control their own emotions.

- **Hypersensitivity.** Hypersensitivity is most common in paranoid individuals, (Chapter 23). The hypersensitive individual can react aggressively to even the most inoffensive and harmless attempts at communication, particularly if they are engaged in any conflict with your agency.

- **Authority complex.** When you try to set limits or say "no," these individuals become very frustrated or outraged, refusing to comply with rules. Rules and limitations are, in their view, oppressive or humiliating. Their attitude is simply an expression of their hatred for authority.

- **Electric tension.** The interaction between you and aggressor results in you feeling an electric tension. This is the feeling you get before a thunderstorm hits. We cannot underscore highly enough that you must ALWAYS trust this feeling, this intuitive sense that you are approaching a dangerous situation (Section II).

Changes in Cognition

As an individual escalates in their aggressive behavior(s), they are priming their bodies to posture, to intimidate, to fight, or to flee. In addition they will change their cognitive state in a variety of ways:

- **Cognitive distortions.** These are thinking patterns where the individual makes broad, negative assumptions. For example, an individual misses a single meeting with HR and assumes he/she will be fired. Therefore, when he/she sees the Security Professional, he/she is already convinced of the injustice they believe will be perpetrated upon them.
- **Interpersonal cognitive distortions.** This occurs when the individual infers the worst of what the Security Professional is saying. For example, "Tia, you have to stop cursing on the worksite. You run the risk of one of the employees making an official complaint. This is an easy thing to correct, and I don't want to see you get in trouble." And her response is, "WHAT? YOU ARE GOING TO TRY TO GET ME FIRED???!!!!!"
- **Becoming less amenable to reconciliation or negotiation.** The individual focuses increasingly on dominating the situation, on winning the argument, or taking out their frustrations on the object of their anger, rather than trying to find a peaceful resolution. They focus on being "right" and not on the facts.
- **Deterioration of concentration and memory.** This causes difficulty in the individual's ability to communicate, or to solve problems.
- **Deterioration of judgment.** As their information processing skills deteriorate, their judgment consequently becomes worse and worse. They cannot evaluate what is really in their own self-interest.

Figure 42.1 Example: Poor Judgment When Angry

A Security Professional was assisting in escorting the wife of an employee off the premises. She was a somewhat unstable woman, and was furious with her husband for taking out a car loan without consulting with her, so she took the argument to the worksite. On the way to the parking lot car, furious, she told the Security Professional, "This isn't fair. Not only does he make important family decisions without me, but he also took my stash of crystal to work with him." The result of this was that the husband, the sole source of income for the family, lost his job.

Changes in Patterns of Verbal Interactions

As an individual escalates in aggression the Security Professional should be aware of changes in verbal interaction. Below are some of these changes:

- **Silence.** Potentially aggressive individuals may lapse into a morose, sullen silence, often accompanied by signs of physical agitation such as hunched shoulders, knitted brows, and glaring at the floor or at other people.
- **Sarcasm.** Sarcasm can be considered to be hostility shaded in humor or passive-aggressive phrases. Sarcastic individuals may jeer at you, or sneer scornfully, demeaning your position.

- **Deliberate provocation.** Angry people will do or say things to upset or irritate you deliberately. Provocation is a challenge, an attempt to elicit a response from the Security Professional that will justify them in becoming increasingly hostile, if not violent.
- **Playing word games.** Some angry individuals will deliberately twist or misinterpret what you say trying to confuse you, or make you question your own memories of previous encounters. They will frequently misremember or "forget" directives, and then try to blame you for this. This is why proper note taking and documentation is vital.
- **Abusive or obscene language**. The use of abusive or obscene language should put the Security Professional on guard immediately, especially if the language is threatening or portends a violent act. In these cases the individual uses language to shock or stun the recipient, causing you to focus on what they are saying, and not on what they are doing (such as moving ever closer, or surreptitiously reaching for a weapon).

Figure 42.2 Obscenity as Abuse or as Punctuation

Note: That some individuals use obscenities as "adjectives" and "punctuation." An individual may swear to illustrate their own emotions and ideas with no intention of using their words as a form of attack. Although your senses may be heightened by their use of vulgarities, the Security Professional should respond in a calm manner, perhaps asking the individual to refrain from such talk. However, the Security Professional must be able to distinguish between true aggression and simple speech patterns, as you may end up escalating what was actually a non-threatening interview, even though foul language was being used.

- **Repeated demands or complaints.** By making constant demands of the Security Professional, the individual is looking for a pretext to legitimize their sense of grievance, creating an issue they consider to be worth fighting about.
- **Clipped or pressured speech.** Some individuals couch their aggression by appearing to be overly polite. They often use very formal or stilted language, presenting themselves as being in control when they are actually seething with aggression or a sense of injustice. This is often the hallmark speech of someone with paranoid traits (Chapter 23).
- **Implicit threats**. As with threatening sarcastic remarks, any implied threats made by an individual must never go unanswered or ignored. An individual who boasts of past acts of violence, or who warns the Security Professional that they might not be able to stop from reacting the same way in the future, must be dealt with expeditiously. Depending on the severity of the threat, this can range from a report to HR, to security staff either escorting the individual off the property, or calling the police.

Changes in Physical Organization

The following are possible changes in physical organization that an angry individual may exhibit as they escalate into aggression:

- **Facial expressions.** These can vary quiet a lot, depending on the mode of aggression. Facial expressions will be discussed in more detail in Section IX. The following list is not hard-and-fast, but there is a real likelihood of heightened aggression when the person displays:

  a. **Clenched teeth.** This is an attempt to contain or control intense emotions.

  b. **Bared teeth.** This is a threat display. You may have noticed certain people smiling who are really baring their teeth.

  c. **Hooding of the eyebrows and lowering of the chin.** These are automatic behaviors in anticipation of a physical confrontation.

  d. **Frowning.** This is often associated with anger.

  e. **Staring eyes.** Staring eyes can be an attempt at intimidation or manipulation; targeting the other as prey, particularly if there is tension in the cheeks and all around the eyes

  f. **Biting or compressing the lips.** These manifestations are associated with barely controllable intense emotions.

  g. **Quivering lips.** These are associated with fear or unhappiness.

  h. **Tightening the lips.** These are associated with an attempt to control or contain intense emotion.

  i. **Pulsating veins in the neck.** These are associated with building anger and rage.

  j. **Dilated pupils in the eyes.** These are associated with drug intoxication.

  k. **Avoiding all eye contact.** This when coupled with other expressions of aggression, is associated with planning an attack, hiding intentions of an attack, or, paradoxically, an attempt to disengage so that they will not be forced to fight.

- **Voiding.** When angered, some people have an urge to void themselves, clearing their bodies for the fight. Nausea and vomiting can occur with reduced blood flow to the gut. Other people feel a need to urinate or an onset of diarrhea. These behaviors occur when an individual is in a state of intense fear or otherwise full of adrenalin.

- **Breathing.** Individuals who are gearing themselves up for an attack often take deep breaths, which can be slow or fast, depending on how quickly their anger is escalating.

  a. **Shallow, rapid, and irregular pattern.** Those going into defensive aggression, fearing they will be harmed, usually breathe in a shallow, rapid, and irregular pattern, almost like panting or gasping. Some hyperventilate, and they may become violent out of a terror induced panic.

  b. **Deep pattern.** Individuals who want the confrontation (the belligerent), and are looking forward to it often breathe very deeply, from the abdomen through the chest.

  c. **Smooth easy pattern.** Psychopathic individuals and others who are "professionals" at violence often maintain a smooth easy breathing pattern throughout.

Changes in Actions

As an individual becomes increasingly *tense and agitated*, they may try to discharge the tension by pacing, often typified by rapid jerky movements.

- **Deliberate rejection in word and deed.** Some individuals simply pay no heed to the requirements of their place of employment or service, and ignore any and all attempts made by the Security Professional to enforce compliance. Their behavior makes their intentions, and their feelings toward authority, abundantly clear, and nothing you do will change their non-compliant behavior and/or criminal activity.
- **Posturing.** As an individual moves up the scale of aggression they will begin to posture, inflating their chests and spreading their arms to make themselves look bigger, invading their victim's personal space, pacing, smacking their fist in their hand, breathing faster, etc. They may move in quick jerky starts and stops, moving toward their victim and then back again repeatedly, as if working themselves up to attack. These actions are an effort to intimidate, prior to adopting a fighting pose.

Figure 42.3 Example: Flashing Weapons: An Act That Is Both Posturing and Implicit Threat

A customer enters a store, and stands in the center of the display area, arms akimbo with a curved knife thrust in his waistband. As people begin glancing at him in alarm, he takes the knife out and begins spinning it around, somewhere between twirling a baton, but also with cutting gesture. While doing this, he makes eye contact with various people, smiling, winking, and sneering. Police are called.

- **Positioning.** Individuals looking for a fight or confrontation square off directly in front of their target, while those looking for a victim tend to move to the corner of the person, trying to obtain an angle on them so that they can attack more easily.
- **Fighting pose.** A combative stance, as opposed to posturing, is often a crouch, with the chin tucked in and the hands raised. In some instances the individual may brandish a fist or a weapon. Be aware, however, that those most skilled at violence can often attack from a position of complete relaxation.
- **Relaxed pose.** One subset of aggressors, the predatory (Chapter 54), tends to *relax* when they are preparing for an attack. They are at home with violence, like a tiger or a snake. These individuals sometimes smile while making eye contact with you.
- **Trespassing and power testing.** An aggressive individual may intrude on your personal space, "accidentally" bumping into you. They may also repeatedly violate your personal space boundaries, getting too close and then backing away, either to establish dominance or test your response. The individual may also test their victim's willingness to defend themselves by picking up, mishandling, or even breaking their possessions.
- **Visual sexual assault.** Male individuals, in particular, will use their eyes to trespass on women, running their gaze over their bodies in what can only be considered a "visual rape."
- **Displacement activities.** Individuals may hit, kick, or throw objects in an effort to discharge tension, as a threat display, or as a "warm up" to an attack.

- **Making a dramatic scene.** The individual "acts crazy," either to get closer to you than you would let someone who was purposefully targeting you, or to get you so preoccupied with calming them down so you lose sight of larger tactical concerns.

The Edge of Attack

An aggressive individual is on the edge of attack when the following are exhibited:

- **Skin Tone.** Angry individuals have a flushed face: the pale skinned turn red, and the dark skinned turn even darker. In essence, blood at the surface of the skin is a threat display, as if to say, "See how angry I am!" If they blanch—light skinned people turn bone-white, and dark skinned people get a grayish tone—this indicates RAGE. The threat is not potential: it is NOW.

- **Pacing, muttering, kicking, etc.** Increased pacing, while muttering, is arousing, bringing one-self closer and closer to the edge or attack. Some individuals engage in more and more displacement activity: hitting, kicking, and throwing things.

- **Internalizing all signs of assault**. Others will *internalize* all signs of incipient assault, and thus, when it occurs, it seems to appear instantaneously. Right before the attack; however, these people often stop breathing a moment. This is often accompanied by a "quiet," the "calm before the storm," as if you are not there. In the latter case, the individual will sometimes have a "thousand-yard stare," where they seem to look beyond or through you. Some individuals, particularly, but not exclusively the psychotic aggressor, get an eerie smile on their face, one that holds no mirth.

- **Acting Berserk.** As the attack is incipient, the individual can *"lose it,"* shaking, yelling, and acting berserk.

Explosion and the Aftermath

The crisis will be some form of assault, either verbal or physical. As discussed throughout this text you must do whatever you must do to ensure your own safety and that of those around you, up to and including the use of force to control the individual and the situation.

After the explosive episode, the aggressive individual moves to the **resolution** phase in which they gradually, sometimes very gradually, return to baseline. Their body relaxes, cognitions improve, and their actions are less stilted and threatening. After resolution, there is often a **post-crisis depression**, which is due partly to physical depletion one experiences after the rush of adrenaline that accompanies any threatening situation, and which is partly psychological. The individual may be remorseful, apologetic, resentful, or merely withdrawn. This issue of communicating with an individual post incident will be discussed in greater detail in Chapter 57.

SECTION IX

The De-escalation of Angry Individuals

CHAPTER 43

Preemptive De-escalation

Sometimes an individual, mentally ill or not, comes in a little heated, but still rational. He/she is able to be polite to the person at the front desk and is able to wait for their appointment. Nonetheless, they are upset. Sometimes all they need is some clarification or the solution to a straightforward problem. Ask what they want or need. If you have a solution to the problem, explain it clearly to them, give them an idea how long it will take and what they should do in the interim. Always try to explain the process. With the proper information they de-escalate on their own. This is particularly valid with service-level complaints.

If you notice that the individual is truly irritated, however, you should not necessarily attempt to address their irritation immediately. In many circumstances, approach them and try to draw them into a conversation about a benign subject such as the weather, the local sports team, or another area of interest to the individual. Such seemingly harmless topics can be used as an assessment tool. If they resist your trying to help them refocus, this tells you immediately that the situation is becoming serious, and your primary goal becomes one of preventing an escalation of the individual's anger and frustration. It can be at that point that you introduce yourself as a company Security Professional, observe that they are upset and offer your services to assist in solving the situation.

When an employee with whom you are familiar comes in clearly out of sorts, introduce your concern by stating impartially that you believe something is upsetting them, and that they do not appear to be themselves today. Do not pose your concern as a question, such as "What's wrong with you today?" or "Why do you seem so upset? Is there some sort of a problem?" By asking a question, you give the individual an opportunity to simply deny that there is a problem. Instead, use phrases like, "You are really down today. Something is going on." or "You looked really stressed out when your son dropped you off today." These phrases give the individual an opening to present their problem to you without seeming to be interrogated.

If the individual has opened up to you and has begun discussing the issue, use open ended questions regarding possible solutions that require them to respond, such as "I see why you are so upset, but how do you think you can take care of it?" Or "What do you think can be done to resolve this?" Open-ended questions are intended to bring the individual into the conversation by making them consider their options and offer their own solutions. This also gives the Security Professional an opening to suggest other potential solutions to their problem, or to discuss the possible ramifications of the individual's suggestions.

Please note however, that questions should only be addressed to an individual who is mildly upset or agitated, not to one who is truly angry or enraged. The questions are used to "slow down" the individual to make them think. An enraged individual is beyond processing your questions, let alone being ready to think about alternative solutions. Likewise, if you notice that your questions are making the individual angrier, stop asking, because questions demand an answer, and an angry or enraged individual will view your continued questioning as an interrogation or a failure to understand their problem.

Security Professionals should also offer positive feedback and reinforcement for any suggestions or actions taken by an individual to resolve their own issues in a constructive manner. This will encourage the individual to seek productive solutions in the future.

Sometimes, the situation can be resolved simply by allowing the individual to tell their story. There is no need to problem-solve and no need to interrupt. In such cases, listening with attention and respect is all that is needed.

A word of caution is necessary here though. Security Professionals must differentiate between an individual "getting something off their chest" and venting. Venting can be viewed as a form of verbal aggression, albeit toward another individual or entity who is likely not present. Venting in and of itself becomes arousing to the individual. You must step in and de-escalate the individual, directing the conversation to another topic perhaps, before the individual has worked themselves into a state of rage. This type of subject will be covered in more detail in subsequent chapters.

CHAPTER 44

Physical Organization in the Face of Aggression

In Section I, the authors offered safety protocols and procedures ranging from the arrangement of office furniture, risk assessment, and mindfulness. In Section II, we discussed the study of body spacing as a means of honing your intuitive skills. In this chapter, the authors would like to discuss the subject of body language, body spacing and positioning on a tactical level.

How you stand, how you breathe, eye contact, and your gestures are all essential factors in calming aggressive individuals. You can say all the right things, but if you look like you are afraid, irritated, or angry, your verbal interventions and commands will have little to no effect, and the situation will only get worse. You cannot successfully and safely de-escalate an individual if you are overwhelmed by the fear of violence. That fear only gives the aggressive individual power. On the other hand, knowing that you have the skills to manage the aggression the individual might offer gives you the power to negotiate a safe resolution.

Please note that the authors do not wish to give the impression that Security Professionals should be in a constant state of combat readiness, assuming a defensive stance during each interview with your individuals, and going through your day tense and hyper-alert to the slightest threat. Instead, we wish to impart the importance of body organization as a component of personal safety and self-defense.

How to Organize Your Body

The following information will help you organize your body when dealing with aggressive individuals:

- **Move slowly and smoothly.** Agitated individuals startle easily, and any sudden movements or gestures on your part may be interpreted as an attack, or simply surprise the individual into a physical reaction. By breathing slowly and moving smoothly, you intend that the individual mirrors your actions and attitude. Not surprisingly, overt frustration, anger, or hostility toward the aggressive individual will cause them to become more fearful and/or aggressive in turn, increasing the likelihood of a physical altercation.

- **Breathing.** We previously described circular breathing (Chapter 11), and the authors strongly recommend that you master this skill. However, for those who are not able to use circular breathing effectively, a more simple method is to inhale on a "four" count, pause your breath on the "four" count, and exhale on a "four" count.[14] Feelings of nervousness or agitation will appear in your behavior, and may make the situation worse. On the other hand, when you are centered, people tend to feel calmer in your presence.

Figure 44.1 How Breathing Contributes to Calming or Escalating a Situation

Think of Security Professionals on your team who walk into volatile situations and everyone simply calms down. Think, also, of professionals who flame things up the moment they step into the room. Were one to track their respective breathing patterns, you would probably be able to predict what was going to happen observing two or three breaths.

- **Eye Contact.** In most cases, try and establish some type of eye contact. As with the other aspects of body language discussed above, you must be both non-threatening and non-threatened. Glaring at the individual with hostility or darting your gaze around nervously will just serve to make the individual more ill at ease, and may actually cause them to attack preemptively.

  a. Some psychotic individuals find eye contact to be very invasive. Particularly when they are calm, or only slightly agitated, angle your body in such a way so that they do not feel confronted or forced to make eye contact with you. Even with these individuals, however, you must make eye contact to establish control if they escalate into real aggression.

  b. Some individuals may be so frightening that you feel apprehensive about making eye contact with them. Others are so chaotic or manipulative that you find yourself unable to focus on what to do or say when your eyes meet. In situations like these, look between their eyes, at the bridge of the nose or the center of the forehead. You will find yourself far calmer, and the other individual, *if aggressive*, will not be able to tell the difference. You will just appear very strong.

  c. There is a disinterested "no-eye-contact" that can be used with *aggressive-manipulative* people (Chapter 25).

  d. Regardless of the exact nature of the situation or the individual's mental state, never look totally away from the aggressive individual. An attack takes but a split second, especially in close quarters, despite your body positioning and spacing. The individual must be aware that *you* are aware.

- **Stand at an angle.** This is sometimes called a "blade stance," because you stand with one foot in front of the other, the back foot at a 45-degree angle with some space between them, thus angling your body. Do not line your feet up, heel to heel ("L-Stance"). There should be at least a fist or two width's space between where your heels fall on the "east-west" axis. This stance does not have to be overtly threatening, or give the appearance that you are fearful. Indeed, this stance can be calming, as the individual can tolerate your proximity better than if you were standing squarely in front of them, a more confrontational posture. Of course, this stance also allows you to react more easily to an attack. Please note that a "stance" does *not* require you to lock in to one position. Security consultant Jeffrey Slotnick refers to this as "maintaining the 10 and 2 position." In other words, one maintains an angle to the subject at an angle, like the 10 and 2 positions on a clock face.[15]

- **Sit at an angle.** You can and should also sit with a "blade stance" in many situations. You sit on the edge of your chair, with your lead foot flat on the floor, and your other placed on the ball of the foot. You look interested and attentive, but in fact, you can easily get up without the use of your hands or needing to lean forward to get back on your feet.

- **Spacing from individual.** Are you too close to the individual? Security Professionals must not forget that individuals also have a sense of personal space, and some individuals, especially those with a mental illness, may have an *extreme* view of personal spacing issues (Section II). Some of these individuals will see any intrusion into their zone as an attack, and may respond with violence. For everyone's safety, Security Professionals have to carefully consider how close they get to an aggressive or disorganized individual. They will become more agitated, uncomfortable, or uneasy the closer you get. Step back so that the individual does not feel pressured or intimidated, and by all means do not get so absorbed in communicating with them that you are not aware of their distress at your proximity.

- **Spacing by individual.** Is the individual too close to you? Just as Security Professionals must be aware of proper spacing between themselves and the individual, they also have to warn the individual when he/she approaches too closely. In essence, the Security Professional needs to maintain proper spacing for themselves and the individual. If an individual keeps trespassing into your personal space, tell them calmly that you are happy to talk about their problems, but they should step back, because they are standing too close. You should not display any signs of fear or unease. By responding calmly and firmly, you are letting the individual know that you are alert and aware of danger, as well as able to take care of yourself.

Figure 44.2 Author's Experience: Intercultural Rules of Spacing and Eye-Contact

I lived in Japan for well over a decade. It is a truism that people from East Asia do not like direct eye contact as much as people from America. However, I have had some Japanese people stare so deeply in my eyes that I felt like they were counting the wrinkles in my brain.

On another occasion, I was teaching a safety class to a group of security guards, all Hispanic. I was demonstrating the proper physical spacing to accompany verbal de-escalation, and one of the men stood up and said, "Bro, you white guys, you kill me. If you acted like that in the 'hood, no one would want to talk to you. We stand like this." And with that, he walked up, a little off to the side, shook my hand and put the other arm around my waist, in friendly embrace. Everyone in the room was laughing, and I asked, "So, it's midnight, and you are on your rounds here on campus, and that's how you go up to the guy in the hoodie, with one hand in his pocket, peeking in the window at the girl's dorm?" After the laughter subsided, the man pointed at a quiet fellow sitting in the back and said, "Yeah, I know, I know. And that other thing? Jose, over there, he doesn't like anyone standing close to him." (laughter again, then he said to Jose) "We still like you, man. That's just how you are."

So do not assume that someone is close to you "because they are from "x" culture. Someone *from* "x" culture may be getting close to you with the intention of harming you, just like someone from your own. To be sure, you should take cultural conventions into account. At the same time, such individuals are now living in this culture (wherever our reader resides) and therefore, in setting your own limits regarding space, you are teaching them how better to survive in their new home.

Therefore, if someone is too close for your comfort, whatever culture they are from, tell them, tactfully, to move back (so that you can continue your conversation with more ease, and conceivably, safety). Each situation is different. But, bottom line, you should not loom over them nor should they EVER loom over you (or, in a professional context, shake your hand and hug you with the other arm).

- **Quiet hands.** When communicating with an aggressive individual, Security Professionals should minimize hand gestures and other movements that could be misinterpreted as an attack. When adopting a comfortable stance, clasp one wrist with the other hand. Do not clasp one hand in the other because you may begin wringing them unconsciously if you get nervous, making you look scared and perhaps evoking the aggression you are trying to avoid. By clasping your wrist, you broaden yourself slightly. You will feel solid rather than nervous. Furthermore, you can easily bring your hands upward to fend off or block a strike if you have to, without looking like you are ready to do so. There is no apparent fight in your stance, just strength.
- **Use your hands as a calming fence.** Fences lend a feeling of security.[16] Some of us lean on a fence to talk to our neighbor, but we also have a sense of privacy and protection. Similarly, when you place both of your hands, in front of you, palms out, you establish a boundary between you and the individual. The arms should angle from the body at about thirty degrees, and the hands should be relaxed and curved slightly. If the individual comes close enough that their body or hands touch yours, with your arms in this position, there is no doubt that they are intruding on your personal space. Upon making physical contact with you, most individuals will back off. If they do not, this means that they are either no longer aware of personal boundaries, or worse, they are about to attack. You can also use your upraised hands to push away or fend off the individual if you have to. Your hands should be relaxed, and not clenched in a rigid, fighting posture. Your hands and arms should express that you are closed off to physical contact, but open to listening.
- **Talking with your hands.** Another option is to hold your hands at about chest height, palms up, with the back of one hand in the palm of the other. In this case, you can "talk" a little with your hands, moving them in unison. You are moving naturally, but at the same time minimizing your gestures. If you move your hands too much, you will further confuse those in chaotic states, or betray your own anxiety. The advantage of this posture, however, is that your hands are higher, even more ready to ward off an attack.

Figure 44.3 Two Hands are Better Than One

Paradoxically, holding up *one* hand, although weaker from a combative perspective, is more likely to provoke the individual. Rather than a fence, a single hand becomes the leading point of a triangle, your shoulders being the other two points. Many people experience this as if your hand is up to shut their mouth.

- **Do not touch the irritated person.** Do not touch the irritated person hoping to calm them down. There are very few occasions where touching angry people will make the situation better. Such situations do exist with distraught children, perhaps but not with adults, and *particularly* not with aggressive individuals. The only time you will touch a potentially aggressive person should be to shake their hand (on some occasions) or protect yourself.

- **Try to get the individual to sit rather than stand.** Pacing and stomping around is stimulating, and when standing, you are more ready to fight. On the other hand, we associate sitting with peaceful communication. Whenever tactically possible, try and remain seated, and instruct the individual to remain seated also. Should the individual repeatedly rise out of their chair, the situation is obviously escalating. If the individual stands, you should stand as well, because otherwise you are at an immediate disadvantage.

- **If they try to disengage, let them.** Assaults frequently occur when the individual tries to disengage, but the Security Professional insists on working things out *right now*. This is almost always a mistake, as the individual is leaving to calm down. However, if the individual is too enraged, or has overtly threatened to commit an act of violence *after* they leave, then safety becomes the Security Professional's more immediate concern. Under such circumstances the Security Professional must attempt to de-escalate the individual to a more rational emotional state before allowing them to leave the office. Sometimes this will simply entail allowing the individual to "cool off" in the Security Professional's office, or perhaps contacting a family member to come to the office in an attempt to defuse the situation. In some cases, your delaying tactics are in order to enable law enforcement professionals or security guards to arrive at the scene to safely escort them off site.

CHAPTER 45

Tone and Quality of Your Voice
for De-escalation

The following information will help you in using the correct tone and quality of voice for the de-escalation of aggressive individuals:

- **Use a firm, low pitch.** In most situations, try to pitch your voice *slightly* lower than normal; it should also be firm and strong. An angry person will focus on your tone rather than the content of your words. Do not betray any negative or angry emotions. A bored tone with either impatience or condescension is guaranteed to evoke more anger, not less. A calm, low-pitched voice communicates to the individual that you are in control of yourself and the situation. When we are upset or frightened, we may feel out of control of everything, including our own body. Under stress our voices tend to go up in pitch. When you pitch your voice lower, you feel a little vibration in your chest. When you feel the vibrato of your voice in your chest, you get immediate feedback that you have taken control back of your own body, restoring your sense of power.

- **Slow Down.** Generally, you should speak a little slower than the person you are de-escalating. However, do not speak with an exaggerated slow motion quality, or in such a way that they think you are trying to hypnotize them. By slowing down, you are trying to get them to resonate with your slower pace, and also to keep yourself from being swept up in their aggression.

- **Do not be overly "sweet" or condescending.** When communicating with an angry person, do not use a condescending or patronizing tone. Despite their problems, they are not small children. Talking to adult individuals, even those with a mental illness as if they were children, will cause them to become even more angry and agitated, possibly in an effort to prove to you that they are not children.

- **Verbal commands.** You will sometimes find that a lower pitched voice will not grab, and hold the individual's attention. For an individual who is very disorganized or angry, the use of a low-pitched voice will not be as effective as it will not penetrate through the fog of their hysteria or agitation. When necessary, Security Professionals must give the individual a clear, firm, and loud command to cease and desist. Do not yell shrilly or with a pleading tone. Be firm and authoritative, letting the individual know that you are in command, while at the same time offering them an opportunity to negotiate a safe resolution to the crisis.

Figure 45.1 Example: Clear, Firm Command Voice

Our company has an annual sale, where various products are sold at very low cost to staff. Employees are made aware of the date, time, and types of products, and start to line up outside the building about 4 AM, hours before the opening of the sale. Security was present, but once the doors were opened, we were immediately overwhelmed with hundreds of employees trying to enter to buy. Because of the poor planning of the event, people later in line got to watch those in front buy cases of products, followed by announcements that one product after another was running short, only an hour into the sale, which had six more hours to go. As employees became angrier, a mob mentality began to set in. There were three Security Professionals present, one of whom was a retired Army Master Sergeant. Before the situation could get out of hand he raised his booming voice and almost immediately restored order, instructing employees how to proceed and behave. Additionally, he restricted the number of employees who could enter the room, and had company representatives adjust the volume of purchases per employee.

- **The use of a dramatic voice.** Sometimes the best tactic is to use a dramatic voice, loud and somewhat enthusiastic, using charisma to grab attention. Make your voice a little louder, and use charisma to grab attention.

Figure 45.2 Example: The Dramatic Voice

A mentally ill woman is upset because she thinks people in the utility company lobby are laughing at her. You say, "Claire, I SEE you are upset! I'D be upset too if I thought those people were laughing at me! Now COME ON over here!" Indicate with your body where you want her to go, moving as if you are absolutely certain she will comply. "C'mon. I want you to tell me EXACTLY what happened—EVERY word! Let's go over here where no one can bother us!" You show her that not only are you giving her your complete attention, but the drama means that she is important, the center of the action. By moving her somewhere else to talk, you remove her from the scene that is upsetting her.

- **The battle cry.** There are almost no situations where you should be yelling at the individual. There is one exception however. When the individual is moving toward you to attack, or is otherwise presenting immediate danger to another, you should roar like a lion to startle and freeze the individual's motion momentarily with commands like "STAY BACK" or "STEP AWAY," so you can evade, counter, or escape. The way you do this is as follows:
  a. Open your eyes WIDE!
  b. Slam your stomach BACKWARDS, trying to connect your navel and your spine.
  c. Tighten your throat. (This will be a little painful to some people, leaving a raw throat for the next day, but it's worth it if it saves you or someone else from harm.)
  d. **ROAR** a command.

Figure 45.3 Wording in a Battle Cry

When someone is moving towards you with hostile intent, do not command that they "Stop." They may comply and still be too close to you. Command that they "STEP BACK" or "MOVE BACK."

The command "STOP" is used to arrest an action that will, in itself, result in harm. For example, if the person is about to jump in front of a car, or throw something.

CHAPTER 46

Across the Spectrum of Anger

All of the de-escalation techniques outlined in this section are for individuals between 20 and 95 on the aggression scale. They are contraindicated with an enraged individual who is between 95 and 99.

Figure 46.1 Methods Used to De-escalate Angry People Do Not Work With *Enraged* People

In fact, they will very likely further escalate the situation. Imagine trying to "validate" a berserk methamphetamine intoxicated psychotic, "I see you want to rip my brains out of my skull and smear them on the walls. You've been having a rough day today."

Conversely, using strategies that are suitable for enraged people (control tactics) with merely ir-ritated or angry people will flame them upwards *into* rage. Imagine coming home and your spouse tells you that she is not happy that you forgot the groceries in the trunk of the car, and you say, "Step back. Give me five feet right now!"

In any case, the Security Professional must first center themselves before stepping into the center of the conflict and establishing control of the situation and the individual. (If you have properly trained in the procedures in Section III, centering is an almost instantaneous act.) Once the individual is under control and their anger has cooled, you can attempt to resolve the situation that led to the aggression.

If you do not establish safety for yourself and others, you can be of no assistance to the individual, or anyone else. This does not mean that you should cease talking with, reassuring, or negotiating. What the authors mean is that everything you do must have a tactical basis. In the sections that follow, the reader will be introduced to a variety of de-escalation techniques, some of which may appear to be polar opposites of each other. Some are applicable over a wide range of circumstances, whereas others may only be useful in very specific situations. Think of them like the scales and octaves of music that must be mastered so that you can improvise freely.

Remember, de-escalation is about resolving everyone's problem, which obviously includes you and the individual. Your problem is the agitated individual, while their problem is attempting to obtain a goal of some sort. After all, ***individuals become angry and violent because they want something***. Mentally ill individuals, however, can present a somewhat different problem regarding de-escalation as opposed to "regular" individuals, because their fears, concerns, and outbursts may be due to their mental illness, and not necessarily their desire for something specific. In other words, their problems are internal, although at the moment of crisis, this may be difficult to distinguish. Successful negotiations will work to solve everyone's problem, although the individual is not likely to achieve exactly what they want at the moment.

- **De-escalate, then solve the problem.** Your focus should be on what the individual is doing, and not the cause of their anger. You cannot solve a problem with an angry person. Remember, the individual sees the conflict as a win-lose proposition. They will view any negotiation or agreement as a loss of power. For this reason, first eliminate the anger, and then engage in problem-solving.

- **Authority presence.** The Security Professional's presence can be enough to calm an individual down. "Presence," however, does not merely mean that you are "filling space." It means that you have established through your stance and demeanor, an authority that cannot be ignored.

- **Watchful waiting.** A crisis always requires a moment-by-moment decision on the best course of action. Sometimes, all that is necessary is that you remain centered and ready, as the individual calms down without any assistance from anyone else. This does NOT mean that you ignore them, but from time to time, the best control tactic is letting them control themselves.

- **Trust your hunches.** As the authors have noted several times throughout this book, Security Professionals should pay attention to their intuition and "gut feelings." If you have a vague sense that something is wrong with the individual, you are probably right. Pay close attention to the individual's behaviors, both verbal and non-verbal, and simultaneously undertake a mental threat assessment. What do you see? How is the individual interacting with other people? Have they been having any problems recently? What is different now from the way they act normally?

- **Be what you want them to be.** Speak to them calmly, control your breathing, and maintain an upright and non-threatening posture, all the while remaining ready to respond to any attack. Your intention is that the individual will template to your behavior and demeanor. This is not an unattainable goal. In a crisis situation people tend to mirror the behavior of the most powerful individual with whom they are interacting. If the Security Professional is out of control, the individual will feel even more threatened, and become even more aggressive. If you are calm, however, you can imbue the situation with that calm.

- **One point of contact.** When de-escalating an individual, only one person should be communicating with them. This becomes more relevant the angrier they become. Trying to talk to two or more people at once, particularly if *they* are not in complete agreement, will cause the angry individual to become more and more confused, as well as making him/her feel surrounded and overwhelmed.

Figure 46.2 Establish a "One Point of Contact" In Advance

You must already have established clear protocols for this type of situation. Many security situations deteriorate when a Security Professional is attempting to calm the angry client or employee and another person from HR, management, or another branch of the company insists on interjecting his/her comments, either because they are upset and want to argue, or they mistakenly think they are being helpful. This is **always** very dangerous.

- **You can tell me, you do not have to show me.** As elementary a suggestion as this might sound, the following illustrates the power of this intervention. An individual, very upset, begins swearing at a Security Professional on the phone. She replies, "Al, it is absolutely clear that you are upset. Furious! And I am able to help you with this. But I cannot and will not do that when you swear at me. You can tell me why you are upset you do not need to show me."

- **Demonstrate empathy.** Empathy is not the same as sympathy, that feeling of sorrow for the person's plight. Empathy simply means that you understand, what other people are feeling based on their physical organization, what they say and how they say it. Or "What you are saying really makes sense." We thereby demonstrate that we grasp what the individual is experiencing without necessarily agreeing with it. However, do not say, "I know how you feel." An aggressive person will feel that you are putting yourself above him, claiming to be able to read his mind, or simply respond, "You have no idea what my life is like."

Figure 46.3 Too Much Empathy Is Counterproductive: Use It Tactically

Do not overuse this or you will sound like a parody of a therapist. Like everything else we have discussed, it is a tactical communication to be used sparingly at just the right time.

- **Be Professional.** Some Security Professionals act in far too friendly and informal a manner. Professional distance gives the subject of your attention a clear understanding of the true nature of your relationship with them.

- **Team up with them.** Incorporate them into your "team" by using the word "we." When they accept this unconsciously, they begin to feel that they are working with you, not against you.
  a. "Let's you and me sit over here."
  b. "Yes, we do have a problem. Let's see what we can do to figure this out."

- **Give praise.** Give praise for their good ideas or positive acts. Do not be over-effusive, but highlight any positive moves the person makes. However, praise is not a "put up," to make them feel good, as if a few mere compliments will solve everything. "Ride" the praise into a problem-solving solution.
  a. "I like that idea! I think we can make it work. You have a few phone calls to make."
  b. "I like how you decided to ignore that guy in the waiting room. You are making some good decisions lately. Honestly, if you can handle the kind of grief that guy was trying to give you, you can handle this situation in your work unit."

- **Humor.** This is the ability to see a situation from another perspective, can sometimes work like magic. However, you must be very careful; it only is helpful when the other person is at irritated, rather than in a state of strong anger. If they are too upset or agitated, their response to a joke or humorous comment is likely to be, "You are making fun of me." Or "This is serious. You think this is a joke?"

Figure 46.4 Author's Experience: Humor for Self-Defense

Many years ago, one of the authors was a member of a mixed-race group when one of the men, an ex-con with a history of assaults, started singing a little song, "I got a bullet here for every white man here, because everyone should die." I smiled at him and said, "That won't work on me. I can only be killed by a silver bullet, followed by garlic and a stake through the heart." I looked at him blandly, and he gave me a momentary hard stare. Then we both broke into laughter, and the atmosphere in the room lightened considerably.

- **Honesty is golden.** In any interaction, with any individual, Security Professionals must be honest and forthright; never making promises (or threats) that you cannot keep; and keeping the ones you do make. This is especially true when de-escalating an angry and potentially aggressive individual. Do not try and fool the individual or agree to their demands in the heat of the moment. If you do suggest a solution, be clear as to what the limitations are, both on company policy and on your ability to make something actually happen.
- **Do not try to win. Try to establish peace.** Try to resolve the situation so that the individual can separate with pride intact. Even if they have not achieved their original goal, the individual should at least have a certain amount of respect for the professional way that you handled the situation. If they subsequently feel cheated or betrayed they will likely be non-compliant in the future due to the personal animosity they feel for the Security Professional.
- **A private space.** As a general rule, de-escalation is best accomplished without an audience, although this is sometimes unavoidable. Whenever possible, the individual should be escorted to a more private area in the office (although your fellow professionals should be close by and ready to respond to any threats or actual assault), free from the view of any onlookers, such as a waiting room full of individuals. If this is not possible, then the waiting room should be cleared until the situation is resolved.
  a. Disorganized individuals may be frightened by onlookers.
  b. Enraged or more predatory individuals may become excited by the crowd or begin to attack others who are present.
  c. "Bluffers" may be afraid they will lose face. Therefore, in front of others, they feel they have to remain aggressive or obstinate.
  d. Manipulative individuals will use the crowd to their own advantage, by acting out to an even greater degree in an attempt to turn the onlookers against you.

CHAPTER 47

Diamonds in the Rough: Essential Strategies
for the De-escalation of Anger

Codes for Living: Following the Access Route

People often have a code or a series of codes by which they live. Some of those codes are based on the culture into which they are born, and others are based on the culture or lifestyle they adopt.

The heart of their code is often a phrase or a couple of words that sums up their deepest values. When people talk about themselves, their codes of living are often woven throughout their speech. This is especially true with an angry person, whose reason(s) for their outrage is often their belief that their code is being threatened or compromised:

- They perceive that others are demanding they violate their code.
- They believe they are facing a choice that forces them to violate their code.
- They take offense when others do not conform to their code.
- Another's actions require them to respond, lest they violate their code.

Angry individuals will very often proclaim their values and code for living in their explanation or tirade, and Security Professionals should be able to identify their core metaphor in one or two words or phrases.

Figure 47.1 Example: Codes for Living

Person one. "I'm a man. He can't talk about me that way."

Person two. "Think of how I feel. If someone did that to you, wouldn't you be upset?"

Person three. "Are you saying I'm not going to get my Cobra extended? It doesn't matter what HR says. I worked here 27 years. I did the job. You are not cutting me off just because of some new rule. You owe me!"

Person four. "I was standing there all alone. Everyone was looking at me. Talking about me!"

You should be able to describe their code in one or two words. What is most important to each of these people in the above examples? Person one's is pride. Person two's is caring for others or empathy. Person three's is mutual obligation. Person four's is fear of being shamed.

Using the Code to Reach the Person

The code is an access route to the individual. When you incorporate it in your response, you are recognizing the individual's values (however misguided or anti-social). This is what the individual often means by "respect." This connection, however tenuous, allows you to work with the individual toward a resolution. See the examples below:

- If you discern that personal integrity is a core issue of concern, frame your responses and suggestions with the same theme. "I wouldn't want people talking about you as a man who can't control himself."

- To the young individual who believes someone treated him with disrespect: "Man, I can see how angry you are. I'd be angry too if someone said that to me, but if you try to hurt him, you'll end up losing your job. Yeah, I know you think he *disrespected* you, but if you assault him, you would be letting him *own* you. He says three words, and your response means you lose your place here, where you have got a fine future. Is that what you want?"

- Sometimes a core metaphor is situational, something as ostensibly benign as the weather. "Look, Frank, it's a hot day, I'm tired, and I guess you are too. I don't care who's right here, really. I just want to finish this paperwork so you can get that appointment with EAP. The computers are down, so we have to figure out some other way to get through to them. Gosh, these days are nasty. Here we are, all stressed out just because we're both hot and tired."

Break the Pattern

You may find yourself in the same argument(s) over and over again, and often with different individuals! In order to detect any patterns or behaviors that may have affected your communication with an individual negatively, Security Professionals can easily perform an **After Action Review** of their own actions and responses in past disputes, noting their "hot buttons," as described in Chapter 10. An honest attempt at self-reflection may reveal patterns of behavior, personal style, even personal codes, that have had a detrimental effect on your interaction with a particular individual, or group of similar individuals.

At times however, you may be forced to more dramatically break the pattern of interaction between you and an individual, by doing or saying something that makes continuing the dispute absolutely impossible. In many cases, you will use a dramatic voice or display somewhat uncharacteristic or unexpected behaviors. This technique is not recommended for "routine" episodes of de-escalation, and most definitely not as an opening in any encounter. However, breaking the pattern can be effective because many individuals expect their targets to react in a somewhat predictable manner to their displays of anger and/or violence. By reacting in an unanticipated manner, you can throw the individual off balance. This tactic can work with very angry individuals. It sometimes takes the fight out of the interchange like suddenly letting out the air from a tire. Here are a few examples of breaking the pattern from one of the author's own experiences as well as those of some associates:

Figure 47.2 Experience: Breaking the Pattern #1

A man came into a clinic, drunk and belligerent, looking for a fight. I came out and said, "Man, WHAT have you been DRINKING? Me, I like Ten Canes Rum. Whoa, *(holding up two hands and yelling boisterously)* Not your turn yet! I'm talking about my rum! Ten stalks of sugar cane for one bottle of rum. It is SWEET as sin and gold as a tiger's eye. What have YOU been drinking?" He blearily looked at me and said, "Whiskey." I said, "What KIND of whiskey. I need to know WHAT you have been drinking! Man, I love my rum. I go home, take 2 ice cubes and put them in a glass. When the rum hits that ice, I hear a crack as clear as the bell in a church and I know everything is going to be alright!" Within five minutes, we were sitting on two chairs, laughing and talking about our favorite drinks.

Figure 47.3 Experience: Breaking the Pattern #2

A very aggressive, manic individual, after darting quickly around my office while verbalizing very dangerous fantasies, whirled around and said to me, a grin of delight on his face: "You are scared, aren't you?" I blurted out, "Yes, I am," (this response, from early in my career, was clearly a mistake I wouldn't make today). He then started to stalk menacingly toward me. Realizing I was in danger, I jumped up, and yelled in a dramatic voice "You know what I'm scared about? I'm scared what's happening to kids today! They are being murdered in wars throughout the world. But we don't even have to go that far! They are cutting school lunches and little children who go to bed hungry are not even being fed in schools!!!!! I'm scared what's happening to kids today!" With a look of shock on his face, he dropped into a chair, and said, "I like kids. What are we going to do about that?"

Figure 47.4 Example: Breaking the Pattern #3

A police officer was arresting a hostile man, who was trying to avoid having handcuffs put on him. The methamphetamine-intoxicated man yelled an obscene accusation about the professionals assumed sexual predilections. The professional jumped back and said, "Goddamn it! You make one mistake 20 years ago, and they never let you forget!" The man held up a hand and said, "Whoa, whoa brother. That's okay. These things happen to everyone. It's okay" and turned around, offering his hands to be cuffed.

Figure 47.5 Example: Breaking the Pattern #4

A police officer was arresting a drunk when he called her that word that, more than any other makes women incensed. With a look of puzzlement on her face, she said, "Jimmy, do you spell that with a 'K' or a 'C.' I need that for my paperwork."

"K," he replied.

"Jimmy, if you are going to use big boy language, you should at least know how to spell it. It starts with a 'C.'"

"It does? Damn, they didn't teach me that one in school."

Determining the time and necessity of breaking the pattern may seem like magic, but instead, this is a intuitive skill that is developed with time and experience. Because future behavior is unpredictable, Security Professionals cannot prepare an array of specialized catch-phrases ready to disarm an aggressive individual. This technique is pure improvisation, grounded in the same strong and powerful calm that we have written about throughout this manual. If you consciously try to be overly creative, or if you are excited about what a cool or funny thing you are about to say, you may indeed say something witty, but it will be at the wrong time, to the wrong individual. When you are in control of yourself, with the mainline skills of de-escalation at hand, such improvisation will simply emerge.

Some Guidelines for Limit Setting

As soon as you draw a line, it will become the main focus of your interchange. Do not ever set a limit that you cannot enforce or one that is not reasonable and simple to understand. Your tone of voice should be matter-of-fact, rather than critical. Simply remind them of the rule or set a proper limit (a new rule, so to speak). Only set reasonable limits that the person can do. If you cannot explain clearly why the limit is necessary—at least to your peers—then it is not a good limit.

Silence

Sometimes, the most powerful thing you can do is to be silent. Be sure that you are not being passive-aggressive, fuming in silent anger, or appearing to ignore or dismiss the individual. Instead, you should wait, quietly and powerfully. Such silence can evoke curiosity, anxiety, or a desire for a response. Keep your facial expressions calm, your posture centered, and carefully listen. Nod your head calmly as you listen, doing so slowly and intermittently. In many cultures, including the United States, nodding your head too rapidly indicates that you want the other person to hurry up and finish, or worse, just shut up.

Silence, however, is not that easy, particularly for the person who is suffering the brunt of another's anger. There are three ways to listen silently, and two of them will make people very angry.

- **Contemptuous silence.** You are tired of the dispute, or tired of the individual. You fidget, you sigh, and most significantly, you roll your eyes upwards to one side, and twist one corner of your mouth. In almost every culture, this facial expression and behaviors express an attitude of contempt, and are guaranteed to provoke anger or rage.

- **Stonewall silence.** When you stonewall, you ignore the individual, or otherwise make it clear that you wish they would shut up. Your demeanor shows that you have no interest in what they have to say or why they are saying it. You can to do this inadvertently by entering notes into your computer while the individual is talking, or by taking a phone call during the interview. Such dismissive behavior can evoke anxiety or anger in the individual who wants to get through to you, only to find that there's a "wall" in the way. As a result, they will do anything to "get through to you," including trying to tear down that wall. In addition to upsetting the individual, such indifferent behaviors on the Security Professionals part will also increase risk, and decrease your ability to defend yourself from attack because your attention is improperly focused on your computer screen or your telephone conversation, instead of where it should be: on the individual. Security Professionals are encouraged to take short notes on a piece of scrap paper or the individuals report form, and transcribe more detailed notes of the interview into the case file after the individual has left the office.

- **The right way to listen: Interested silence.** When you have been listening quietly, the individuals often interrupt themselves to ask, "Aren't you going to say something?" or "Don't you have any ideas?" If they don't stop, and continue to talk and talk, you may have to interrupt them. Do this by advancing a hand slightly at waist level or a little higher, fingers curved, palms down (you don't want the individual to interpret your hand movement as a "shut up" gesture). You should also lean toward the individual slightly, indicating that it's your turn to speak. If they don't notice your hand gesture, put both hands up in front of you in a "fence," and tell them to stop a moment, in a voice that is loud and holds a little humor. "Joey, Joey, wait a minute. You gotta give me a chance to say something! Listen to me a second! After interrupting the individual, the first thing you should do is to sum up your understanding of what he/she just said. This proves that you were indeed listening to them, and are interested in solving their problem. Once you have summed it up, you can either go into problem solving-mode, or, if they are still heated, shift into "tactical paraphrasing" (Chapter 48).

CHAPTER 48

Tactical Paraphrasing: The Gold Standard
with Angry Individuals

What is paraphrasing?

Paraphrasing is perhaps the most important technique for calming <u>angry</u> individuals. You sum up in a phrase or sentence what they have just said in a paragraph. If you paraphrase accurately, you have established that you have "gotten" it that far, so they do not have to repeat it, or try to say it in other words. It is like peeling off a single layer of an onion so that you can be shown the next layer. If you do not demonstrate that you "get" it, the individual will feel compelled to repeat and/or elaborate that layer of the problem with more and more intensity. As they get more intense, they usually get more irrational, and their ability to communicate breaks down even further. The wonderful thing about paraphrasing is that you do not have to be "smart" and interpret anything. You simply have to listen carefully.

Returning to our image of an onion, as you peel off each layer, they get to the next layer that is driving them. They might start out complaining about HR staff being late for an appointment, and that paraphrased, tell you that they are afraid they will lose their job, and that paraphrased, tell you that their wife left, and that paraphrase, start talking about suicide.

Paraphrasing establishes that you are truly listening and have understood what they have said. There is another component, however, where we take a slightly activist approach. We select what we will sum up from the complex, multi-faceted communication that the individual has just given us, choosing the healthiest aspect of what they have just said.

This method is "self-correcting," whereas passive summation can make things worse. If you sum up an angry person's worst impulses, they will find themselves in agreement with you: you have lined up with what desires destruction. If you sum up an aspect of what they have said that is in the direction of conflict resolution, you will draw out of them that which does wish to resolve the conflict. On the other hand, if they are, in fact, bent on mayhem, they will correct you by escalating what they are saying, believing that you are not getting the message. Remember, they are trying to communicate! All you have to do is sum up what you understand from what they said. When you get it right, they go to the next layer.

Figure 48.1 Example: Correct and Incorrect Paraphrasing

Angry employee. I am so mad at my manager that I could just wring her neck!"

- Incorrect paraphrase: "You want to murder Ms. Christie."
- Correct paraphrase: "You are *really* furious with her!"

If you have, in the second example, accurately paraphrased the meaning of the employee's intention, you will naturally go on to the next layer of his complaint:

Angry Employee. "You will not believe what she did. I've spent three months on the Xenex project. So she talks to advertising and they have some bright idea on how to market things, but this means I have to scrap the last three months of work and start over!"

If, however, the second example is *inaccurate*, the employee will correct you with more vehemence, in this case necessitating an immediate emergency response.

Angry employee. "No, not really furious. I honestly want to loop a belt around her neck and slowly strangle her. Seriously! She better not be on-site when I get back to my work area."

Remember: If they are talking to you, they are trying to communicate. Effective tactical paraphrasing brings out more information from an angry subject, often more accurate than you can acquire through interrogating questions.

Why not simply ask the person what's going on? If they want to tell me, why don't they just answer the questions?

Asking questions is usually not a good idea with really angry individuals. They already believe you have to "get" what they are saying, and a question shows that you do not. Still angry and now frustrated at their failure, this makes them try harder, albeit with less organization and coherence than before. Over and over, they experience failure: they cannot get through to you! When anger is combined with a sense of powerlessness, the individual feels like he/she is "losing" to a more powerful other. In essence, they experience a question as a demand for an answer, putting you in a dominant position.

Figure 48.2 The Problem With Questions

You surely have experienced how irritating questions can be. Imagine coming home after a bad day. You are hot, tired, and frustrated. You walk into your house, drop your gear on the floor, sigh loudly, and walk toward the shower. Your spouse says, "Did you have a bad day?" Isn't this irritating? Isn't it *obvious* you've had a bad day? After all these years together, and he/she doesn't know when a bad day just walked into the house! On the other hand, imagine your spouse observing you and saying, "Bad day, huh?" You continue walking towards the shower, and say, "I don't want to talk now. I just want a shower. I'll talk to you later." You are not "forced" to explain yourself.

How to Use Paraphrasing Successfully

The following will help you in paraphrasing successfully:

- It is very important that your voice is strong. You speak to the individual as someone who has the power within to take care of his/her problem, not as someone who is fragile or volatile (even if he/she is).
- You must contact the strong aspect of the individual, the future looking side, that which is striving for strength, looking for integrity. If you contact the weak, or the insecure, you may foster regression to a less mature level of action. Childish action is often impulsive or violent.
- Sometimes, you can use a dramatic summation, "You are really ticked off!" Here, you sum up the individual's mood with your voice and posture, in addition to what is being said.

Figure 48.3 Example: Paraphrasing With an Angry Employee

Shoshona. "I am so sick of that guy. Charlie Mahon. I'd file a complaint for harassment, but no one would believe me!"

Security Professional. "You are really upset!"

Shoshona. "No! I'm f***king furious!"

Note: When you sum up imprecisely, the other usually corrects you. This is as if she were tuning up the signal rather than arguing with you.

Security Professional. "You are talking about the engineer in Building Four."

Note: You can include extra information. In this case, you are demonstrating that not only are you tracking her, you know who she is talking about.

Shoshona. "What a creep! He disgusts me."

Security Professional. "So far I've heard the words 'creep' and 'harassment.' And that you are furious. But you also said you thought no one would believe you."

Shoshona. "Yeah. I don't know what to do with it. I go to the lunch room and he's always there, a table or two over, eating. He's always got this smirk on his face, and he shoves the food in his mouth and acts like he's having an orgasm, all the while trying to make eye contact."

Security Professional. "You are sure that it's directed at you!"

Shoshona. "Yeah, I'm sure. He's even moved his seat so he can get close to me."

You just got the story without a single question. At this point, you can start tactical planning with her; for example, having one of your team sit at a nearby table and observe his actions.

Core

We know we have reached the core level when there is no more "progress." The individual *spins his wheels*. They may use different words, but they say essentially the same thing over and over again. Others express relief at being finally understood; some individuals exhibit an intensification of emotion, because you have reached that which is most distressing. When you reach core, and it is clear that you are on the same wavelength, you can begin problem-solving. This can be as follows:

- Further paraphrasing, where you show greater and greater understanding about what they are upset about.
- A summation of the core problem, followed by a puzzled "why?" For example, "You have been working here seven years. You love the work. Jackley has shown contempt for the organization since the day of his hire. We are aware that material has been stolen, and we are quite sure that it is him. I can understand why you do not like to talk about other employee's affairs. What I am confused about is that, given he claims that you are the one who is stealing things, why you continue to remain silent about this. I truly do understand the code about not "snitching." I understand, too, that part of your code is that a man owns up to his own sins. So I do not understand how that code would lead you to throwing away your future here, when you are only honoring half of it, because as far as we know, you haven't done anything wrong—and he has! We have to figure out a way that you can clear this up without feeling that you have violated a code that Jackley does not even believe in."
- With some individuals, you have, by paraphrasing them every step of the way, established that you are a person of trust. In some cases, you can now be quite directive, because we often are willing to accept advice or even instruction from people we trust.
- With others, we are ready to engage in a collaborative process of problem-solving, trying to figure out a way to solve the situation that is in the best interest of everyone involved.

Do Not Waste It

Paraphrasing is almost a cliché, so much so that we can imagine some of you rolling your eyes when you read the title of this chapter. This technique is too important to abandon, and at the same time, it must be used carefully, that is, **rarely**. If the individual is not getting angry and requiring you to use de-escalation tactics, do not use paraphrasing. Simply talk with them.

If there is a crisis, however, and the individual does *not* believe they are understood, *now* paraphrasing comes into its own. Paraphrasing can have an almost electrifying effect with an angry individual. Imagine the feeling when you try to pull a splinter from under your fingernail, and after ten long minutes of aggravating struggle, you get a hold of it finally and pull it out of your nail bed. That is the sense you get when, angry and desperate to be heard, you realize that the other person "got it."

Figure 48.4 How to master paraphrasing

As you as you view paraphrasing as a 'specialized,' pseudo-counseling technique, you probably won't want to do it—and you won't be good at it anyway. When you are hit by adrenaline, dealing with an angry, perhaps mentally deranged individual, you will stumble over your words if you try to remember to say things like:

- "So what you are sharing with me is . . ."
- "What I hear you saying is . . ."

Don't do this! Many people will find you irritating, and you will be in your head at a time where you must be aware of what's going on in front of you.

You are, in fact, a master of paraphrasing. You do it all the time simply keeping a conversation going, saying things like:

- "Your kid flunked out, huh?"
- "You're not getting a raise."
- "You hate that guy."
- "She's the one."

In short, the natural statements you intersperse in any conversation are perfect paraphrasing. However, because you do this unconsciously, it's hard to tap into as an *emergency technique*. It's easy to perfect, however. Consider this—how many conversations do you have a day? Twenty? Thirty? Forty? <u>In each and every conversation, at an arbitrary moment of your choosing, decide to paraphrase the next thing they say.</u> Just once. Your conversational partner won't even notice. But because you made a conscious decision to do this, your brain notices. That means you have practiced that skill twenty to forty times a day. Consider how good your defensive tactics or skills at evading an attack would be if you executed twenty, thirty, forty perfect repetitions a day—it would become automatic! Similarly, if you do this every day, you will be able to step into crisis oriented paraphrasing without hesitation. It will be so natural to you that you do not even have to think about it.

CHAPTER 49

Big Mistakes That Seem Like
Such Good Ideas at the Time

Unlike report writing, where the Security Professional has ample opportunity to refine and edit their work, de-escalation requires improvisation in a very fluid and dynamic situation, often with volatile and unpredictable individuals. In such a highly charged atmosphere, where clear communication is necessary to prevent any misunderstandings, Security Professionals must think quickly, but calmly, before speaking.

By maintaining an emotional distance, and not reacting personally to anything the individual may say, you will be less likely to escalate an already heated situation. Conversely, Security Professionals cannot be overly obsequious, or claim to relate personally to the individuals problems, as any personal comparisons will just anger the individual further.

Many mistakes are very obvious, and the moment something leaves our mouths we think, "Uh-oh. I shouldn't have said that!" Fortunately, this can be prevented rather easily by taking a moment to gather your thoughts before responding to what the individual has said. Sometimes you can hold up your hands to give them pause, gather your own resources, and then reply.

Some mistakes are subtler. On certain days, you may be tired, not feeling well, or are distracted by family matters perhaps, and de-escalating an angry individual is the last thing you wish to do. Not surprisingly, risk increases when you are at less than your optimum ability and awareness. Your timing will be off, you will choose the wrong wording for what you intend to say, and you will be off-center. On occasions when you are not at your best, you actually need to be more alert, and in control of yourself.

The following topics are areas of which the authors feel Security Professionals should take note, so as not to make a mistake that leads to an escalating encounter with an angry individual.

Ingratiation

Do not try to ingratiate yourself with the individual; do not pretend that a potentially aggressive situation is not developing by continuing to engage the individual as you would normally; and, do not ignore the aggressive behavior in the hopes that the individual will eventually calm down on their own.

One of the paradoxes of ingratiation is that Security Professionals who belie their professional integrity by allowing the individual to control their interactions often present themselves as having a "special rapport" with a person who, in fact, intimidates them. Oddly enough, these same Security Professionals, who try to avoid conflict are often suppressing a lot of anger at being controlled. They displace this on those who call them on what they are doing. Thus, one of the first signs that the Security Professional is ingratiating themselves is an attitude of self-righteousness, a defense mechanism that enables them to avoid questioning the violations of their own integrity. The following factors are also signs of ingratiation:

- You worry about "how things are going" between yourself and the aggressor, and act or react on that basis.
- You are sometimes ashamed of your actions, or believe that you are acting in a cowardly fashion.
- You believe you are caring and nice, and react with shocked outrage when the aggressor is unkind, cruel, or disrespectful toward you, as if you and that person has made some sort of transaction that they have now betrayed.
- You allow the other person to speak to you in overly familiar or rude terms, such as dude, buddy, pal, babe, sweetheart, etc.

The Mistake of Mind Reading

Sometimes, Security Professionals will try to connect with an individual by telling them how they must feel, by confessing to having the same issues, or claim to have gone through a similar situation. As noted elsewhere, personal comparisons normally make the individual even more indignant at your assumed familiarity. Statements like, "I know how you feel," "I know you love this job," or "When I...," are statements that the angry individual may not agree with at all. They then decide to prove you wrong by demonstrating that they are NOT what you just said they are.

The Mistake of Allowing Venting

Venting is an expression of energy, such as going for a run after a difficult day, or chopping wood until fatigued so that you can "let go" of an unpleasant incident. However, generalized aggression expressed verbally in front of others (tantrums), or aggression expressed about one person to another is also designated by this same term.

In Chapter 43, we referred to letting an individual "get something off their chest." This is not the same as venting. The purpose of the former action is to get finished with something by talking about it. The purpose of venting is to stoke oneself up into higher levels of aggression.

Many people have a false idea about aggression, and imagine it to be some kind of psychological fluid that builds up pressure inside a person. When we vent (hence the word), these people believe that we get rid of the anger and then become peaceful, similar to a valve releasing pressure from a water line. Aggression is not a fluid; it is a state of arousal. Just like any other state of arousal—sexuality, happiness, excited interest—additional stimuli elicit more arousal. When a person shouts, yells, complains, kicks things, or the like, they are stimulating themself to greater and greater aggression. Therefore, if you allow an individual to vent angrily, the more aroused, and hence, angry they become. This only makes de-escalation more difficult.

When you let an individual vent about other people, they perceive that you are giving implicit approval to their verbal complaints and abuse. However, when they get so angry that they start to become dangerous and *then* you object, they will turn on you, feeling betrayed. Thus, if an individual begins to vent, de-escalate and control them.

Obvious Mistakes We Should Not Make, But Do Anyway

Although some of the items included in the following list have been discussed before in this book, they are repeated here as a reminder to the reader of the seemingly minor, yet crucial, details of de-escalation. Security Professionals should not:

- Make threats or promise consequences they cannot keep. The failure to follow through on promises made or consequences threatened will also serve to undermine authority with the individual after the incident has been resolved.
- Bombard the individual with choices, questions, and solutions, as this will only overwhelm the individual, especially if they are suffering from mental illness.
- Ask an upset individual "why." Asking a "why" question demands an answer or an explanation from the individual, something they may be quite unwilling, or unable, to do. "Why" questions should only be used when you have used paraphrasing to reach the core problem successfully (Chapter 48).
- Talk down to the individual as if they were stupid or ignorant, or, conversely, in an overly solicitous manner. Do not roll your eyes or sigh heavily while the individual is trying to communicate with you. Do not interrupt as they speak, particularly to correct what they are saying. On the other hand, interruption of aggressive verbalizations or pointless monologues on the part of the individual IS the right thing to do.
- Analyze their behavior while de-escalating. Problem-solving and evaluations can be completed after safe de-escalation.
- Share the individual's private information in front of others.

Figure 49 Be Mindful of "Hallway Consultations"

Consider who may be within earshot of your conversations, either with other individuals or with your fellow professionals. If individuals overhear you discussing the details of another individual's situation they may think, "If they talk about that person like that, they are probably talking about me in the same way."

- Take things personally when the individual attacks your character or professionalism. The measure of the true professional is NOT taking things personally.
- Allow the individual to trespass on your personal boundaries, or violate theirs. The safety issues inherent in personal spacing issues are quite obvious. Safety is enhanced when one enforces a strong, professional hierarchical relationship with the individual.

- Touch, push, or try to forcefully move the individual from one place to another, or point at them in a threatening manner. In fact, Security Professionals would be well served to limit any personal contact with all individuals to the obligatory handshake, and even that minimal contact is not necessary. The only time when Security Professionals should lay their hands on an individual is in the rare event when they are defending themselves physically, or, if it is your responsibility, physically moving an individual from one area to another, or off the premises.

- Adopt an authoritarian or demeaning attitude, particularly in front of their peers or other onlookers, including fellow professionals. Authoritarian attitudes and behaviors are some of the most common precipitants of assault by individuals.

SECTION X

Managing Rage and Violence

CHAPTER 50

Preface to Rage

Rage and anger are not merely different in degree; they are different modes of being, just as water, once past the boiling point, becomes steam. Frustrated individuals, posture or otherwise act angrily to establish dominance, or to force agreement or compliance from others. If nothing else, their goal is to communicate their feelings, although, due to their lack of interpersonal skills, their mental illness, the effects of drugs and/or alcohol, or just plain old frustration, they often resort to anger in an attempt to make themselves heard.

The reader will recall that anger is denoted as falling between 20 and 95 on the aggressiveness scale (Chapter 40). This represents a very broad range of arousal, ranging from mildly irritated to truly irate. Rage however, occupies a much smaller fraction of the scale, from 95 to 99, with 100 signifying an act of violence. When in a state of rage, the individual desires to commit mayhem. Enraged individuals are in a "threshold" state, escalating themselves until they have overcome any moral or personal constraints that may prohibit them from committing the ultimate expression of rage—violence.

Therefore, all of the strategies described in the previous chapters dealing with the angry individual are more or less useless with one who is truly enraged. In the office setting, the enraged individual should quickly elicit a response from the rest of the staff. In fact, the authors would hope that the Security Professional will have already called for assistance through the use of code words or other early warning systems as the individual becomes noticeably angrier. At the very least, raised voices and angry outbursts should draw a "show-of-force" (Chapter 4) to the interview room well before the individual is actually enraged.

Security Professionals need to recognize what type of rage the individual is expressing, because there are different verbal control strategies to deal with each. Fortunately, an enraged individual's behavior is quite obvious, and after reading this section of the book, you will be able to identify what type of rage the individual is exhibiting rather easily, allowing you to employ the appropriate strategies to control them.[17]

Figure 50 IMPORTANT CAUTION

Here, and in several other areas of this book, we have used animal symbols to aid in the understanding of various types of rage or other behavior. For example, we use the image of a leopard or a shark in describing predatory rage. These are thought devices, and are not intended to be used in either paperwork or communication to describe such individuals. In our hypersensitive times, such a reference to a specific may be misconstrued as stigmatizing an individual as "being like an animal." Nothing could be further than the truth; the images are to assist in understanding modes of behavior, not character. Nonetheless, such images should remain aids of understanding, not terms of reference.

CHAPTER 51

Chaotic Rage: A Consideration of Rage
Emerging From Various Disorganized States

Signs of Chaotic Rage or Delirium

Chaotic rage is typified by profound disorganization of cognitive and perceptual processes, and can be engendered by severe psychosis that has "crossed over" into a delirium state, mania, intoxication, drug withdrawal, severe intellectual/developmental disabilities, senile dementia, overwhelming emotions, or as a result of brain injury or trauma. Enraged disorganized individuals are often very impulsive and unpredictable, striking out in all directions. They are also often indifferent to, or unaware of, pain or injury to themselves. They may not be coordinated in their actions, but they are fully committed, meaning that they have no fear of injury or consequences to hold them back. However, trained individuals, be they military, prize fighters or simply seasoned street fighters, combative reflexes are almost instinctive, and thus, even though they are cognitively shattered, they can still throw punches and kicks with accuracy.

Unlike a classic psychosis, the most salient characteristic of chaotic rage is the near impossibility of establishing *any* lines of communication with them. They may utter cascades of words making no sense whatsoever, or grunts, moans, and mumblings. Others make sentences based on rhymes, puns, or cross-meanings, their brains capriciously linking words together based on sounds, not meanings. Delirious individuals may laugh or babble, completely at variance to the seriousness of the situation. They may speak in repetitive loops, fixating on one subject, which could be real, hallucinatory, or such a manifestation of their disorganization that you do not even know what they are talking about.

Delirious individuals can easily become quite frightened or irritable, especially if they are overwhelmed with stimuli, such as a large number of onlookers or the presence of several Security Professionals or law enforcement professionals. They may begin yelling, screaming, lashing out physically, or engaging in self-injurious acts such as scratching and gouging their own flesh, striking themselves repeatedly, or banging their heads against the wall or ground. Such behaviors should be considered a medical emergency, and proper medical attention must be summoned as soon as possible. Ideally, EMTs should stage nearby while the Security Professional and possibly other law enforcement, are establishing the safe de-escalation and resolution of the crisis. As this can be a sign of a life-threatening emergency, individuals manifesting chaotic rage must be transported to a hospital.

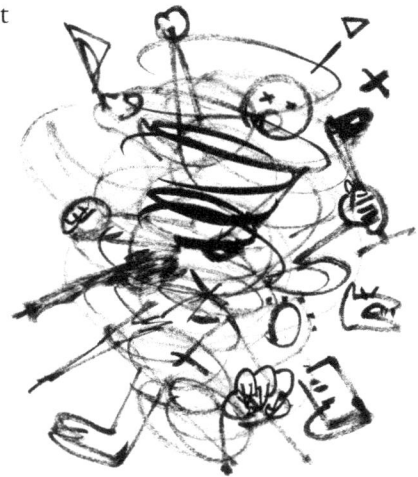

De-Escalation of Chaotic Rage

Disorganized or delirious individuals are among the most difficult to de-escalate verbally, because comprehension and coherent cognitive processes are among the first faculties chaotic individuals lose. Because of their impulsiveness and unpredictability Security Professionals must be on guard against a sudden attack.

One person, usually the supervising Security Professional, needs to take command and control of the situation and direct other professionals as to what they should do, including clearing the room of unneeded personnel, providing site security to prevent others from entering the area, phoning for police and emergency medical assistance, etc.

Use calm movements, and a firm but reassuring voice. Chaotic individuals often experience poor motor control, vertigo, disorientation, etc. Slow movements and soothing tones of voice help orient them physically and emotionally. Use simple, concrete commands with no more than a single "subject" in each sentence, as complex sentences or detailed instructions will be confusing, overwhelming, or threatening to the individual. Repetition is always helpful. Disorganized individuals in chaotic rage states are sometimes susceptible to being deflected to another topic, although in this case, it is unlikely when they have entered fully into chaotic rage. You can sometimes fabricate a theme that catches their attention and seems to engage higher thought processes, delaying their outburst of rage until help can arrive.

Figure 51.1 Example: Distraction of a Person in a Chaotic Rage State (Buying Time)

A paramedic approached a chaotic man who was standing on the edge of a highway, and said, "Ike, what are you doing here. I haven't seen you since high school." As he kept rattling off fictitious memories to the man, whose name was *not* Ike and whom he had never seen before, the delirious man gazed into his eyes in confusion, rocking back and forth in rhythm with the paramedic's words. The paramedic was successful in capturing the man's attention, which kept him from dashing into traffic, until police could arrive. To illustrate how dangerous this situation was, the moment the police tried to physically ease him back from the highway, the man exploded into a violent attack, requiring a number of police professionals to subdue him.

Use tactical paraphrasing to validate and acknowledge their confusion and/or fear. For example, use phrases such as, "Really scary, huh?" Or "You are really worried, aren't you?"

One of the last things we "retain" is our name, so use their name, repetitively, interspersing it frequently in your commands in order to get their attention before initiating attempts to redirect them to another activity. This can be very helpful with combat veterans experiencing a "flashback." [18]

Be very cautious about touching chaotic individuals, as this may be experienced as invasive, or even as an attack. Security Professionals should make physical contact only as a means of self- defense or to prevent the individual from harming themselves or any other people present.

As has been described earlier in Chapter 28 on Disorganization, use simple, concrete commands with no more than a single "subject" in each sentence. Repetition several times is almost always helpful. Use only one thought at a time, as complex sentences will be confusing, and thus threatening or irritating. For example, say slowly, "Sit down, William. Sit down. Sit down. William, sit down."

Minimize such distracting behaviors on your part as extraneous body movements. Your movements should be calming and also only be those useful in helping the person understand what is going on. Because of their difficulty in attending to what you say, non-verbal communication is a paramount concern. A calm reassuring presence, manifesting both strength and assurance is your best hope of helping to stabilize an individual in chaotic rage.

Figure 51.2 Disorganized Individuals Are Among the Most Difficult to De-escalate

Words and coherent cognitive processes are the first thing that disorganized people lose. You must, therefore, be prepared to evade a sudden attack, and further, be prepared, throughout, to use physical control tactics to ensure your safety as well as others.

Catatonia: Special Considerations

Catatonia is a very rare, very bizarre condition in which an individual stays in a fixed posture, not congruent with injury or seizure. Catatonia is caused either by mental illness (schizophrenia) or an organic condition (drug use for example). The catatonic individual's posture may be quite awkward or twisted, seeming to require great flexibility. A classic symptom of true catatonia is "waxy immobility," whereby if someone else moves their body or limbs, the individual maintains the posture into which they were moved. Such individuals will often be totally unresponsive to speech, touch, even pain, and there seems to be no way to establish any communication with them.

Considerable caution is needed in dealing with immobile individuals, for several reasons. First, they may be injured or having a seizure and are in need of medical attention. A second consideration is safety. One way to regard catatonia is to view the individual as exerting 100 percent of their will to *not* interact with the outside world. Trying to help, you may be tempted to make physical contact or speak forcefully in an effort to get them to respond when they are unsecured. This can be a disastrous mistake. Imagine the incredible exertion of will required to maintain immobility for hours, even days, without movement, without response, without even blinking in some cases. Now imagine disturbing this equilibrium. The result is what is clinically called "catatonic rage," a state that really can be considered one form of excited delirium (below). The catatonic individual shifts from 100 percent stillness to 100 percent explosive motion. One of the authors can recall an incident where a law enforcement professional's career was ended by such an individual who, all of 110 pounds, grabbed hold of his arm and yanking as if he was cracking a whip, ripped through all the ligaments of his shoulder and shoulder blade.

Although you may think the individual is unaware, they *can* hear you. Therefore, speak calmly and respectfully. Individuals can have very long memories of being shamed, and if you speak about or treat the catatonic individual as an object rather than as a person, you may evoke a terrible sense of humiliation. In their frozen state, they may not be able to respond immediately, but months or years later, someone or something may trigger an episode of postponed rage. Beyond that, everyone, even a person in a coma, deserves to be treated with respect. Even if it seems that the person cannot hear a word that you are saying, act as if they are listening to every word. Whenever an individual is immobile and unresponsive, Security Professionals should summon medical attention.

Excited Delirium Syndrome

Excited delirium is a rare condition at the extreme end of the hyper-aroused wing of the delirium spectrum. Etiology can be varied, but it is most commonly associated with long-term use of stimulants; particularly cocaine and methamphetamine. Single doses of such drugs as PCP, Ketamine, pyrovalerones such as methylenedioxypyrovalerone (so called "bath salts"), and very rarely, psychedelic drugs such as "magic mushrooms," can cause chaotic rage states. It is also associated with extreme manic or psychotic excitement, and can be precipitated by a variety of purely medical conditions. It is typified by some, if not all of the following: a sudden onset of extreme agitation; pervasive terror, often without object; chaotic, sudden shifts in emotions, disorientation; communication difficulties, including screaming, pressured incoherent speech, grunting, and irrational statements; aggression to inanimate objects—particularly shiny objects like glass and mirrors; hyper-arousal with unbelievable strength, endurance, and insensitivity to pain; hyperthermia accompanied by stripping off clothes; and most notably, violent resistance to others, before, during, and after arrest or restraint.

Accompanying their almost unbelievable level of physical arousal and resistance to both physical and mechanical restraints, is respiratory and cardiac arrest. ***These people die!*** The usual pattern is that they struggle with incredible power and then, suddenly, they stop moving. Or sometime after becoming quiet, either in a stupor or in seeming normality, they go into cardiac arrest. This can look remarkably similar to a seizure, also a very dangerous syndrome.

If they have not been already called, get an emergency medical team on scene now! Correct protocol demands that EMS should be staged, and ready to intervene medically the ***instant*** the individual is physically subdued. Furthermore, Security Professionals (or police) should NOT transport the person either to the hospital or jail, unless there is no other option. Ensure that EMS transports the person. If the individual dies in your personal vehicle or a corporate vehicle, YOU will be deemed responsible! The only time you should transport such a person is when it is proven and documented that EMS was not available, and you had to do the transport.

Such individuals can be appallingly dangerous both to others and to themselves. We cannot emphasize strongly enough that this is a medical emergency manifesting as physical danger, and usually requiring police and emergency medical intervention to secure them so that they can be treated.

Always summon law enforcement and emergency medical aid, alerting dispatch to the type of situation you are facing. You will, almost surely, be unable to verbally de-escalate the person in excited delirium, but if they are not presenting an immediate assault risk, make the attempt using the principles delineated above until emergency responders arrive. Why?

- You may be able to de-escalate them.
- You may be able to gain partial compliance that may delay things, enabling you to "buy time," allowing sufficient emergency personnel to muster, making the restraint that will be necessary to get them help more feasible.
- By getting the subject focused on you, they stop moving. This will make it substantially easier for those who are empowered to use higher levels of physical force (police or in some facilities, Security Professionals) to physically intervene.

Figure 51.3 Excited Delirium or Chaotic Rage?

Most individuals who go into chaotic rage are <u>not</u> in an excited delirium, but given the ever-increasing abuse of stimulants (methamphetamine, cocaine, etc.) that are the most common precipitants of this condition, it is important that you are familiar with the signs, symptoms, and "best-practice" interventions.

Remember: Protocol must dictate that you call for both police and emergency medical assistance. Your intervention will, in almost all cases, try to keep everyone safe while emergency personnel arrive. That said, there are times when Security Professionals must intervene physically, either because they are properly equipped (e.g., with Taser) and empowered to do so, or because safety concerns <u>demand</u> that they act now.

Greater knowledge about this syndrome has led to several new problems.

a. The protocol for excited delirium is to subdue them as quickly as possible to get them the medical attention they need, as well as protecting everyone from the appalling violence they may enact. As most mentally ill individuals, including severely disorganized people, are NOT in excited delirium states, this protocol can seem to directly contradict the model of verbal de-escalation we have offered here. In brief, with most mentally ill individuals, take extra time to talk them into compliance; with individuals manifesting excited delirium, subdue them as quickly as possible. However, a careful reading of this text reveals a graduated set of interventions, including how to approach a disorganized individual, even one manifesting chaotic rage. As we have emphasized throughout the text that assessment is behaviorally based, any dangerous behavior on the part of the person of concern should elicit a well-practiced physical response.

b. Because Excited Delirium has finally begun to be recognized by the medical community as a genuine medical syndrome, this complicates things for Security Professionals. Psychosis, unlike schizophrenia, is a general term. Therefore, it is usable. However, if a Security Professional uses the term Excited Delirium, he/she can be accused of diagnosing the person. Therefore, we recommend the use of the term **Chaotic Rage** to describe such individuals. It is fully descriptive, encompassing both the disorganization AND the agitation that such individuals display. Furthermore, the professional is not required to make a distinction between a person with genuine excited delirium from a mushroom intoxicated naked man running onto your property from a distraught grief-stricken employee in a chaotic state. All parties can use this descriptive term without running the risk of being either over-specific or diagnosing in the street.

c. This term will help Security Professionals, on a behavioral basis, to distinguish chaotic rage from either lower levels of disorganization or psychosis so that best practice interventions can be used.

CHAPTER 52

Terrified Rage

Figure 52 Chaotic Rage and Terrified Rage Can Overlap

Be aware that the line between terrified and chaotic rage can be very fine. The terrified person, overwhelmed, can shift into chaotic rage. When facing an individual in a state of either pure terror or terrified rage, be prepared, therefore, to shift to protocols suitable to assisting individuals in chaotic states (Chapter 51).

What does terrified rage look like?

Terrified individuals believe that they will be violated or abused. They appear apprehensive and furtive, looking halfway ready to run, halfway ready to strike. Their voice can be pleading, whiny or fearful, and their eyes are often wide-open or darting from place to place. However, wide-open eyes do not always indicate fear. When fearful, the muscles under the eyes are slack, giving the face a pleading look. Even through the terrified individual is looking in your direction, they do not, usually, look *into* your eyes, nor do they want you to look into theirs. The enraged, aggressive individual with wide-open eyes, on the other hand, displays tension around the eyes. Furthermore, they do, often, look penetratingly into your eyes or *through* you.

The mouths of some terrified individuals gape open slightly, as they breathe in panicky, short gasps, while others press their lips together in a quivering pucker. Their skin tone is often ashen or pale. Some make threatening gestures with a flailing overhand blow, while others primarily use a fending off gesture, as if trying to ward off attack. Their body posture can be described as concave, as they pull away from you or hold themselves tightly in fear. Terrified individuals also exhibit heightened levels of physical arousal, accompanied by panting, sweating, or trembling. They may back themselves into a wall or corner. They also may yell, seeming to be threatening and pleading simultaneously, using such phrases as, "Stay back! You get away from me! I will hit you!! I will! You stay back!" There is a hollow quality to their voices, as if it has no "foundation." This is due to the tightening of their abdomen and diaphragm, so that not only their breathing, but also their speech is high in their chest.

What causes terrified rage?

Severely frightened individuals often suffer from paranoid delusions, a fear of the unknown or terrifying hallucinations. At other times, they are afraid of a loss of control or of being laughed at or humiliated. Some are afraid that they are in terrible trouble with some agency, be it police, the courts, or mental health professionals. Finally, for any one of a number of reasons, they are simply terrified of you. ***Imag-***

ine a snarling wolf cornered, backed up against a cliff face. It is a frightened animal with fangs: do you think that what it really needs right now is a hug?

De-Escalation of Terrified Rage

Your goal here is to reduce the individual's sense of danger. Maintain a safe, distance and relax your posture. Make sure your movements are unhurried, and that your voice is firm, confident, and reassuring. If direct eye contact is reassuring for the individual, do so, if intimidating, do not. How will you know? Notice if their body relaxes or tenses in response to your eye contact or its lack. Of course, you should never take your eyes *off* of them: merely that you should not look penetratingly into their eyes if they are terrified by the eye contact.

Initiate a litany of reassuring phrases, speaking slowly, with frequent pauses: "I know you are scared, that's okay. Put down the chair, you don't need that. I keep it safe here. You can put it down now. I'm way over here. Go ahead. Sit down. I keep it safe here."

Do not say, "I'll protect you" or "I won't hurt you." Many individuals who go into terrified rage have been hurt by people who said those kinds of phrases. However, when you say "I keep it safe here," you are telling them, "This is my territory and no one, including you, will be hurt on my territory. I am taking responsibility, and because of me, you will be safe." Furthermore, by saying something similar to what they expect to hear, yet somehow different, you cause a "glitch" in their thought process. "What did he say? He didn't say, 'I'll keep you safe.' What's different in what he said?" By getting the individual questioning what you said, you cause him/her to "re-engage" the parts of the brain that actually think things through as opposed to just react.

The individual's body language will also indicate that they are calming down. Their breathing will get a little shuddery or be expressed in short high-pitched gasps. They may slump into a chair or onto the floor as if physically exhausted, even beginning to weep. Maintain your reassuring litany, and slowly approach them. If they show signs of becoming frightened again, pause, move back slightly, and continue to speak to them reassuringly. As you approach the individual, move in half steps—for example, move the right foot a full step, then bring the left foot *up* to the right foot. Pause. Move either right or left foot forward, and then bring the other foot forward *up* to the lead foot. Pause. The advantage of moving this way is that you stay balanced, in case the individual attacks suddenly. Additionally, if the individual becomes startled or reactive, you can ease backward, creating more space between you.

CHAPTER 53

Hot Rage

When you think of an individual who is on the edge of violence, hot rage usually comes to mind. Imagine being faced with an individual who is yelling and screaming, brandishing their fists or a weapon, and threatening to do harm; they throw things, tip over desks, and engage in other forms of violent behavior. Such behaviors are often thought to be instinctual, a product of our primitive "flight or fight" response to danger. However, instinctual aggression is usually uncoordinated and flailing, and falls under the category of terrorized or chaotic aggression.

Hot rage, however, is coordinated: a learned behavior, trained through repetition, learned through modeling, and reinforced through success. This does not mean that hot rage is the equivalent of the actions of a professional fighter, who coolly and calmly prepares his/her line of attack and focuses aggression on the opponent. Instead, hot rage should be considered a pseudo-instinct, a deeply ingrained combination of primitive drives and trained actions. Such pseudo-instinctual behaviors are actions that have either been repeated so often, or are so ingrained in powerful early experiences that they function almost like reflexes. Over-arousal also leads to deterioration in judgment, and at higher states of arousal, even basic cognitive processes, leading the individual to fall back on these behaviors that function, to some degree, automatically. For example, some individuals with a long history of abuse lash out in rage whenever frightened, with no ability to evaluate whether or not they are currently in danger. At the same time, they target where best to hit, and frequently, choose a time and a place where they believe they have the best chance of success.

On a more functional level, a good street fighter who loses his temper does not necessarily lose his coordination. He does his best to knock his opponent senseless, but he automatically takes a stance with chin tucked in, shoulder rolled forward, and punches with his entire body lined up so that the power of the blow is amplified by his body weight and the torque of his hips.

General information about hot rage

The more often someone goes into a state of hot rage, the more comfortable they are with their rage, and the easier it becomes to be violent. Hot rage is often a behavior that has led to short-term success in the past, such as scaring and beating a selected victim either for criminal gain, or just for the fun of it. In a state of rage, such an individual has no concern about longer-term consequences, much less guilt. For some, there is a sense of liberation, even a paradoxical kind of joy when they peak into rage. All one's fears and insecurities disappear, and one is left with only the ecstasy of the pure act. For this reason, some desire rage, because that ecstatic state is, to them, the best thing they ever feel.

Displacement is a common factor of hot rage. The individual's anger is displaced, at least temporarily, toward an inanimate object instead of you, or another individual. This also includes picking things up and slamming them down, throwing things, punching or kicking walls, furniture, or other nearby objects. More predatory individuals use displacement as a tactic to make the target of their aggression more fearful, while warming themselves up for an attack.

Figure 53.1 Example: Hot Rage

A customer comes into a store because his phone was unable to make or receive calls. The sole employee was working with another customer, but took a couple of seconds to explain to him that the network was experiencing issues and the only thing to do was wait until they were resolved. The customer said something about expecting an important call, cursed and stormed out of the store. He then whirled around, took his phone and threw it as hard as he could against the front door while other customers were coming in and out of the store, then sped away almost hitting a couple of parked cars in the process.

Hot rage is also associated with peer group influence and masculine display, a primitive attempt to dominate access to or eliminate perceived competition, status, or other objects of desire. This can be especially problematic if the individual begins acting out in front of a group of onlookers, coworkers, or family, where to save face, he believes he must act aggressively toward anyone representing authority.

Some therapeutic professionals claim that hot rage is a result of frustration, but frustration alone does not usually elicit rage in normal people. The individual is more likely to become enraged when their frustrated desires are coupled with something personal, as when they believe another person is impeding them. Hot rage can be a "transference" in which the Security Professional becomes the emblem of everyone who ever controlled them or put them down, an agent of an oppressive society, or simply a legitimate target to express hatred and violence.

There are various types of hot rage, each typified by almost unendurably intense feelings. We distinguish three subtypes: Fury, Bluffing, and Aggressive-Manipulation.

Figure 53.2 Extreme Example: Hot Rage into Violence

A man sees a fellow employee walk down a hallway, and passing a woman, grabs her on the buttocks. She yells in outrage and he laughs. He intervenes, saying, "That's totally out of line." The other man shoves him and says, "Mind your own business. She wants it."

The man later describes hearing a high-pitched noise in his ears, and his vision turning black-and-white. He comes to himself astride the man, pounding his face with his fists.

General De-Escalation of Hot Rage: The Ladder

The primary method of de-escalation for hot rage is called "The Ladder." This is an ideal technique for someone who is beginning to get threatening. It is used only for rage, that gray zone between anger (even extreme anger) and violence. The individual is no longer trying to communicate with you, and they are right on the edge of assault, in a sense, doing a war dance to work out inhibitions to committing violence.

Figure 53.3 Never Compromise Safety

Do not hold back from any action to keep yourself and others safe if the individual does become violent. Escape, evade, and fight back, if that is what you have to do.

The technique itself is simple. Identify the most dangerous behavior and repetitively demand that it cease. Use short sentences and easily understood commands. Once they stop that particular dangerous behavior, identify the next problematic behavior and use the same technique; continue until the individual is de-escalated. This technique is only effective right before, during, and after the peak of the crisis because it is a control tactic rather than a "Lining Up" de-escalation tactic. Control tactics will provoke rage in a merely angry individual, someone we might have over-estimated, due to his/her loud tone, or dramatic behaviors. **As described earlier, facing an enraged individual causes us to experience fear in a way that anger does not.** The danger is NOW, not merely a possibility should the situation continue to deteriorate.

Establishing a Hierarchy of Danger

The general hierarchy of dangerous behaviors, from most to least, is as follows:

1. Brandishing an object or a weapon in a menacing way. NOTE: If they are too close, or are trying to use the weapon, this is violence, not rage.
2. Approaching or standing too close to you with menacing intent.
3. Kicking objects, punching walls, or throwing things (displacement activity).
4. Pacing, stomping, and inflating the body in an aggressive manner (posturing).
5. Shouting or talking in low, menacing tones.
6. Language that is intended to violate, demean, or degrade.

The Ladder is not merely a verbal intervention. Like any other control tactic with an aggressive individual, you must move as needed to maintain the optimum space to both defend yourself, and exert maximum influence upon the aggressor. If they are very close, or threatening, your hands should be up, prepared to ward off any attack, but also as a gesture that is both calming and dominant. On other occasions, you should, as previously described, clasp the wrist of one hand with the other hand.

Give the individual a straightforward command to stop their most dangerous behavior. By keeping things so simple, you can use your mind to look for escape routes, where weapons might be, or how to get help. By holding to an demand that the most dangerous behavior cease, you are displaying clarity and strength to the aggressor, as well as helping them focus their mind on the most problematic thing they are doing. You should not scream or shout: that will not get through, and will increase their aggressive energy. Rather, your voice should be strong, low and commanding (Chapter 45).

After a couple of repetitions, always add, "We'll talk about it when you ..." followed by the same command. Once that behavior is stopped, pick the next most problematic behavior (the next "rung" of the ladder), and command/require that it stops. If the aggressor does calm down and stops all the aggressive behaviors, including assaultive language, THEN set a firm and direct limit.

This is not the time to try and think of something brilliant or life changing to say. By keeping things simple, you can continue to look for escape routes, identify potential weapons, and attempt to get help. You should intersperse your sentences with their name frequently, using this to pace and break the rhythm of your commands, as well as "calling them back" to a more personal interaction. In addition, by holding to a demand that a specific behavior cease you are displaying clarity and strength to the individual, as well as helping him/her focus their *mind* on their most problematic behavior, then the next, and on down the rungs of the ladder.

Continue working your way down the rungs until the individual is no longer in a state of fury. If the individual re-escalates to a higher and more dangerous activity, simply return to that rung of the ladder and begin again. Remember to stand and use your voice as described in the previous sections.

The last "rung" is probably swearing or other obscene language. Remember, some individuals swear as punctuation, without any hostile intent. They may be crude, but they are not trying to be verbally violent. *For example, "Security Professional, I'm sorry, I was just mad at my f**king daughter, and s**t, you happened to arrive at just the wrong damn moment."* If that kind of language offends you, it is something you will deal with at another time, during moments of calm. However, if the swearing is an attempt to violate you, it <u>must</u> be dealt with in proper order. **Do not, however, focus on the language, no matter how vile, if the person is *doing* something dangerous**. Remember that predatory individuals will use language to shock, distract, immobilize or terrorize. Their behavior is far more dangerous than anything they are saying.

Figure 53.4 A Level Calm Voice for the Witnesses

All witnesses will have heard your commands. Because you will have calmly repeated the same order in a strong, non-abusive voice, there is a better chance that they will be <u>good</u> witnesses should this situation deteriorate further into a physical confrontation. You will have been heard, repeatedly, commanding the person to comply with an order that they repeatedly ignored or refused.

Figure 53.5 Caution: The Ladder Should Only Be Used With an Enraged individual

Using this technique with an angry individual, even an extremely angry person will cause them to escalate into rage. In most cases, de-escalation tactics suitable to dealing with angry people are sufficient.

Figure 53.6 Example: The Ladder

Your voice is firm, low pitched and commanding, as you "descend" down the rungs. In the following scenario, each statement is, of course, in response to something the aggressor has done or said. Do not talk too fast. Pause between each phrase. Use command presence, not hysteria!

- "Step back. Step back. Robert. We'll talk about it when you step back. Robert. Step back. Step back, Robert. We will talk about it when you step back."
- "Stop kicking things. Robert. Stop kicking things. We'll talk about it when you stop kicking things."
- "Robert, I cannot follow you when you pace around. Sit down and we can talk. Sit down, Robert."

Notice the paradoxical message, that you cannot "follow" them. Of course you could, if you wanted to. This is another example of what we call a "brain glitch," the same as we do with the individual in Terrified Rage, when we say, "I keep it safe here." You are trying to catch their attention as they try to make sense of what you said. We want them thinking again, trying to figure out what you said and why you said it. We want the part of the brain that thinks things through taking over from the part that is driving them towards violence.

Imagine, however, that they have stepped forward again, thus ascending to a higher "rung" on the ladder.

- "Step back! Robert! Step back and we'll talk. We will TALK about it when you step back, Robert. Step - - - - -back."
- "Sit down Robert. We will talk about it when you sit down. I cannot talk when you are walking around. We will talk about it when you sit down."
- Lower your voice. I cannot hear you when you yell that loud. Lower you voice and we will talk."

Here is a second paradoxical communication: of course, you can hear an aggressor who is shouting loudly. Once again, you are trying to create a "glitch" where he tries to figure out what you mean when you say you cannot hear him when he is yelling.

- "Talk to me with the same respect that I talk to you. We will talk about it when you stop swearing. Stop swearing. Robert. We will talk when you talk to me with respect, the same way I talk to you."

Remember, people often swear as punctuation. They have no hostile intent whatsoever. If the individual is swearing in this manner, it is not a problem

However, if the swearing is an attempt to violate you, it must be dealt with in proper order. However, do not focus on the language, no matter how vile, if the aggressor is doing something dangerous. Remember that predatory individuals will use language to shock, distract, immobilize or terrorize. What they are doing is far more dangerous than anything they are saying.

Hot Rage Subtype #1: Fury

What does fury look like? Furious individuals are very tense, looking as if they are about to explode. For a mental image, imagine that if they are of big stature, think of a grizzly bear, if they are smaller, think of a wolverine. In either case, the image suggests an animal that will tear you to pieces if it perceives danger, if provoked, or if cornered. Many individuals, both those with a mental illness and those without, display fury, and it is particularly common among those who have suffered head injuries. Furious individuals may show some of the following physical manifestations of their rage:

- Their skin tone is flushed as they become angered, turning red or purplish in color. As they become even more enraged however, their skin blanches, and they turn pale if light skinned, or if dark skinned, they get a grayish tinge, as the blood pools in the internal organs.
- Their voice, whether loud, or low and quiet, has a menacing and belligerent tone.
- They often pace, inflate their upper body, hit or kick objects, or strike their hands together ominously, punching one fist into the other hand.
- They tend to stare into your eyes directly, glowering from under their brow, with a furious and hostile look on their face.
- Their eyes will appear red or inflamed; usually their eyes are wide open, with tension around the eye sockets and facial muscles.
- Physical arousal, blood pressure, and muscular tension all increase. You may notice veins popping out of the skin, particularly around the neck.
- They may display a smile that shows no humor or joy. Others snarl, or compress their lips with a twist, as if they have a foul taste in their mouth. Still others bare their teeth, or clench their jaws so tightly that the muscles stand out in bunches.
- They are very impulsive, and unconcerned with possible consequences.
- Their breathing is often loud and straining.
- They may claim to be disrespected, humiliated, or shamed. Others will allege that they are not getting their questions answered and their problem solved, or that no one listened or cared. They may rant about "the system" and claim that they are out of alternatives or solutions.

- At their most dangerous point, they may become calm, breaking off eye-contact, or adopting a thousand-yard stare.

Control of Fury

When confronting a furious individual your posture and tone should be confident, commanding, even imposing. Maintain direct eye contact, and frequently use their name. Stand directly in front of the individual, using a blade stance, but out of range of an immediate blow. This best prepares you to escape along tangents to his attack, to ward off blows, and if necessary, to fight back. With the blade stance, you are already "chambered" to do this. As described earlier, your hands are either up in a fence, or the wrist of one arm is clasped in the hand of the other in front of you at waist level.

If you stand too close you will appear to be challenging them, too far and you will be seen as fearful: a potential victim. You may have to move forward or backward to maintain this spacing. In either event, move smoothly, without flinching or making any sudden or threatening gestures. When you move with a relaxed body, you are more ready to protect yourself, yet you do not appear as if you are trying to initiate a physical altercation.

Your voice is strong and forceful. Do not, however, shout. Instead, keep your voice low- pitched and calm, dropping it into your chest where it resonates, as enraged people, in particular, react violently to threatening or angry vocal tones. The only time you would shout is a "battle cry," that lion's roar of outrage and strength that you use only when you are trying to stop an actual attack.

You will use the Ladder in its most orthodox form, with your voice pitched low and powerful. You should feel it vibrate in your chest. The individual will exhibit one of only three actions:
- They keep on coming; you will do what you have to do to ensure safety.
- They get close and when you tell them to step back, they say, "make me;" you will do what you have to do to ensure safety.
- They comply. When individuals in hot rage comply with the command to step back, they usually do so yelling and screaming, "you can't tell me what to do!"

Once you have them de-escalated, you must maintain control. Only after setting very strong limits would you shift into problem-solving, even with a mentally ill individual. Otherwise, they will assume that the best way to get a reward, your attention, or help is to abuse you.

Hot Rage Subtype #2: Bluff Aggression

In keeping with the systems analogies when describing the furious individual, the aggressively bluffing individual is like a gorilla beating his chest, a display of aggression designed to keep you at a distance. There is a sense of bluster rather than the pent-up pressure of the enraged individual.

However, their manifest behavior appears much the same as the individual displaying fury, hence the terrifying image of the enraged gorilla. At 50 yards, could you tell the difference between a charging gorilla and a charging grizzly bear? Both are huge, hairy beasts that apparently mean you harm. In all likelihood, the gorilla would prefer to be left alone, rather than engaging in combat, but he postures as if he wants nothing more than tear you to pieces. If he perceives no other alternative, he will do so.

How can you tell the difference between a furious individual and a bluffer if their behaviors are so similar? When facing a furious individual, fear is your natural and likely response. You instinctual mind, that part of you that places survival above all else, demands your immediate attention, and it uses fear to accomplish this. An aggressive bluffer, in a state of hot rage, may also elicit fear, but this fear will be accompanied by another emotion: you will find yourself a bit irritated, thinking how stupid (yet potentially dangerous) this incident has become, and if the bluffer were not with his friends, or in another case, if his wife had not chosen to taunt him as being less than a man, this dangerous situation would never have developed.

The enraged bluffer *often* displays aggression for the benefit of friends or family. On many occasions their friends or family members have provoked them to "prove" they are tough. In reality, they are actually frightened that they will be found out as being frightened, intimidated, or as succumbing to authority. These individuals can become quite violent if they feel they resist your commands and efforts to de-escalate them to impress their audience.

Sometimes bluffers are alone, but they still have an audience, an image inside their own head to which they believe they must conform. You will often hear this in their self-talk as they amp themselves up. "You don't know who you are talking to. Do you believe this guy? Do you have any idea who I am?"

Some worksite bullies, having a long record of violence, actually function day-to-day in "bluff mode." They are in a perpetual quest to prove to others, and even more so, themselves, that they are not frightened or insecure. As a result, they repeatedly solicit situations where they must either intimidate others or resort to violence.

One thing which lone Security Professionals simply must not do is to try and "out tough" the individual by refusing to back down or leave the scene. This is merely bluffing behavior on your part, and the individual's audience will only amplify their calls for the individual to be even more resistant. As the authors have stated many times throughout this book, do not personalize any of your encounters with aggressive individuals, and if professional prudence dictates that you should retreat, then do so!

Figure 53.7 Example: Bluffers Sometimes "Hide" Behind the Professional and Increase Their Threat Display

Security Professionals responded to a report of a fight in progress between two employees in the company gymnasium. On arrival, there were two men squared off, and 20 others standing watching. There was no physical altercation, only verbal name-calling and angry language and behaviors. As professionals entered the room, one of the "combatants" saw them and began a more aggressive stance, knowing professionals were there and would interdict, protecting him if things actually got physical. The other "combatant" did not see the professionals, and his level of anger grew substantially, as he responded to the others perceived escalation. This would have resulted in a physical fight had professionals not intervened. *In other words, you cannot establish command presence, unless people know you are there.*

Control of Bluffing

Security Professionals need to recognize that the aggressive bluffer is not really in confrontation with you; they are *pretending* that they are, either for an audience, or sometimes in an attempt to bolster their own self image. These individuals are quite dangerous because they may believe they need to prove themselves by refusing to back-down. Another aspect of bluffing is that when frightened, the bluffing individual will move forward, toward you, so that no one will see how frightened they truly are.

If you cannot simply retreat, <u>de-escalate and control using the Ladder, much as you would with an individual in Fury, but with a much more relaxed and even friendly tone</u>. Your eye-contact, too, is matter-of-fact, as if you are having a conversation rather than a confrontation. Rather than having your hands in front of you (either clasped or in a fence position), open your hands, slightly to the sides, palm up. You can still protect yourself just as easily, but your posture appears non-threatening, more open and relaxed. Your body language expresses, "there is no fight here." Remember, these individuals will attack out of the fear of being "found out" by their peers. Your task becomes helping them to save face, rather than issuing forceful commands and instructions. In doing so, you will greatly reduce the risk of violence. However, Security Professionals cannot allow the individual to *win the encounter* with concessions or agreements, and there must be some form of consequence subsequent to the resolution of the crisis. The imposition of punishment or consequences can come at a later date, if that is the most tactically sound way to handle things.

Figure 53.8 The Bluffer's Strut

When you have done things well, aggressive bluffers often strut back with a smirk, sometimes glancing around, and making eye-contact with onlookers. This is for the benefit of the audience, and their own self-image. They are trying to show that they are not afraid, and in control of the situation.

When exerting verbal control on the enraged bluffer:

- Do not point out their fears in front of others. They will feel the need to defend their honor.
- Do not try to be more forceful than they are, or appear overly domineering or condescending, as their self-image may require them to strike out.
- If they are not responsive to a more low key approach and continue to escalate, you may have a furious individual (see above) who happens to be in front of other people or a bluffer who has shifted into fury. In this case, you "turn up the dial," adopting a more powerful tone and stance, and shifting into the more forceful version of the Ladder technique for the furious individual.
- Remember, the individual's audience is what makes them dangerous. If possible, removing them from their audience will often result in the individual calming down on their own. For this reason, Security Professionals should prohibit employees from coming to meetings with a retinue of friends and family.

Figure 53.9 Example: Speaking to a Person Who Was in Bluff-Rage After You Have Them Under Control

"Bernard, I'm glad this worked out with no one getting hurt. Had you not chosen to sit down and talk, you very likely would have ended up being arrested. Staff was just about to call police. No. Listen to me for a minute. I'm not disrespecting you; that's why you and I are over here talking instead of in front of them *(indicating the onlookers)*. I'm telling you, it was a very near thing. Again, I'm glad this has worked out that you and I are standing here talking."

"Next time, though, don't do this in front of them" *(Referring to his friends or family for whom he was on display, and actually put a little contempt in your voice when you say the word "them," as if to indicate that Bernard is better/cooler/stronger than those people he is trying to impress.)* "Come to me and talk to me one man to another" OR "one woman to another" (One adult to another in male-female conversations). You shouldn't put your personal business in front of them."

You will observe him "puff up," feeling flattered. You then continue, "Okay, are we clear for next time? Good. Now as for this time…." Then set the same types of limits as you did with the individual in a state of FURY, which will often include the phrase, "You must leave the building. HR will call you and your union rep tomorrow to set up another appointment." They can accept a direct message when their ego is built up enough to take the hit.

Hot Rage Subtype #3: Controlling Aggressive Manipulation

The following will be helpful when trying to control individuals using aggressive manipulation:

Information about aggressive-manipulators. This is a strategy, not a symptom of illness. Such individuals are calculating, trying to monitor the effects of their actions. They are not constrained by feelings of honor, integrity, or pride; their goal is win any way they can. Sometimes, you can tell when you are being manipulated ("played") because you are confused about why the individual is upset, or the purpose of his argument. The aggressive manipulator changes either his/her mood or the subject of the complaint frequently, displaying some or all of the behaviors of manipulative and psychopathic individuals (Chapters 25 & 26).

Aggressive-manipulative individuals may have a long history of losing control, particularly when their desires are frustrated, or when they believe they are not given what they feel they are entitled to.

These individuals may approach you with flattery, or a plea for something, explaining their dilemma in great detail with talk of their suffering. Once their request is denied, however, they blame or criticize you for their troubles, inferring that your refusal will result in furthering their suffering or cause them irreparable harm. They might try to make you feel guilty, or begin to demean you, then shifting to subtle threats of violence. They may talk in an arrogant manner, trying to make you look incompetent to others or make you think you are stupid. They often claim to be a victim, basing this on either real or imaginary issues. Furthermore, they may use their "status" as a member of an oppressed or victimized class of people as a means of intimidating others, making their demands in a whiny, accusatory voice. Such individuals will recall past grievances, adding their current crisis to the list of prior accusations. They will tell you how you are just like someone else who wronged them. They ask frequent or repetitive questions. They try to frighten you or make you feel uncertain of yourself.

Manipulation does not mean false threat, and manipulative individuals will often harm others. The difference between such an aggressive-manipulator and those in a state of pure fury is that the furious individual's inhibitions are swept aside by their rage. You will often hear terms like "He just lost it" to explain such behavior. The aggressive-manipulator, on the other hand, attempts to monitor your responses and the situation as a whole to assess if their actions and behaviors will be successful. Although the individual's behavior may be calculating, that does not mean they are in control. As they become more and more agitated, their judgment deteriorates, and they may concoct a rationalization for violence that makes sense to them in the moment.

Control Tactics. Individuals who use this strategy attempt to twist your feelings and emotions, making you doubt yourself, making you ashamed or scared, for example, to get what they want. Do not buy in to it. If you recognize this strategy early on in your interaction with the individual, you can often verbally cut it off at the onset. If, however, the manipulative individual begins to escalate his/her strategies, you may have to use the Ladder as a means of control and de-escalation. In this case, however, your tone of voice should be matter-of fact and slightly detached.

Making eye contact enables another person to truly see you as you are, and in return, see them as well. Aggressive-manipulative individuals do not care about you, and they use apparent feelings of contact and intimacy to "read" and control you. They are interested in gaining information that they can use to their benefit. Similarly, they will use their own eyes to create a false sense of trust, as it suits them to confuse you, misdirect your attention, or dominate you. Rather than making eye contact, look past one ear.

Figure 53.10 Disinterested Use of the Eyes With the Aggressive-Manipulator

Do not look away. While looking past an ear, you can still see what they are doing. If you look away, you will be assaulted and not even know it is coming. This disengaged look, done properly, indicates that you will not participate in the degradation that manipulation creates.

Ladder for aggressive manipulators. If your attempts at control and de-escalation of their manipulative strategies are unsuccessful, the individual may escalate into a rage state. What distinguishes this from pure fury is that, even now, they continue to read and monitor you for advantage: are they intimidating you; have they succeeded in distracting or throwing you off balance so that you are open to an attack; have they got you trying to "bargain" your way to safety? Eventually, they will begin to "lose it," as it becomes more apparent that their strategic application of intimidation is unsuccessful. Furthermore, they get increasingly frustrated because they believe their manipulation *should* be working, primarily because it has worked so well for them in the past.

In essence, aggressive-manipulative rage is a merger of hot rage and predatory rage (see other chapters in Section X). When dealing with such an individual Security Professionals should:
- Stand relaxed and ready to evade a blow and counter the attack.
- Express flat disinterest in their demands, accusations, and complaints.
- Use the repetitive commands of the ladder technique. Your vocal tone should be flat. Do not negotiate. Do not discuss other matters as long as the manipulative behavior continues.

Figure 53.11 Locking Eyes: THE LOOP

If the individual escalates into *fury*, or if they continue to be otherwise non-compliant, turn your head to look directly in their eyes, roll it slightly up and then down as if sighting a weapon. Speak powerfully and directly, just as you do with the individual who is in a state of fury. If you have ever raised a teenager, you have almost surely done this. In essence, once you make eye-contact with the aggressive-manipulative individual, treat them as you would the furious type.

With the aggressive-manipulative individual several things can happen when you attempt to control their rage:

- Your flat disinterest indicates that they cannot "get to you." After trying several different avenues, they give up, leaving in frustration, shifting to another strategy, or sagging in defeat.
- In more heated situations, they will flare into a fury (or pseudo-fury).
- When you "lock in" eye-contact, they may "bounce" off into another tactic—sudden tears for example.
- If the behavior does not stop immediately upon being "hit" with your eyes, this means that an attack is imminent. You will shift into the de-escalation techniques used for controlling fury, or take appropriate action to ensure your safety in the event of violence.

CHAPTER 54

Predatory or Cool Rage

Thankfully, this type of aggressor is rather rare. They are intimidators who threaten with vague innuendoes or explicit threats. Their aggressive behavior is calculated, but unlike the manipulator, violence is often their first choice rather than one of many options. The predatory individual may deliver threats in cool, dangerous tones, often *after* a clear and strongly stated demand. Then they offer you a chance to avoid injury if you comply. A variant tactic is to pretend being out of control. This is in contrast to a genuine attack, an action that they may be eminently capable of and willing to carry out. Our symbol for them is either a leopard or a shark, depending on if they present as "warm-blooded" or "stone cold."

While these individuals seethe with hostility and/or contempt for others, they have developed these emotions as a deliberate weapon of terror, perhaps even enjoyment. Paradoxically, their physical arousal is often low. Their heart rate can actually go down and they can be charming and engaging, even as they prepare to commit an act of violence. This disconnect between appearances and intentions can cause Security Professionals to lower their guard, particularly if they are investigating the person's alleged aggression against others, because they may have a hard time believing that such a seemingly nice guy is ready and willing to terrorize others psychologically, or hurt them physically.

They actually have no inhibitions regarding their aggression other than tactical calculation or self-interest. They have no capacity for sympathy, empathy, or guilt, and many experience low levels of anxiety in situations that would frighten ordinary people. Every time they intimidate someone successfully, their behavior is reinforced, and they view non-action on your part, either during the confrontation or afterward, as either weakness or of tacit approval, thereby increasing the likelihood of similar behavior in the future.

The best response is a combination of overwhelming force and respect.[19] The former is obvious. Never be in a situation where you are vulnerable with such an individual. "Respect" means, simply, that you make your control "institutional," not "personal." When you are dealing with them, try to architect things, so that they perceive themselves as not having a problem with you, personally; their problem is between themselves and the company as a whole. You should not set yourself up as an individual target.

Principles: What to Do When You Do Not have Overwhelming Force

Your basic task is to demonstrate that you are not prey, and that the individual's attempts at intimidation will simply not work. Most predatory individuals do not wish to interact with someone whom they *cannot* intimidate or otherwise control through emotional abuse or physical posturing. Instead, they seek more conciliatory and subservient victims, where their chances of success are great. When engaging a predatory individual, Security Professionals should remember the following:

- Stand or sit ready to move. Be poised, but do not appear fearful or too defensive.
- Avoid gesturing or expressive movements. Fear often causes your movements to be awkward, and the individual will see this as confirmation of their control over you.
- Be open and strategic in everything you do: the way you position your body, your voice, and your posture. The predatory individual is well-versed in reading body language and assessing weakness. Protect yourself openly, and do not change your actions based on what they say, that is, their efforts to put you at ease or promises of compliance. Another tactic the predator may use in these circumstances is to use anything you do against you, either deriding you or pretending that you are out of control, paranoid, or acting strangely. Ignore all that, and openly act to keep yourself safe.
- Do not make explicit or unrealistic threats, such as "If you come near my family, I will kill you!" That tells the predator what you will not do. In his mind, if you really meant it, you would do it now. An explicit threat is an empty threat.
- Do not over-react to vague threats, or he/she will interpret your reaction as a victory. If, however, the individual makes an explicit threat to harm you then they should be taken into custody by police (after you have removed yourself from the situation safely).
- Do not comply with any of the individual's orders or demands that you *should not* carry out your professional duties and responsibilities.

Cryptic Consequences: To Extricate Yourself When You Do not Have Overwhelming Force

Keep your voice matter-of-fact, and give clear and direct statements of *potential* consequences. If you can, smile. These consequences are of a special type, clear, but cryptic, that is, "You know what would happen if you did hit me." In this case, do not tell him what would happen. Let his imagination take over. These vague consequences are a mirror of his/her own method of intimidation, and he/she may likely react to you as "not prey, not edible, not worth the trouble."

If he/she says, "What are you talking about?" you should reply, "You know exactly what we are talking about." When the predator responds to your cryptic consequence with questions or with confusing statements that would make your statement illogical, simply say, "You know what is going on here. You know what is happening." You may have to intersperse your vague consequences with ladder commands if he/she escalates his/her behaviors.

Try to minimize eye contact. However, you need to look directly at him/her, so look between the eyes, or look at him/her with a flat stare (imagine turning your eyes to buttons. He begins to look like a cut-out or silhouette). Your eyes are flat as buttons, with no attempt to "penetrate" or make contact; you should make sustained eye-contact only if in a fight for your life. Then, you must shift focus, trying to penetrate his/her eyes as if you were a laser beam.

Do not over-react to his/her threats, or he/she will interpret your reaction as a victory. If you and your family have been threatened (whether the tone is velvet or harsh), you must do everything necessary to keep everyone safe (Chapter 58). You may have to be on your guard for a long time. Such incidents are often just words, or a one-time incident, but on other occasions, they can go on for a long time, with further threats, stalking, or other dangerous behaviors that require you to muster all professional skills and assistance to ensure that you and your family are safe.

Figure 54.1 Cryptic Consequences: A Tool Rarely Used

You ONLY use cryptic consequences with the openly predatory, that most rare of people, and ONLY when they are escalating into predatory rage, and only when you do not have sufficient force or backup otherwise control them. In other words, it should never happen, but you need to know what to do if it does.

Figure 54.2 Example: Interaction With a Predatory Individual When the Security Professional Is Blocked From Exiting a Room: a Predator Leaning in the Doorway

Predator: "Look, this is very simple. I think you and I can agree that you misinterpreted what I said about 'taking out' my manager. I don't know where you got the idea that I meant I would hurt her. I was talking about making a complaint to the union. Look, I understand. You must have been having a bad day, and you over-reacted. This can be fixed very easily. Just call HR and tell them that you didn't quote me accurately, that you've been overworked lately and misjudged the situation. See, I bet you love your family as much as I do. You've got your child in a good school over at Echo Lake. Actually, it's amazing, that's one of the last schools in this area that still lets the kids out for recess . Oh, sorry, I'm a little off track. What I'm saying is that I bet you would be devastated if anything happened to your family. I'm the same. The problem is that what is happening to my family is you! And this is a problem you could fix, unless you are really sitting there telling me that you want to destroy my life and that of my family by messing up my career here. IS THAT WHAT YOU ARE SAYING??!!!!"

Security Professional. *(With a little smile and a strong, confident voice)* "I am really glad we are having this conversation, because it's good that we both understand each other."

Predator. "So you'll make the call."

Security Professional. "Oh, you know what's going to happen."

Predator. "Suppose you tell me."

Security Professional. "There's no need to do that. You know exactly what's going on."

Predator. "Are you threatening me?"

Security Professional. "I don't know where you got that idea. In fact, we both know the situation here."

Predator. *(Walking away)* "You think this is over. You better watch your back."

To reiterate, you do not have to prove that you are bigger, tougher, or more dangerous. Merely establish that you are on to his game, you are not someone who will be victimized, and that there will certainly be consequences for their actions. Predatory individuals are likely to disengage if you do not react to their threats as they wish.

CHAPTER 55

De-escalation of Developmentally Delayed Individuals

There are probably few situations where it would be necessary for a Security Professional to verbally de-escalate an enraged developmentally disabled individual. One possibility would be if some members of your custodial staff are developmentally disabled.

The preferred de-escalation tactics are not remarkably different for developmentally disabled individuals, but if you use language that is too sophisticated, you may provoke the person to more frustration and anger by making them feel stupid. In addition, many developmentally disabled individuals are subject to magical thinking, and their beliefs about the world, and their own powers and vulnerabilities often do not conform to reality. Sometimes, Security Professionals can use these beliefs to help calm them, as you would with a child. On other occasions, one must be aware of these beliefs to keep the situation from escalating out of control.

If you try to control a developmentally disabled individual based on their physical age and appearance, say a 250 pound, 35-year-old male, for example, things can go wrong very quickly. Instead, speak to them at their emotional age. Most of our associates have found that once we make eye-contact, we can usually estimate the emotional age of the developmentally disabled person very quickly, among small child, young kid, pre-teen, or teen. However, regardless of the individual's emotional age, you cannot permit their apparent childishness to compromise your physical safety. As with children, developmentally delayed individuals can be quite impulsive and unpredictable.

Security Professionals can still use tactical paraphrasing (Chapter 48) with an enraged developmentally disabled individual. In this case, however, do not just sum things up calmly. Use a more dramatic voice, over-emphasizing certain words. For example, "YOU are REALLLLLY upset about that schedule change! You really don't want to change schedules!" Your tone is a combination of drama and enthusiasm. In essence, you are trying to catch their attention with charisma, a kind of energy in which you change the dynamics of the relationship through your voice and demeanor. Your dramatic voice validates how important the situation is to the individual. They themselves in interaction where there is no "fight" coming from you. Rather, you draw them in to a dynamic where, although conflict is absent, the relationship is still of compelling interest.

Following the crisis, which was undoubtedly frightening and confusing to them, Security Professionals can certainly acknowledge and validate their feelings. For example, "Mark, that was really scary. I'm glad that's over. I want you to sit in this chair now. Yeah, know you were scared, but it's over now." A detailed critique or discussion, however, may be a mistake. Developmentally delayed individuals are often cognitively impaired, and this also affects their memory. They are unlikely to recall or retain what happened, and emotionally, they may react to your debriefing as a new attack. Your concern should be behavioral stability (no new attack) and reassurance because they are very likely afraid that you will punish them for their behavior.

Figure 55.1 Author's Example: An Assault from a Developmentally Disabled Woman

A developmentally disabled woman once grabbed my finger, trying to break it. I neutralized her attempt by shifting the angle of my hand as she yanked, and as she was at the emotional age of about eight-years old, rather than commanding her to "let go!" I said, "I know you want to hold my hand. You don't have to twist my finger. We can hold hands as much as you like. Sure, we can hold hands." She suddenly let go and dropped to the floor, crying.

Figure 55.2 Review: De-escalation of the Developmentally Disabled Person

Speak to them at their emotion age, not their chronological age.

Use tactical paraphrasing, summarizing not only what they are apparently thinking, but what they are doing. Use energy and enthusiasm in your voice, to catch their attention without sounding harsh or aggressive, just as you would when redirecting a child.

CHAPTER 56

Feeding Frenzy—Mob Rage

Figure 56.1 Mob Rage IS Violence

This discussion covers both the rage state and the possibility of violence. Pack (Mob) Behavior can easily escalate and therefore, it is impossible to separate out rage from violence in this discussion.

Mob behavior amplifies hot rage exponentially, with one person's behavior and arousal amplifying that of those around them. The more people there are, the more likely that they will coalesce into an enraged mob, a beast of many heads, but one terrifying, destructive mind. Individually, members of a mob will display any or all of the types of rage we have discussed throughout this section. Aggressive bluffers may try to entice those he/she is trying to impress into violence. Sometimes, mob frenzy is created and stoked by one predatory individual who uses the mob as a weapon or distraction. When faced with such a situation the best possible solution is to escape and summon help from the police. However, if escape is impossible attempt to control the mob by:

1. **Demonstrate overwhelming force.** Quite simply, the most powerful method of de-escalation is a demonstration to the mob and its members that they will be stopped. Each member of the mob suddenly feels alone: "the first to go down." We are aware that this is the extreme end of the spectrum, but all the possibilities must be named when considering such a terrible situation.

2. **Isolate the leader.** Isolating the leader as the one individual who will face the consequences. All of your psychological energy should be focused on the leader. This is particularly effective when the leader is hiding *behind* the power of the mob. If you perceive that the leader is manifesting manipulative, bluff, or predatory rage, make it clear that whatever happens, they will not emerge unscathed. The goal is definitely not to shame them, especially before the mob. Instead, presenting yourself with a quiet, grave, yet powerful calm, and allowing the leader to save face is essential if you have any hopes of causing him/her to draw their forces back.

3. **Build up the leader's ego.** Build up the leader's ego by clearly identifying them as one worthy of conferring with. This is for the purpose of either drawing him/her away from the group, or appealing to his/her grandiose narcissism. If their goal is to appear important in the eyes of the mob, you may have given him/her what they really want, without the need for violence.

4. **Break the pattern.** As discussed in Chapter 47, you do something so unexpected or outlandish that none of the individuals in the mob knows how to react.

Figure 56.2 Author's Example: Breaking the Pattern When Facing a Mob

About 40 years ago, while hitchhiking, I was malevolently dropped off in a very dangerous area of a city during a very volatile period of racial strife. A crowd began to coalesce around me. I grabbed a stick I found on the ground, began cackling and shrieking like I'd lost my mind, and began dancing and whirling down the street, attacking moving cars with my stick. Everyone pulled back. I continued for about ten blocks until I reached a safer area.

To review, the best option when facing a mob is to escape and summon police assistance. If you do intervene, be aware that you may have to fight for your life. Your best hope, were this terrible situation to develop, is to go "berserk." Fight like a wolverine in a trap: with teeth, claws, and anything else you can use, tear your way free, trying to maim your attackers as savagely as you can. The goal is to become so appallingly violent yourself that each member of the group wants to get away from you. As they recoil, hopefully, an escape route will open up.

SECTION XI

Managing Rage and Violence:
The Aftermath

CHAPTER 57

The Aftermath: What Happens to the Aggressive Mentally Individual After an Aggressive Incident?

Rage and even more so, violence, are an exhausting experience, both emotionally and physically. Many people get the "shakes" after such an incident. So much blood has "pooled" inside the core of their bodies to prepare for combat that they feel cold and start to tremble. Some misinterpret this as fear or cowardice—it is simple biology, the body recovering from the experience that the person has just experienced.

Most individuals have a significantly impaired ability to remember what happened in sequence. They may have a patchy memory of a few events. Much of the rest of the incident is a blur. Although they may be remorseful, they usually do not remember what happened, how it started, or who was responsible. Even more drastically, they can lapse into a state of defensive confusion where they no longer recall what happened at all, or they distort the incident in their memory completely, thereafter taking no responsibility whatsoever.

Others may feel profound guilt. This might be positive, were it to lead them to reflect on their own responsibility, but for most people, this guilt is so noxious that they project responsibility onto the person who "makes" them feel guilty. Thus, they soon shift to resentment and begin to blame the other person.

Humiliation, the feeling of having one's faults or vulnerabilities involuntarily or forcibly exposed to others, is quite common, and here, too, many people become defensive. People described humiliation like being flayed and exposed, and some react to this by becoming enraged all over again. Their thinking seems to be, "If I feel this bad, someone must be doing it to me." What is almost universal is a post-crisis fatigue, a combination of the depletion of energy stores in the body and the cumulative effect of all the mood and cognitive changes described above.

Managing Risks Post-Crisis

In many situations, you must enforce consequences on the perpetrator of the rage or assault. If this is the case, Security Professionals must clearly convey the processes and procedures to the individual. In situations not so severe that police have arrested the person, security has escorted them off the premises, or the employee got fired on the spot, it is necessary to undertake some kind of debriefing.

If the person is stable and willing to talk, set clear and unambiguous limits regarding future behaviors. Without the imposition of limits and the reiteration of consequences for violating them, the individual will simply repeat their aggressive behavior. Through de-escalation you have established control over the individual, and you must not relinquish that control simply because the crisis has passed. Reassure the individual that you are not out for revenge, but neither will you pretend that nothing serious happened nor are you going to reward them just because the aggression is over.

If the individual is really frightened or devastated by what happened, the first priority is reassurance and orientation. With individuals who are disorganized, psychotic, or otherwise in a fragile mental state, you may have to explain to them what has happened, what is going to happen, and why. With individuals who do not have the mental capacity to really understand the details or implications of what happened, the best approach to take is to be calming and reassuring.

If the individual has the cognitive ability to understand, the incident should be reviewed with the individual in order to clarify and reiterate the consequences of similar behavior in the future. Discuss with the individual what other tactics they might have used to get what they desired, assist them in recognizing patterns that lead to aggression and how to avoid such situations in the future, and return the individual to a sense of dignity and integrity.

Any sanctions or requirements regarding an aggressive employee's behavior should be signed. Establish a time frame in which corrective actions will be taken. This should also include a clear understanding on what management, HR and/or security will do to follow-up on the situation.

CHAPTER 58

Managing Threats to Your Family

By threatening your family, aggressive individuals can create within you a sense of helplessness and desperation. The threat is usually empty, made in the heat of the moment or as means of additional defiance when being arrested, or meant to terrify. You must, however, take any such threats seriously, because it is almost impossible to know when the threat is real or not. And, truth be told, a bit of preventative planning and education of your family members as to their need to be aware is never a bad thing. As in the work environment, the development of a safety plan is not enough; your plan should be reviewed regularly with your family. You should do the following:

1. Inform your family of any threats and of the need to take protective action. In regard to children, your responsibility is to explain everything they *need* to know, but no more. Furthermore, if you display your own fears excessively, you will only frighten your family members. To this end, we strongly recommend that you acquire two books by Gavin de Becker: *The Gift of Fear* and *Protecting the Gift*.[20]

2. **Inform local law enforcement.** Police professionals will assist you in drawing up a safety plan as well as considering what, if any, action they can take on your behalf.

3. **Review home security.** Are you a soft target or a hard target? A soft target is easily accessible, predictable, and unaware of danger. A hard target is not easily accessible, or predictable. Adequate lighting and the use of quality locks, doors, and windows will limit the ability of an intruder to enter your home. Consult with your local police department as to how to make your home more secure. Some departments will be more willing than others to send a professional out to walk through and around your home to inform you of security gaps. There are also excellent books on home security available. Consider a home alarm system.

4. **Firearms.** Should you decide to purchase a firearm for home security, then each member of your family *must* attend a firearm safety and instruction course, and firearms should be stored and cared for accordingly.

5. **Dogs.** In many ways dogs are a better security option than a firearm. Unlike humans, a well-trained dog, particularly certain breeds, will not hesitate to act when they perceive a threat. Dogs will also provide you with an early warning system, detecting sounds and smells that you cannot. Further discussion of dog breeds and training is well beyond the scope of this book, but dogs can be one of the most important aspects of home security.

6. **Scan your surroundings.** Your family members must learn to scan their surroundings and note anything out of the ordinary. Remind family to report suspicious people and cars.

7. **Inform employers and schools**. Do this so they are aware of the identity of the potential assailant. Make clear to school officials exactly who is allowed to meet or pick-up your children.

8. **Change your routine.** As much as possible, travel by different routes and at different times. Be unpredictable.

9. **Safety in numbers.** Neither you nor your family members should be the last person to leave the workplace or school. Enlist co-coworkers, coaches, teachers, etc., to be part of a team.

10. **Notification of travel plans.** Notify your office and family of travel plans, and ask that they not reveal any travel plans or other schedules.

11. **Be careful about giving out personal information.** This can be difficult with children, as they happily exchange information with their friends or others. Remind them to be careful of strangers, and to report any such inquiries. Do not forget about social networking sites such as Facebook and My Space, and other dangers of the Internet.

12. **Plan an escape route.** Figure out the best ways to escape from the home and rehearse this with family members. You can combine this with fire drills, something the children are already familiar with from school.

13. **A safe haven.** Arrange with trustworthy neighbors to a) watch the neighborhood for the person(s) of concern near your house b) a safe haven for your family to go if your home – or they – are under attack.

14. **Plan how to ask for help.** Plan how to ask for help if in public and how best to call for help if needed. If your children are alone and there are no nearby police cars, the best stranger to ask for help is a *woman*, as women are far less likely to be a threat. Of course, this is not the case if a woman is the threatening individual.

15. **Code words.** Teach your children a code word or challenge that must be answered by strange individuals. This includes neighbors, and in some cases, relatives. For example, a person approaches your child after school and says, "Tasha, your mother and father were injured in an automobile accident. The police told me to take you to the hospital! Please come with me now." Your child should have been taught to keep his/her distance, looking for escape routes as she asks "What's the word?" If the person does not reply immediately the child should run to a safe haven and describe the individual as best they can.

16. **Post emergency numbers near each telephone extension.** Establish safe havens to escape to in times of danger. If possible, enlist your neighbors in your safety plan.

CHAPTER 59

Conclusion

Security Professionals encounter a variety of individuals in a variety of situations and circumstances. By understanding the traits and characteristics of potentially mentally ill, volatile, and aggressive individuals as articulated in this book, professionals place themselves in a better tactical position to establish a safe resolution of the crisis situation.

It is important that you regularly review and practice the safety and de-escalation methods in this book. Just as you automatically snatch your hand away from a hot stove or blink your eyes when a small object flies toward them, these skills must become so familiar to you that they seem as reflexive as instincts.

As important as it is to incorporate this information into your own repertoire of skills, it is equally important, as time and circumstances dictate, to engage HR and managers in advance to conduct a risk and threat assessment. Armed with such information, Security Professionals can better position themselves to deal with these events.

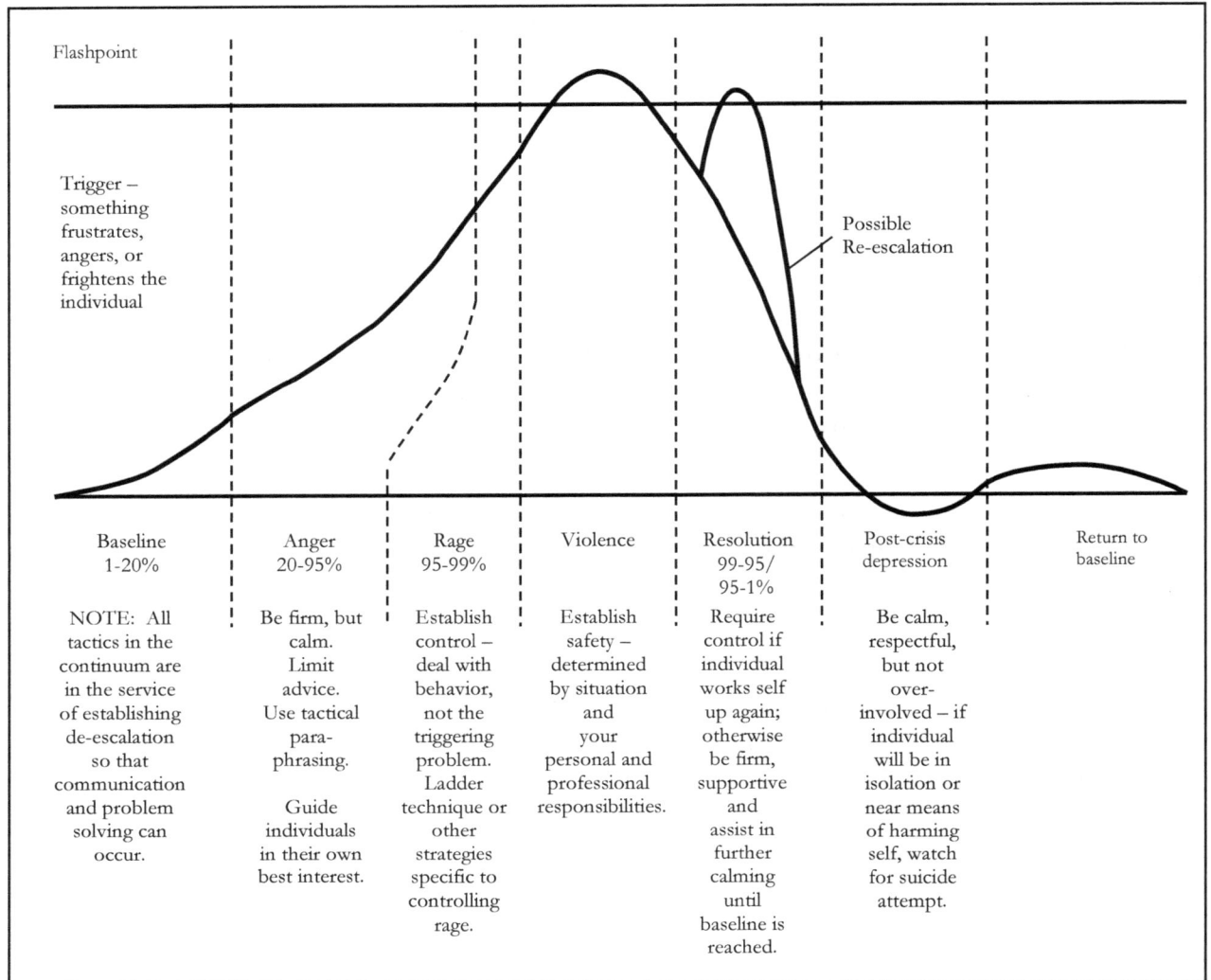

Flashpoint

Trigger –
something
frustrates,
angers, or
frightens the
individual

Possible
Re-escalation

Baseline 1-20%	Anger 20-95%	Rage 95-99%	Violence	Resolution 99-95/ 95-1%	Post-crisis depression	Return to baseline
NOTE: All tactics in the continuum are in the service of establishing de-escalation so that communication and problem solving can occur.	Be firm, but calm. Limit advice. Use tactical para-phrasing. Guide individuals in their own best interest.	Establish control – deal with behavior, not the triggering problem. Ladder technique or other strategies specific to controlling rage.	Establish safety – determined by situation and your personal and professional responsibilities.	Require control if individual works self up again; otherwise be firm, supportive and assist in further calming until baseline is reached.	Be calm, respectful, but not over-involved – if individual will be in isolation or near means of harming self, watch for suicide attempt.	

SECTION XII

Staff Working in
Specialized Roles

CHAPTER 60

Newly Hired Security Professionals

General Programmatic Issues

It is essential to make clear to new employees that a culture of safety is the primary focus of your agency. Therefore, newly hired employees should

- be included in meetings regarding individuals who present risk;
- be included in the *regular* training for show-of-force and defensive tactics;
- be included in instruction on how to set up a safe office, which should be reviewed by a supervisor;
- become familiar with all emergency policies—one training/supervision session should go over these procedures. The supervisor should verify that the new professional understands and can enact these procedures fully;
- voice any concerns, and direct all "what should I do if…?" questions to the supervisor, trainer, and/or safety professional, so that they feel prepared to work;
- clearly understanding that the ethos of the agency is
  a. "Ask for supervisory advice whenever you are not sure of something."
  b. "Ask for supervisory advice whenever you are concerned or frightened."
  c. "Ask for supervisory advice whenever you find yourself off-center or angry due to an interaction with a person."
- be mentored by seasoned professionals (Senior staff is expected to be available to assist new employees regarding safety issues.);
- have senior professionals or supervisors sit in on their work—not only to give advice on their interview skills, but also to give advice regarding actions *that* enhance or impair safety;
- Clerical and support staff often have a front-line role with potential aggressors, at least when they walk into the agency. Therefore, they are the first to assess risk in a presenting individual and often bear the full brunt of aggression in its initial stages. Therefore, Security Professionals need to understand that treating support staff with respect is a safety issue, and an absolutely mandatory requirement in your company. The ethos of respect, in which staff should always feel free to express concern or misgivings, applies equally to support staff. It is essential that they, too, have a full voice.
- be familiar with the various personality types and how to handle an encounter (This must be aligned with agency or corporate policy and procedure.).

Preparing for Problems That Might Happen Before a Newly Hired Security Professional Is Fully Trained

Staff can be trained quickly in show-of-force procedures, because they do not require verbal de-escalation skills. As any agency using show-of-force strategy should be having a weekly or bi-weekly drill in the procedure; different units can do this in five minutes, as part of staff meetings and they will quickly get up to speed. Given attrition levels within the security field, it is imperative that your agency has regularly scheduled training to keep current, and so that new professionals be trained as soon as possible.

Staff can be trained to direct people to clear an area. You should use scenario practice to do this until you are sure that they can express themselves with tactful, strong authority. This is also a very quick way to begin to assess the capacity of your new staff people to handle themselves in a crisis. If they cannot step into a situation and take authority, they cannot solve a crisis.

Newly hired staff should also be taught how to call 9-1-1 properly (or the equivalent emergency number in your country). They should be instructed on how to handle an emergency, and then expected to alert other individuals within your agency when an emergency occurs, including notifying them to escape or lock-down.

Whether you staff has sophisticated de-escalation skills or not, there are two items that new staff must learn right away that will carry them through most situations:

- The policies and procedures of the agency regarding safety in this section.
- How to center and calm oneself in crisis. Centering procedures should be taught as part of orientation (Section III).

The time an incident occurs is not the time to train for it. Anticipate incidents that may happen in your organization and prepare for them. Practice for them, understand roles and responsibilities, acceptable actions, and the capabilities and capacity of your Security Professionals.

CHAPTER 61

Support Staff: Managing Aggressive Individuals in the Lobby and on the Phone

This chapter could be considered a "stand-alone" section for support and clerical staff. But All the Security Professionals in your company should read it as well. If you do not know what is expected of support staff, you will not be able to work in harmony with them. Support staff, particularly those who work at the front desk, are in a difficult position. Some agencies include support staff in both training and safety procedures. In such circumstances, your agency policies and training may supersede some of the recommendations made here.

The following will postulate that support staff is not provided with the necessary level of training in de-escalation to empower them to undertake the management and control of an aggressive individual from "start to finish." This is certainly a subject of debate. On one side are those who argue that crisis situations require specialized training, and that de-escalation and crisis intervention are not part of the support staff's job description. There also may be liability issues if such an important task is delegated to someone without the proper credentials. On the other side is the understanding that many support staff have years of experience in managing aggressive behavior that they have learned, literally, on the front lines of the company. Furthermore, there is a legitimate concern that if supervisory or Security Professional personnel are delegated to step in on behalf of support staff when encountering a belligerent or aggressive individual, instigators will soon learn that they can "move up the food chain" by abusing the people at the front desk.

The discussion that follows will be under the assumption that support staff has a limited but vital role in the de-escalation of aggression, but once a certain threshold is met, the Security Professionals and/or the supervisor should step in.

System Issues Regarding Face-to-Face Encounters

What follows in this section are ideal principles, based the sources listed below:
- Interviews with other threat assessment professionals.
- Our own experiences as both employees and customers.
- On-site threat assessment, which we generally carry out by: a) simply sitting or otherwise observing a work environment and noting any factors that seem to agitate individuals; and b) asking clients, customers, and other individuals what about an organization angers or otherwise upsets them.

A variety of considerations may make some of the principles enumerated here, impossible to implement. *The decision to NOT implement, however, should be an informed one. The following will help you make an informed decision:*

- **Lobby layout.** The lobby should be a place where people feel welcome and comfortable. If people are made to feel unwelcome, they will behave accordingly. Therefore, the carpet or floor should be clean, furniture should be comfortable, and magazines (address labels removed or blacked out) should be reasonably current.

  a. A well-kept place is "territory." It is, in fact, more difficult to behave in an aggressive or disorderly manner when the environment is clearly "owned" and one experiences oneself to be a guest on someone else's territory.

  b. No one "owns" a sloppy, unkempt, uncomfortable or dirty environment. It is obvious that no one takes responsibility for it or cares for it. In such an environment, people have "permission" to act in a more disorderly fashion because no one cares.

  c. On the other hand, if the lobby is too cold, sterile, and impersonal, people experience a sense of isolation. They find themselves facing an apparently uncaring, distant institution, and some will act in all-too-human ways to make sure that they are recognized as "counting for something."

- **Front desk layout.** Some consideration must be made to the placement of the front desk. If there is any glass, is it well-secured, and/or Lexan, or safety glass. The desk should be wide enough so that an aggressor simply leaning forward cannot grab the support person behind it.

- **Access to assistance.** Given that support staff are expected to secure assistance when an aggressor is presenting with threatening behaviors, they must have **ABSOLUTE** assurance that they will get an **IMMEDIATE** response when they call for help. Some agencies have a direct line to a designated Security Professional to protect the reception area. Others have a button system. <u>The bottom line is that if the safety plan includes rapid response by trained staff, then this must be guaranteed.</u> There should be occasional, random tests of the system to assure that security staff will respond as needed. Although some might find this inconvenient, it is no different from a "fire drill" or other test of the emergency response system.

- **Empowerment.** Support staff should be encouraged to report anything that appears to be amiss, and their observations must be treated with respect. If their concerns are belittled or ignored, they will, quite understandably, stop reporting. If a particular employee is too reactive or frequently misjudges situations, either seeing danger at too low a threshold or not seeing a threatening situation developing when it is right in front of them, this should be considered a training issue for that specific person, not an indication that support staffs' concerns should be ignored.

- **Alerts.** Support staff should be made aware of:

  a. Individuals who present any particular concern or risk.

  b. Individuals whose behaviors are odd or eccentric, but do not pose a risk. That way, the front desk person can sort out something that is out of the ordinary for that particular person, given that their baseline, non-threatening behaviors are always "out of the ordinary."

- **Cultural training relevant to aggression.** Staff need basic training so that they are familiar with styles of behavior that, unfamiliar to them, might be misinterpreted as aggressive. However, such training should NOT include "reframing," in which aggressive, intrusive, or sexualized behaviors are "contextualized." Here, offensive acts are claimed to be acceptable because someone asserts that they are derived culturally. *The basic standards of human decency are held in common by almost all cultures.* Attempts at cultural relevancy or understanding should never allow abusive or threatening behavior.
- **Show-of-force training.** Different agencies may use support staff in different roles when a "show-of-force" is needed. But whatever role they are expected to fulfill, support staff must have sufficient training so that they, without any hesitation, can mesh with other personnel in helping to calm the situation down.
- **Police.** When a crime is being committed: assault, harassment, or any other in which imminent risk is occurring support staff must be trained to call 9-1-1 properly (or equivalent emergency number in your country) for assistance. Such training includes what to say, succinctly, in order to get police there immediately.

Threat Assessment for Support Staff

This is the basic information that support staff should know. If they observe any of these behaviors or characteristics, they should call for assistance as soon as possible, to circumvent any potentially dangerous escalation.

Support staff should note:
- **Any weapons.** This includes such ordinary objects as canes, bags, books, if the individual is wielding them in a threatening way.
- **Intimidation towards others in waiting room.** Staring with hostility, abusive language, or threatening behaviors towards other people.
- **Scapegoating.** An individual in the waiting room may vent, pick-on or otherwise be aggressive to a child, spouse, or others in the waiting room.
- **Fear.** The individual seems to be quite afraid.
- **Reactivity.** The individual who snaps at support staff with aggression, particularly when asked reasonable questions.
- **Low frustration tolerance.** The individual who becomes frustrated when requested to wait.
- **Intoxication.** Staff should always be alerted if a person in the lobby shows signs of intoxication.
- **Mood swings.** Staff should be alerted if the person shows rapid changes in behavior—from elation to anger to fear to withdrawal.
- **Atypical behaviors.** Staff should be alerted when a person, familiar to the front- desk personnel, is behaving in a way quite different from their baseline behaviors.
- **Trespass.** The instigator who trespasses on support staffs' space and does not cease when a limit is set. This includes leaning inside the desk, waving hands in support staffs' faces, or trying to take paperwork from them.

- **Electric tension.** Information on aggressive behaviors will be presented in other training modules. However, any time support staff feels a shot of adrenaline, a sense that something bad is about to happen, *even when they cannot explain why*, they must call for assistance. Better an occasional false alarm than allowing one developing emergency to go unattended until it is too late.

Self-Control for Support Staff

- **A simple breathing method to calm oneself in crisis situations.** Let the belly expand on an inhale to a moderate four count; hold for a four count; and exhale, letting the belly drop back into the rib cage for a four count. Continue. Use this breathing when you anticipate a crisis developing, while enmeshed in the middle of a crisis situation, and to de-compress after the situation.
- **It is not personal.** Staff must be trained that difficulties with aggressive individuals are not personal issues, no matter what they say or do. Support staff must understand that if they do not take things personally, they will actually have far more control over both their own responses and the aggressive person's behaviors.
- **Professional pride.** It should be a mark of professional pride to be able to move people through screening and waiting procedures expeditiously and compassionately so that they are calmer *after* interacting with support staff.
- **Bracketing.** Part of training for support staff should be an awareness of one's own "buttons." A discussion with your staff about the subject of their hot-buttons is *not* a request for revelation about what their issues are. Rather, they should be educated to maintain a "background" awareness regarding what causes them to lose their temper, so that they are prepared for these events when they occur.

Education

Although support staff will not be responsible for full de-escalation, they need to be educated in the following subjects that are discussed in other sections of this book.

- **The Cycle of aggression.** In addition to helping support staff, assess when a problem is occurring, we have found that knowledge of the escalation cycle is invaluable in helping people keep calm.
- **Why someone would be aggressive.** Empathy, the understanding of what is going on within the person, is one of the primary routes to non-violent communication, particularly with the mentally ill individual. It is very difficult to be compassionate or understanding when one cannot comprehend why other individuals would act the way they do.
- **Recognizing aggressive behaviors.** This is an expanded version of risk assessment. When one is not surprised by another's behavior, one can anticipate and act, rather than merely react.

What Not to Do and What to Do Instead

What not to do and what to do are listed below:

- **Do not shout at an aggressive person.** It is important to keep your voice strong and firm. The only time you should yell is to call for help or to stop an assault in progress. When you are trying to calm down an aggressive or upset person, try to pitch your voice a little lower so that it is "in your chest." This will serve to show your strength and authority and will also help you keep calm.

- **Do not talk down to anyone**. Such behaviors are listed as follows:
  a. Do not roll your eyes.
  b. Do not show your frustration by sighing.
  c. Do not ignore someone who is talking to you. It is fine to say, "Please sit down, I'll speak with you in just a moment;" for example, or "I've already told you that you have to speak to a Security Professional about this." But do not simply turn your back on people or act as if they are not there.
  d. Do not talk to them "through" the paperwork. Instead, speak to them as a person with clean, direct, eye contact.

- **Keep your problems to yourself.** Everybody has problems in life. As a professional, leave your problems at the door. If you find you are unable to do this—if things that are worrying you intrude into your work—consult with your supervisor to figure out best how to take the pressure off. This is a safety issue. If you flare up at a person, or conversely, are overwhelmed by them, you are at greater risk for possible harm.

- **Do not ignore problems.** Do not hope that a problem will go away if it is ignored. It is better for you to address it now when it is a minor situation, perhaps for example, asking for someone to sit down and wait quietly, or to lower their voice. If it is a bigger problem, then you should call professionals who are designated to deal with dangerous situations. Do not be embarrassed or otherwise hesitant to disturb the Security Professional. If you are over-reacting, you will get support through more training. If, however, you aren't taken seriously, then the problem would be the fault of the professional, not you. A simple discussion with your supervisor should help with that kind of problem.

- **Do not be bossy.** Authoritarian attitudes are one of the biggest precipitants of aggressive behavior.

- **Guard their privacy.** Do not speak loudly about their confidential information. If you have to discuss something confidential, either to tell the person something or in response to their question, keep your voice low. If other people can overhear you, either find a quiet area to talk, or if that is either not possible or safe, tell the person that you will inform a professional, and they will get their answer soon.

- **Do not point.** if you want someone to back up, for example, put BOTH hands up, close to your chest, and request that they move back.

Strategies for Front-Desk Staff
Although not expected to do de-escalation of aggressive behavior, front-desk staff are responsible for trying to help mildly upset individuals calm down. Here are some basic principles to follow:

- **Do not make things a power struggle.** Whenever possible (most of the time!), make requests rather than give orders.

- **Leave people alone if that is what they want.** There are times that we believe we must get certain information. If the person is resistant or suspicious, do not push it. Simply inform the responsible staff that certain information you need is outstanding.

- **Eye contact.** Calm, direct, and open eye contact is best. If the person is uncomfortable with this, limit your eye contact *without looking downwards*. Instead, detach, moving your eyes to the side, and then return to making eye contact occasionally.
- **Names.** People have different styles, but it is often helpful to use a person's last name rather than their first. Let them invite you to use their first name.
- **Paraphrasing.** When people are upset, it is very hard for them to answer questions. Help them calm down first. With paraphrasing, all we do is sum up what they said in different words. If you sum things up accurately, you have established that you have "gotten" what they said thus far, so the upset person does not have to say it again.
- **Get the whole story.** Do not problem-solve until you know what they are trying to tell you. Otherwise, you will be seen as either interrupting, which is rude, or not interested. Paraphrasing will help you get the story in a minimum amount of time.
- **Non-threatening requests.** Make a non-threatening request that the person has a high likelihood of complying with.

Communication Problems Between Support Staff and Security Professionals

- **Treat support staff with respect.** It is an absolute requirement that Security Professionals treat support staff with respect. Examples of disrespect would include:
  a. Comments that discount support staff's observations or views by citing Security Professionals alleged greater experience on the street, in the military, or in the security field.
  b. Responding to support staff's safety concerns with a statement prefaced by such patronizing phrases as, "From a security point of view...."
- **Boundaries.** Security Professionals should not demand something outside of either protocol or support staffs' scope of employ particularly if they are in front of a problematic individual.
- **Buffering.** Security Professionals must not use support staff to pass messages to troublesome people, run interference, pass bad news, or otherwise use support staff to avoid speaking with the person directly. Security Professionals must never use support staff to "hide behind their skirts". Examples would include:
  a. "Tell him/her I said...."
  b. "Tell him/her what the case plan is...."
  c. "Tell him/her he/she is supposed to...."
- **Triangulation.** Security Professionals, when notified by support staff of an aggressor's presence, should attempt to give support staff a message when they will be available. If they are delayed, Security Professionals must not triangulate, saying to the person, "I didn't know you were there," or "They forgot to call me."
- **Phone tree system.** Support staff MUST have a phone tree system so that they are assured of immediate response from professionals whenever they call due to an aggressive individual in the lobby who is confronting support staff.
- **Established plans for monitoring individuals.** Sometimes Security Professionals may have set up a plan regarding a person's contact with the agency. Support staff should NOT be expected to monitor or enforce such plans.

Support Staff and the Phone

Because of the distance between folks, people will often say things on the phone, or even worse, by email that they would never say in person. Aside from all the information in the previous sections, what follows is specific to phone contacts.

- **Support personnel are NOT required to accept abuse, verbal violence, or obscenity.** Callers should be informed, calmly, of how they are expected to communicate and warned that if they continue their abuse, the call will be terminated. If the abuse continues, hang up the phone. Document with exact quotations.

- **Dealing with verbal abuse.** There are two kinds of swearing. If they are the kind who swears for "punctuation," you should ask them to stop, if it offends you. If the verbalizations are abusive, however, terminate the call and notify security. Support staff must be expected to take responsibility to set firm limits with the caller on how they will speak to you. In some cases, for example, more emergent circumstances, there needs to be tolerance for such language.

- **Orient the Caller.** "New" callers, with upset or grievances should be informed that support staff do not solve problems—they give information—and it is a firm expectation of the agency that callers should not expect the support staff to comply with requests that should be directed to the Security Professional or other staff. Furthermore, it must be made very clear that support staff must be treated with respect.

- **Threats.** If a person makes threats, the call should be terminated immediately and Security Professionals informed. Again, in some cases, such as a suicidal person, or where threats are being made to do actual harm, it is necessary to get as much information as possible. Bomb threats are another example; the more specificity, the higher the threat level.

- **Personal information.** Do not reveal personal information. Furthermore, if a caller is flirtatious or otherwise requests personal information, inform security. *Document with exact quotations.*

- **Overly personal remarks.** Set firm limits. Inform the caller that you do not accept personal remarks. Terminate the call if they continue, and report to security and your supervisor. Try to give as much detail as you can whether the remarks were merely inept attempts to flirt by a socially clueless person or something more predatory. *Document with exact quotations.*

- **Unavailability.** When staff is not available, the best thing to say is "He/she is unavailable right now." If you have a good prediction of when he/she WILL be available, give it to the caller. Ensure that calls like this get through to Security (is there someone else who could help?). Things a receptionist should not say include:
  a. "He isn't back from lunch." This implies that the professional is taking his time, and is therefore a selfish person.
  b. "I think she's still having coffee." Do not share personal information.
  c. "He/she is in the middle of a big problem or a crisis." This implies that the office has problems and this may make the person anxious. It also implies that what the caller is telephoning about is not as important.
  d. "She/he went home early." Creates both resentment and envy. They need the professional, but the professionals are unavailable.
  e. "He/she is not in yet." This is also infuriating. He/she is late when the caller needs them.

If, however, the needed person is not going to be available for several days or more, try to either get an idea of the problem and pass the information to the professional's back-up or connect immediately to the back-up.

- **Putting callers on hold:**
  a. When you ask to put them on hold, get a response before doing so. If the caller is irate, and attempts to continue to argue with you, state, "I must put you on hold now" and do so. If you are connecting them with another party, be sure to inform that person that the caller is irate.
  b. When you reconnect with the caller, do not apologize after putting them on hold. Instead, thank them for their patience. You did not do anything wrong.

- **Close-ended question to end a call.** This is used when the call is relatively straightforward, but the caller still seems unsatisfied. "Is there anything else I can help you with before I hang up?"
  a. Do not use this if the call has become tense or aggressive, as the other party may think you are being sarcastic.
  b. There are some people, however, who will seize any opportunity to continue talking.
  c. If you *have* used one closed–ended question and answered it, it is time to end the call now.

- **Get rid of negative energy before answering the phone again.** Particularly after an intense call, take a break—even thirty seconds. Stand up and stretch or otherwise get rid of some of the tension you may have incurred so that it is not transferred into your next call.

- **Do not just say, "I don't know."** Commit to finding out the needed information and give the caller an idea when you will return with either the answer or a status report.

Appendixes

APPENDIX A

Frequent Precipitants in Incidents of Worksite Violence

There are a number of excellent threat assessment instruments that attempt to codify various factors that lead an employee or customer to present with a greater potential for violence. The authors strongly recommend that your agency or company use such instruments, because they put all involved in threat assessment (literally) on the same page. What follows below is something simple, but equally important: a common-sense list. Based on our experience, these items should always elicit concern. It is startling to both of us the number of times that the items below, seemingly so obvious, are completely ignored. At minimum, these are more than "red flags"—treat them as sirens blaring.

- Any time sanctions are levied towards an employee
- The termination of employment
- Threats from others
- Domestic violence brought on the worksite
- Relationship conflicts on the worksite
- Lack of consequences when rules are broken
- Vague or inconsistent rules
- Rigid, <u>excessive</u> application of rules
- Lack of staff training or skill
- Broken promises to employees or customers
- A lack of opportunity or choices
- Character problems on the part of staff: intimidating, withdrawn, impatient, rude, angry, or burned-out

APPENDIX B

The Viewpoint of OSHA

OSHA recently cited a hospital in Connecticut for failing to provide its employees with adequate safeguards against workplace violence. OSHA found that the hospital's workplace violence program was incomplete and ineffective at preventing workplace violence. As a result, OSHA cited the hospital for an alleged serious violation of OSHA's general duty clause for failing to provide a workplace free from recognized hazards likely to cause death or serious injury to workers, in this case the hazard of employees being injured by violent patients.

OSHA's citation encompasses several suggested means of abatement that the hospital could pursue to address the workplace violence issue. They are applicable far beyond this particular hospital. These included:

- Creating a standalone written violence prevention program for the entire workplace that includes a hazard/threat assessment, controls and prevention strategies, staff training and education, incident reporting and investigation, and periodic review of the program.
- Ensuring that the program addresses specific actions employees should take in the event of an incident and proper reporting procedures.
- Ensuring that security staff members trained to deal with aggressive behavior are readily and immediately available to render assistance.
- Ensuring that all new hires are screened for a potential history of violence.
- Putting in place administrative controls so that employees are not alone with potentially violent individuals.

Workplace violence programs in organizations should consider the following for their programs, in addition to what has been articulated in this book:

- When creating your plan, use people with a background and the training to develop a sound, comprehensive plan.
- Policies based on the plan, or plans based on policies need to have legal and HR review.
- Workplace violence intervention should be targeted at troubleshooting what potential problems exist to develop intervention plans. Predictive analytics, statistical probabilities, should be developed where practical.
- Train the Security Professionals on a scheduled basis to develop and maintain knowledge, skills, and abilities in interacting with the various types of personalities articulated in this book.
- Ensure that there is a review or after-action of any significant interaction.

Further References Regarding OSHA Guidelines

http://www.osha.gov/Publications/OSHA3148/osha3148.html

http://www.opm.gov/Employment_and_Benefits/WorkLife/OfficialDocuments/handbooksguides/WorkplaceViolence/p3-s5.asp

APPENDIX C

Security Assisted Termination Request Form

REQUEST FOR SECURITY ASSISTED TERMINATION

Name: _____

Business Unit: _____

Date: _____ Time: _____ Phone: _____

Name of Person Being Terminated: _____

Position: _____ Office Location: _____

Date of Termination: _____ Time: _____

Location of Termination: _____

Reason for Termination: _____

_____

HR Manager: _____

Manager: _____

Any threats? (Describe specifically) _____

_____

_____

_____

Any other concerns? (Be specific) _____

_____

_____

_____

Any weapons known? _____

_____

Security escort needed?_____ To Office:_____ To vehicle: _____

Collect card key:_____ Collect parking permit: _____

Endnotes

[1] See Rhodes, Richard. (1999). *Why they kill: The discoveries of a maverick criminologist.* New York: Vintage, on the work of sociologist Lonnie Atkins, who coined the phrase "violentization," to describe the process in which a victim of violence becomes a perpetrator. Atkins focused on the family, but violentization can also occur later in life.

[2] Ibid.

[3] One of the authors observed an informal study by a neurologist at a youth detention facility. He noted signs of closed head injury (through neuro-psych evaluation) in approximately 50 percent of the male inmates.

[4] Many hospitals and other social service agencies have changed the title of this operation to a "show of support." This is not mere political correctness. It is an attempt to create a specific mindset that is most appropriate to de-escalating a vulnerable patient, where, to some degree, the Security Professional becomes part of the over-all treatment team. Of course, in other settings, "show-of-force" is the proper term. Consider, based on your particular venue, what is the better term.

[5] Ekman, P. (2003). *Emotions revealed.* New York: Times Books, Henry Holt and Company, LLC.

[6] You will sometimes see the same thing with people for whom English is not a first language.

[7] One of the best books on manipulation is: Allen, B., & Bosta, D. (1981-2002). *Games Criminals Play: How you can profit by knowing them.* Berkeley, CA: Rae John. Although it focuses on a prison setting, as well as having examples written in some remarkably outdated slang, it is an excellent resource.

[8] Babiak, P. & Hare, R. (2006). *Snakes in suits: When psychopaths go to work.* New York: HarperCollins.

[9] Arieti, Silvano (1974). *Interpretation of Schizophrenia* (2nd ed.). New York: Basic Books, Inc.

[10] Other major categories of stalkers are:
   - **Relational stalkers.** Often an extension of a controlling or violent relationship, this stalker is either keeping tabs on his/her partner, or pursuing them once they have left.
   - **Obsessive stalkers.** The classic stalker, he or she has a hyper-focus on the victim as prey, not necessarily to kill or even harm, but always to control. Like ordinary obsessive-compulsive disorder, this stalker can be quite aware that the victim does not desire contact, and may be afraid of or hate him/her. But just as the germ-obsessed obsessive MUST wash his hands 50 times, despite *knowing* that they are clean, the obsessive stalker has to have the attention of his/her victim.
   - **Psychopathic stalker.** Such an individual may certainly have been in a relationship with or be obsessed with his/her victim. In addition, there is considerable "ego" involved—this stalker's psychological energy focuses on self rather than the victim. A true predator, he/she is doing something they enjoys, simply because they can (for amusement), or because the victim, in some way, offended them (for revenge).

[11] Our thanks to Aaron Fields of the Seattle Fire Department for this example.

[12] An actual incident. The engineer was killed trying to jump clear when the manic person wrecked the train.

[13] Researchers note that a mixture of alcohol and cocaine is particularly dangerous, as the body synthesizes them together into a new substance, cocaethylene. Retrieved from http://jpet.aspetjournals.org/ content/274/1/215.abstract

[14] One of the authors first heard this method presented by author David Grossman. Also see his exemplary book: Grossman, D. (1996). *On Killing: The psychological cost of learning to kill in war and society.* Santa Ana, CA: Back Bay Books.

[15] Jeffrey Slotnick. Written communication.

[16] We owe the image of the hands as a fence to Geoff Thompson, who has authored a number of books on his career as a doorman in violent British pubs, as well as exemplary books on self-defense.

[17] The authors owe a debt for some of the basic information in this section to a form of training called PART, thanks to a workshop one of us attended approximately 20 years ago. We have made major changes in their basic 4-part schema, as well as adding a significant amount of new data. Therefore, our approach is, in many aspects, quite different, and it should not be confused with PART's procedures.

[18] Sherwin Cotler, Ph.D. Written communication.

19   See: Salter, A. (2004). *Predators: pedophiles, rapists and other sex offenders: Who they are, how they operate and how we can protect ourselves and our children.* New York: Basic Books. Our gratitude for the formulation of the overwhelming force/respect concept that she presented in a great story during a seminar.

20   See: de Becker, G. (1997). *The Gift of Fear: Survival signals that protect us from violence.* U.S. and Canada: Little Brown; and (1999). *Protecting the gift: Keeping children and teenagers safe (and parents sane)* New York: Random House, New York.

ABOUT THE AUTHORS

Ellis Amdur

Edgework founder Ellis Amdur received his B.A. in psychology from Yale University in 1974 and his M.A. in psychology from Seattle University in 1990. He is both a National Certified Counselor and a State Certified Child Mental Health Specialist. He has written a number of books concerning communication with mentally ill and emotionally disturbed individuals and the de-escalation of aggression.

Since the late 1960s, Amdur has trained in various martial arts systems, spending thirteen of these years studying in Japan. He is a recognized expert in classical and modern Japanese martial traditions and has authored three iconoclastic books on the subject, as well as one instructional DVD.

Since his return to America in 1988, Ellis Amdur has worked in the field of crisis intervention. He has developed a range of training and consultation services, as well as a unique style of assessment and psychotherapy. These are based on a combination of phenomenological psychology and the underlying philosophical premises of classical Japanese martial traditions. Amdur's professional philosophy can best be summed up in this idea: the development of an individual's integrity and dignity is the paramount virtue. This can only occur when people live courageously, regardless of the circumstances, and take responsibility for their roles in making the changes they desire.

Ellis Amdur is a dynamic public speaker and trainer who presents his work throughout the United States and internationally. He is noted for his sometimes outrageous humor as well as his profound breadth of knowledge. His vivid descriptions of aggressive and mentally ill people and his true-to-life role-playing of the behaviors in question give participants an almost first-hand experience of facing the real individuals in question. For further information please see Amdur's website: www.edgework.info

William Cooper

Bill Cooper is a 30-year law enforcement veteran, retiring as Chief of Police. He has subsequently worked for two Fortune 200 corporations, managing Security Operations, Workplace Violence Intervention, Executive Protection, and Policies and Programs. In his unique and highly successful approach to proactively addressing workplace violence, Bill developed a predictive approach, using statistical probability to predict workplace violence, allowing for preemption and mitigation strategies to be implemented.

Bill has extensive experience in his background, dealing with a wide variety of personality types and disorders, most of which are discussed in this book. He has conducted training for Security Professionals in responding to higher risk incidents and has managed and conducted many threat assessments and cross-functional response teams.

Bill is trained in Six Sigma and Lean Six Sigma and teaches graduate school MBA courses. He has been interviewed on radio, television, and for national and local publications. He holds an MBA and a Masters Degree in Public Administration. He is a graduate of the FBI National Academy and the Northwest Law Enforcement Executive Command College. He is also an award-winning speaker.